Ekwall/Shanker Reading Inventory

Ekwall/Shanker Reading Inventory

FOURTH EDITION

James L. Shanker
California State University, Hayward

Eldon E. Ekwall
late of University of Texas at El Paso

Allyn and Bacon
Boston • London • Toronto • Sydney • Tokyo • Singapore

Vice President, Education: Paul A. Smith
Series Editor: Arnis E. Burvikovs
Series Editorial Assistant: Bridget Keane
Senior Marketing Manager: Brad Parkins
Composition and Prepress Buyer: Linda Cox
Manufacturing Buyer: Suzanne Lareau
Cover Administrator: Linda Knowles
Production Editor: Christopher H. Rawlings
Editorial-Production Service: Omegatype Typography, Inc.
Text Designer: Carol Somberg/Omegatype Typography, Inc.
Electronic Composition: Omegatype Typography, Inc.

Internet: www.abacon.com

Library of Congress Cataloging-in-Publication Data

Shanker, James L.
    Ekwall/Shanker reading inventory / James L. Shanker, Eldon E. Ekwall — 4th ed.
        p.   cm.
    Ekwall's name appears first on the earlier edition.
    ISBN 0-205-30441-9 (pbk.: alk. paper)
    1. Reading—Ability testing.   I. Title.   II. Ekwall, Eldon E.

    LB1050.46.E38   2000
    428.4'007621—dc21   99-042224
                                                                             CIP

Printed in the United States of America
10 9 8 7 6 5 4   04 03 02 01

To current and former students in the graduate reading programs at California State University, Hayward. For the past twenty-six years, these dedicated teachers have taught me much of what I know about reading instruction and have continually inspired me by their efforts to bring the gift of literacy to youngsters in our schools.

Contents

Interpretation of Test Results   53

Preparation of Diagnostic Reports   92

Preface

The *Ekwall/Shanker Reading Inventory* (ESRI) is designed for the teacher-candidate, classroom teacher, psychologist, resource teacher, or reading specialist to assess the full range of students' reading abilities. This fourth edition contains an expanded battery of thirty-eight different diagnostic tests in ten different areas. These tests measure oral and silent reading ability, listening comprehension, phonemic awareness, concepts about print, letter knowledge, basic sight vocabulary, phonics, structural analysis, context clues, fluency skills, vocabulary, reading comprehension, and reading interests. This edition includes *new* tests for emergent literacy skills, including five tests for phonemic awareness ability and a test for concepts about print. It also includes a new Quick Check for Basic Sight Words (Test 4a) and a new form for assessing the reading interests of older students.

The ESRI provides flexible assessment to match the needs of the individuals who will use it. The ESRI may be used as a quick screening device for placement of students in groups or classes, for a brief assessment, or for a comprehensive individual diagnosis. In this edition, specific directions guide the novice teacher or the experienced specialist to conduct the kind of diagnosis appropriate for each setting. The examiner's selection of the tests to be used will determine the depth of the assessment. Examiners may use as few or as many tests in the battery as they wish. The four forms at each grade level that are provided for the evaluation of oral and silent reading and listening comprehension enable examiners to use the ESRI to measure students' growth in reading ability over time.

The instructions for both administering the tests and conducting the diagnoses have been carefully refined to make them even more user-friendly. The ESRI also provides the following special features: a crib sheet and flow chart to clarify the administration of the oral reading, silent reading, and listening comprehension passages; a chart to help the examiner identify which reading abilities are measured by the various tests in the battery; and test summary sheets and analysis sheets to enable the user to interpret data and report on the testing in an understandable, systematic way. The ESRI also provides a chart for the prescriptive analysis of all phonics skills, enabling the user to compare the student's performance on all tests given in which phonics skills might be applied. The ESRI takes the reader step by step through the diagnosis of two sample subjects, and then diagnostic reports for each of these students are presented in their entirety.

The passages used for measuring oral reading, silent reading, and listening comprehension do not appear childish to students at any grade level. All passages except those at the preprimer level contain ten questions to enhance the reliability of the inventory. The scoring procedure is based on research and the most commonly accepted criteria for scoring informal reading inventories.

Although all passages were written at specific levels based on widely accepted readability formulas, the user should realize there is less difference between, say, a seventh- and an eighth-grade passage than there is between a first- and a second-grade passage. Consequently, at the upper grade levels factors such as interest and knowledge of the subject matter may sometimes be more important in determining when a student can adequately read a passage than the designated grade level of the passage. Thus the examiner should not become overly concerned about always obtaining a perfect sequence of independent, instructional, and frustration levels on the higher-level reading passages.

Acknowledgments

Appreciation is extended to Alison Kuehner and Kendra Wagner, who assisted in the development of this fourth edition of the Ekwall/Shanker Reading Inventory. Alison created the new reading interest inventory for older students and Kendra drafted the initial versions of the phonemic awareness tests. Thank you to Lisa Alday for her careful and thorough review of the manuscript in its final stages. Thank you to Cheryl Milner, who wrote the passage for the test on the application of phonics skills in context, and to Susan Shanker, who wrote the passages for the tests on the application of structural analysis skills in context.

Thank you to the many preservice and graduate students at California State University, Hayward, who have administered and evaluated most of the tests in this inventory since 1979 and who have participated in the development and refinement of some of the decoding tests since 1974.

Special thanks to Steven Johnson of SCORE and Janet Tinari of the Mahopac (New York) Central School District for their valuable and specific recommendations.

Thank you to the following reviewers, whose thoughtful suggestions and insights are deeply appreciated: Joseph T. Brennan, Duquense University; Linda Fulvio; and Patricia Wilson, Taylor University.

I am extremely grateful to the fine people at Allyn and Bacon who have been unusually patient and helpful to me during the development of this manuscript. I wish to thank my longtime developmental editor Virginia Lanigan and production editor Bridget Keane. Sincere thanks to Bonny Graham of Omegatype Typography, Inc., whose extraordinary talent and creativity made this book better organized, more attractive, and easier to read.

Finally, appreciation is extended to all of the teacher-candidates, graduate students, classroom teachers, and reading and learning disabilities specialists who have administered this inventory, and to the many elementary and secondary students to whom it has been given.

J. L. S.

PART I

Exploring the Ekwall/Shanker Reading Inventory

Description of the Ekwall/Shanker Reading Inventory

The Ekwall/Shanker Reading Inventory (ESRI) is a set of test instruments designed for the assessment or diagnosis of individual students' reading abilities. The ESRI may be used by educators for different purposes. Classroom teachers may use the ESRI to quickly assess students' reading performance. This *quick assessment* will enable teachers to group students for instruction and to guide the selection of reading materials for both instructional purposes and students' independent reading. Quick assessment also helps teachers identify those students who may need more thorough diagnosis or referral to a specialist. Classroom teachers, reading specialists, resource specialists, psychologists, or others with experience administering the ESRI may use the appropriate tests to conduct a *thorough diagnosis* of reading abilities. These tests will reveal each student's performance on all critical reading skills. An analysis of the student's performance on these tests will provide a blueprint for prescriptive instruction to remediate reading difficulties. Pre- and posttesting of oral and silent reading will enable the examiner to measure the student's progress over time.

The ESRI consists of thirty-eight different tests in ten different areas designed to assess the full range of students' reading abilities. These tests are:

1. **San Diego Quick Assessment or Graded Word List (GWL)**
2. **Reading Passages Tests**
   2a. Oral Reading
   2b. Silent Reading
   2c. Listening Comprehension
3. **Emergent Literacy Tests**
   3a. Phonemic Awareness
      3a1. Rhyme Production
      3a2. Rhyme Recognition [Alternate Test]
      3a3. Initial Sound Recognition
      3a4. Phoneme Blending
      3a5. Phoneme Segmentation
   3b. Concepts about Print
   3c. Letter Knowledge
      3c1. Auditory Stimulus
      3c2. Visual Stimulus

4. **Basic Sight Vocabulary Tests**
   4a. Quick Check for Basic Sight Words
   4b. Basic Sight Words
   4c. Basic Sight Word Phrases

5. **Phonics Tests**
   5a. Application of Phonics Skills in Context
   5b. Initial Consonants
   5c. Initial Blends and Digraphs
   5d. Ending Sounds
   5e. Vowels
   5f. Phonograms
   5g. Blending
   5h. Substitution
   5i. Vowel Pronunciation

6. **Structural Analysis Tests**
   6a. Application of Structural Analysis Skills in Context
      6a1. Lower Level
      6a2. Higher Level
   6b. Hearing Word Parts
   6c. Inflectional Endings
   6d. Prefixes
   6e. Suffixes
   6f. Compound Words
   6g. Affixes
   6h. Syllabication

7. **Knowledge of Contractions Test**

8. **El Paso Phonics Survey**

9. **Quick Word List Survey**

10. **Reading Interests Survey**
    10a. Elementary
    10b. Adult

BRIEF DESCRIPTION OF THE TESTS

The first test in the ESRI is a Graded Word List (GWL), the San Diego Quick Assessment. This word list is a series of ten words at each level from the preprimer through the ninth grade. It is designed as a quick check of a student's word recognition and word analysis skills and is normally used to make a rapid determination of the student's independent, instructional, and frustration reading grade levels before administering the oral and silent reading passages and other tests. The GWL enables the examiner to determine an entry point for beginning the oral and silent reading passages. It also can provide an initial analysis of the student's ability to recognize basic sight words and apply phonics and structural analysis skills. Because such a word list does not require a student to read words in context, it cannot evaluate a student's ability to use context clues or to comprehend written material. Although the GWL can be a highly useful screening instrument and can aid in a complete diagnosis, by itself it is an inadequate measure of a student's overall reading ability.

Most informal reading inventories include passages to assess oral reading, silent reading, and listening comprehension. In the ESRI these abilities are evaluated in the

Reading Passages Tests, Tests 2a, 2b, and 2c, respectively. The ESRI includes a complete set of four equivalent reading passages ranging in difficulty from preprimer through ninth-grade level. These passages are designed to measure students' oral and silent independent, instructional, and frustration reading grade levels. They are also used to determine students' listening comprehension levels. As in the administration of any informal reading inventory, students' use of decoding skills, as well as their ability to comprehend, is taken into consideration in the scoring procedure.

Once you determine your students' various reading levels, you will be able to give them appropriate materials for instruction and for independent reading. This is especially important for students who are having difficulty in reading. In addition, you can analyze your students' performance on the reading passages and the other tests in this battery to determine their reading strengths and weaknesses, enabling you to provide specific instruction that will help your students attain their potential as readers. As previously indicated, the inventory contains four reading passages at each level, as follows:

Preprimer-A	Preprimer-B	Preprimer-C	Preprimer-D
First Grade-A	First Grade-B	First Grade-C	First Grade-D
Second Grade-A	Second Grade-B	Second Grade-C	Second Grade-D
Third Grade-A	Third Grade-B	Third Grade-C	Third Grade-D
Fourth Grade-A	Fourth Grade-B	Fourth Grade-C	Fourth Grade-D
Fifth Grade-A	Fifth Grade-B	Fifth Grade-C	Fifth Grade-D
Sixth Grade-A	Sixth Grade-B	Sixth Grade-C	Sixth Grade-D
Seventh Grade-A	Seventh Grade-B	Seventh Grade-C	Seventh Grade-D
Eighth Grade-A	Eighth Grade-B	Eighth Grade-C	Eighth Grade-D
Ninth Grade-A	Ninth Grade-B	Ninth Grade-C	Ninth Grade-D

The A passages are designed to be read orally by the student on the first administration and the B passages to be read silently. The C and D passages may be used for a second administration at a later date, or as supplementary passages to confirm the results of the first administration. As with the A and B passages, the C passages are to be read orally and the D passages silently. Any of the passages may be used to determine the student's listening comprehension level. For this we suggest you employ unused A or B passages on a first administration and C or D passages on a second administration at a later date. If you choose instead to use C or D passages to test for listening comprehension on a first administration, these passages will then be unsuitable for use in testing oral or silent reading at a later time.

The ESRI also includes eight Emergent Literacy Tests, designed to assess students' phonemic awareness, concepts about print, and letter knowledge. These tests will help you determine whether students have mastered the skills required of beginning readers to be successful.

The Basic Sight Vocabulary Tests measure students' ability to recognize and pronounce the words that appear most often in the English language. The ESRI tests allow you to measure students' knowledge of basic sight vocabulary in several different ways. The Quick Check for Basic Sight Words does exactly what the title suggests: It enables the examiner to determine, in less than two minutes, whether a student has mastered basic sight words when reading them off a list of carefully selected sample words. If a student misses even one of the words on that list, the next two tests should be given. These tests thoroughly assess knowledge of both basic sight words and basic sight word phrases. Other tests in the ESRI will demonstrate whether students can read basic sight words in actual reading passages.

Nine different Phonics Tests provide for thorough evaluation of all phonics skills. The first test, Application of Phonics Skills in Context, is a unique test that measures a student's ability to apply phonics skills when reading regular one-syllable words in context. It also serves as a screening test. If a student demonstrates mastery on this test, it is not necessary to administer the remaining phonics tests. For students who do not master the first phonics test, other tests measure the specific skills of Initial Consonants, Initial Blends and Digraphs, Ending Sounds, Vowels, Phonograms, Blending, Substitution, and Vowel Pronunciation.

The Structural Analysis Tests measure students' abilities to decode multisyllable words using a format similar to that used in the phonics tests. The first test, Application of Structural Analysis Skills in Context, consists of two different passages (at two levels of difficulty), which reveal whether a student is able to apply structural analysis skills in the act of reading. Again, if students master this test, it is unnecessary to administer the remaining structural analysis tests: Hearing Word Parts, Inflectional Endings, Prefixes, Suffixes, Compound Words, Affixes (a test that combines both prefixes and suffixes), and Syllabication.

The ESRI contains three optional tests: the Knowledge of Contractions Test, the El Paso Phonics Survey, and the Quick Word List Survey. The Knowledge of Contractions Test evaluates a student's ability to pronounce common contractions *and* reveals whether the student knows the two separate words that compose each contraction. The well-known El Paso Phonics Survey can be used either to confirm findings from the other phonics tests or as an alternative to them. The Quick Word List Survey can be used to verify quickly whether a student has indeed mastered all important decoding skills. If so, it will not be necessary to spend time administering various decoding tests, and you can instead explore the areas of fluency, vocabulary, or comprehension as possible causes of reading difficulty.

Finally, the ESRI includes the Reading Interests Survey. This easy-to-administer survey consists of two forms, elementary and adult, that you may use to assess students' reading interests, experiences, and habits.

Each of the tests in the ESRI will be covered in detail in later sections of this manual. For each test, you will be given its purpose, a description, specific directions for administering and scoring, and thorough information on how you can use the data gathered to evaluate the student's reading performance in the area(s) tested.

WHO SHOULD USE THE EKWALL/SHANKER READING INVENTORY?

The ESRI was designed for use by classroom teachers, reading specialists, resource specialists, psychologists, and others and for the training of prospective and in-service educators. Most reading experts readily agree that the reading grade level of a student can be determined more accurately by the use of a reading inventory of this nature than by the use of standardized achievement tests or other commonly used methods. Furthermore, while administering an inventory such as this a teacher can gather a great deal of diagnostic information that will serve as a blueprint for instruction. The ESRI is also flexible. In some cases, the examiner will employ only the Graded Word List and the oral reading passages to determine the student's reading levels, so that appropriate placement may be made and guidance given when helping the student select reading materials. In other cases, the examiner may wish to perform a brief diagnosis of the student's reading difficulties based on the use of some, but not all, of the tests in the ESRI. In still other cases, the examiner may wish to perform a comprehensive diagnosis of the student's reading abilities based on the administration of many of the tests in the ESRI.

If you are using the ESRI as part of a college course or staff development training, your instructor will guide you in the selection of tests and procedures to be used. Because these tests cover the full range of reading abilities, from emergent literacy skills through fluent reading with comprehension, under no circumstances should an examiner give all of these tests to any one student.

Levels of Assessment

For a quick screening of students' abilities, give Tests 1 and 2a to students individually. These tests can be administered and scored in as little as ten to fifteen minutes per child. If you desire more specific information about your students' reading abilities, the tests listed in the following table may be given for quick assessment.

A thorough reading diagnosis for a struggling reader may require an hour or more. The specific tests given for diagnostic purposes will vary depending on the reading skills of the student being tested. Typically, however, the tests listed in the following table are given in order to gather data for a comprehensive reading diagnosis.

Quick Assessment

Student's reading level	Tests	Test description
Prereaders	Area 3 tests	Provides more information on prereading abilities.
Beginning readers[1]	Test 4a	Tests basic sight word abilities.
	Test 5a	Tests phonics abilities.
More able readers[2]	Test 6a1 or 6a2	Tests structural analysis abilities.

Diagnostic Testing

Student's reading level	Tests[3]	Test description
Prereaders	Test 1 and area 3 tests	Provides more thorough information on prereading abilities.
Beginning readers[1]	Tests 1, 2a, 2b	Tests reading abilities using graded reading passages.
	Test 2c	Tests listening comprehension abilities.
	Tests 4b and 4c	Tests basic sight word abilities.
	Tests 5a through 5i	Tests phonics abilities.
	Test 10a or 10b	Provides information on reading interests.
More able readers[2]	Tests 1, 2a, 2b, 2c	Tests reading abilities using graded reading passages.
	Test 4a	Verifies mastery of basic sight words.
	Test 5a	Verifies mastery of phonics.
	Tests 6a through 6h	Tests structural analysis abilities.
	Test 10a or 10b	Provides information on reading interests.

[1]This level may include older remedial readers who are struggling with decoding skills.

[2]This level may include students who have mastered their beginning reading skills but who may lack fluency and the ability to decode written materials written at a third-grade level or higher.

[3]Tests 7, 8, and 9 are considered optional and are given only in unusual circumstances or when additional information is desired.

Do not be daunted by the apparent complexity of this inventory. Most of the tests in this battery have been used by tens of thousands of teachers and students in training to become teachers. The only tests that are somewhat difficult to administer are the Reading Passages Tests (Tests 2a, 2b, and 2c), and this manual contains ample guidance and special tools to assist you in learning to administer them. Once you have given the tests, you will not find it necessary to reread the instructions in the manual. Both your speed and your ability to administer, score, and interpret these reading tests will improve considerably with experience.

READING/LISTENING LEVELS MEASURED BY THE EKWALL/SHANKER READING INVENTORY

The ESRI measures four grade levels. These include the three reading grade levels: the independent level (sometimes called the "free" reading level), the instructional level, and the frustration level. A fourth level, listening ability, is determined by reading passages to the student and then scoring the student's comprehension of that material. This is usually termed the student's listening comprehension level. A description of the independent, instructional, frustration, and listening comprehension levels follows.

Independent Reading Level

The *independent reading level* is the level at which a student should be able to read without help of any kind from the teacher. This is the level at which one would normally expect the student to read a voluntarily selected library or trade book. The student should accurately pronounce or decode at least 99 percent of the words and should comprehend at least 90 percent of the material.

Most teachers are surprised to learn that students must decode 99 percent of the words to be able to read at an independent level. One of the most important reasons for teachers to give the ESRI is to determine students' correct independent levels and thus guide students in selecting appropriate materials for independent reading. Experts know that students must spend large amounts of time engaged in the act of reading to develop their reading skills. This reading practice is most effective when students are reading materials at their independent reading levels.

Instructional Reading Level

The *instructional reading level* is the level at which a student would normally be reading when required to read a social studies or science textbook, a basal reader, or an anthology without having had a chance to read it previously. The student should accurately decode at least 95 percent of the words and should comprehend at least 60 percent of the material. The instructional reading level is always higher than the independent reading level. Material written at the student's instructional reading level will be too difficult for the student to read independently. Therefore, the teacher should discuss the material with the student and build up the student's background of experience to improve both vocabulary and overall comprehension. New words should also be discussed so that the student will be able to use word-attack skills correctly when encountering them.

Frustration Reading Level

The *frustration reading level* is the point at which reading material simply becomes too difficult for the student to read. The student can decode accurately 90 percent or less of the words and can comprehend only 50 percent or less of the material.

Listening Comprehension Level

The *listening comprehension level* is usually considered to be the highest level at which the student can listen to a passage and comprehend 70 to 75 percent of the material. Because there are ten questions on the ESRI, the lower percentage of 70 is used for easy scoring.

To determine the student's listening comprehension level, you will read passages to the student and ask questions about those passages. The purpose for finding a student's listening comprehension level is to determine whether a discrepancy exists between the level at which the student can *read* and comprehend and the level at which the student can *listen* and comprehend. If the student can listen and comprehend at a grade level or several grade levels higher than that same student can read and comprehend, you can conclude that this individual has good potential for improving in reading ability. Once problems with decoding skills are overcome, the student's reading comprehension would be likely to improve.

The scoring criteria for the independent, instructional, frustration, and listening comprehension levels are summarized below:

Level	*Word Recognition*	*Comprehension*
Independent level	99% or more	90% or more
Instructional level	95% or more	60% or more[1]
Frustration level	90% or less	50% or less
Listening comprehension level	—	70–75% or more

In determining a student's oral reading level, both word recognition and comprehension are taken into consideration. Because we are unable to determine how many words the student recognizes in silent reading, only the comprehension factor is considered in scoring silent reading passages.

In scoring the ESRI, or any informal reading inventory, the ultimate decision about grade placement is usually based on the percentages previously mentioned. However, Johnson and Kress[2] have listed certain behavioral characteristics commonly observed in students at their independent, instructional, and frustration reading levels. These related behavioral characteristics are as follows:

Independent and Instructional Levels

- Rhythmical, expressive oral reading
- Accurate observation of punctuation
- Acceptable reading posture
- Silent reading more rapid than oral
- Response to questions in language equivalent to that of author
- No evidence of lip movement, finger pointing, head movement, vocalization, subvocalization, or anxiety about performance

Frustration Reading Level

- Abnormally loud or soft voice
- Arhythmical or word-by-word oral reading
- Lack of expression in oral reading
- Inaccurate observation of punctuation
- Finger pointing (at margin or every word)
- Lip movements, head movements, subvocalization
- Frequent requests for examiner help
- Noninterest in the selection
- Yawning or obvious fatigue
- Refusal to continue

THE DEVELOPMENT OF THE EKWALL/SHANKER READING INVENTORY

The Graded Word List (GWL)

The Graded Word List (GWL) used in the ESRI was developed by Margaret La Pray and Ramon Ross at San Diego State University. Since it was published in the *Journal of Reading* in January 1969, this list has been widely used and is likely to place a student at the correct independent, instructional, and frustration reading grade levels based on the student's sight vocabulary, phonics, and structural analysis skills. However, this test evaluates neither the student's ability to use context clues for decoding nor the student's ability to comprehend what is read. Therefore, the examiner should use the GWL as a starting point in administering the oral and silent reading passages and for a quick assessment of basic sight word knowledge and phonic and structural analysis skills.

The Graded Reading Passages

All of the passages in the ESRI were written by Eldon E. Ekwall, who attempted to create passages that, according to research, would be of interest to students. Effort was made to control the subject matter so that questions about the content of each passage could not be answered by students who had not read that passage. All of the passages contain ten sentences, except the preprimer passages. Usually there is one question about each sentence. In most cases, the first question is rather easy and is designed to give students confidence in their ability to answer the rest of the questions.

In all of the passages *above* the second-grade level, one question is designed to test the student's vocabulary. This question can often be answered by the student if he or she makes good use of meaning context. In all passages above the second-grade level, one question is also designed to test the student's ability to make inferences. Most of the answers to the inference questions can be inferred from the passage itself. Any student with a good ability to reason should be able to answer these questions even though the answers may not be directly stated in the passage. We do not believe it is fair to expect a student to answer inference questions based strictly on background experiences, because some students with abundant experience would be likely to have an advantage over those with more meager backgrounds.

The initials F, I, and V appear beside each blank on the comprehension questions on the teacher's answer sheet. These initials designate the type of questions being asked. The initial F stands for factual, I stands for inference, and V stands for vocabulary.

In some cases, the examiner may feel it would be desirable to have more inference questions. Research in the area of reading comprehension, however, has shown that it is difficult, if not impossible, to design questions accurately except those that sample vocabulary knowledge and factual information. Furthermore, inference questions are less passage-dependent than literal questions. For this reason, students would be unduly penalized if more than 10 percent of the questions were of the inference type.

The grade levels of the reading passages for preprimer through grade 8 were determined by using the Harris-Jacobson Readability Formula,[3] a formula based on a great deal of research by Albert Harris and Milton Jacobson. The formula is based on the percentage of hard words in the passage (words not on the Harris-Jacobson List) and average sentence length. In writing the passages, the authors adjusted the average sentence length and the percentage of hard words to derive a score that would place the reading difficulty of each passage near the midpoint of each grade level. The grade levels of the reading passages for ninth grade were determined by using the revised version by Powers, Sumner, and Kearl[4] of the original Dale-Chall Readability Formula.[5]

After the initial writing of the passages and the questions about them were completed, the inventory was administered to approximately fifty students. These administrations were tape-recorded and later analyzed to determine whether certain questions were consistently missed by nearly all students due to faulty wordings. Following this analysis, adjustments were made. The inventory was then reviewed by four professors of reading education. Based on these reviews, more adjustments were made. The inventory was then administered to approximately sixty students of various ages, and further minor revisions were made in the content of the passages and the questions about them until it was determined that the questions and the levels of the passages were satisfactory.

The initial version of the inventory contained primer as well as preprimer and first-grade passages. The authors found that although it is possible to differentiate between preprimer and primer passages using a readability formula, it was not practical to include both preprimer and primer passages in the inventory because there is simply not enough difference between the reading levels of preprimer and primer passages to assess the difference accurately for most students. Therefore, only preprimer and first-grade level passages appear in the ESRI. The preprimer passages represent the lowest level at which a student can be said to read, and the first-grade passages represent a medium to high first-grade level.

Time Factors for the Silent Reading Passages

An important aspect of reading ability is *fluency*. One measure of fluency is speed of reading, or reading rate. For this measure to be meaningful, however, the student must also decode accurately and comprehend what has been read. The ESRI provides a built-in measure of reading fluency. As described in following paragraphs, you can determine the student's reading rate on each silent reading passage. Because criteria have already been established for comprehension, you can determine the student's reading rate on passages read at either the independent or instructional levels.

The ESRI includes time factors for the silent reading passages: *slow, medium, fast, median* (the point at which half the students read slower and the other half read faster), and *mean* (average). These categories were developed by administering the ESRI to approximately 170 students at each grade level. Care was taken to select students from various socioeconomic levels in three different school districts.

The times listed are for only those students who comprehended at 70 percent or higher. You may note that even at the same grade level the longer passages tend to take a shorter amount of time to read, in terms of words per minute, than the shorter passages. Studies of the reading speeds of children report a great deal of variation. In addition to passage length, other elements influencing reading speed include interest, prior knowledge, and distractions. The times given for the preprimer level apply to students in the first grade who read the passages during the month of November, and the times given for the first grade and all other grade levels apply to students who read the passages in late February, March, and early April of the school year.

Reliability of the Reading Passages

A preliminary study was conducted in which forty students were administered the A and B forms and C and D forms to determine the reliability of the two forms. Two examiners tested forty students from grades 1 through 9. Half of the students were given the A and B forms first and the other half were given the C and D forms first. All students were given the second set of forms (not previously taken) within a period of one week or less after the administration of the first forms. A product-moment coefficient was calculated between the A and C (oral) forms and found to be .82. The same calculations between the B and D (silent) forms produced a correlation coefficient of .79. One examiner administered forms A and B and forms C and D in grades 1 through 4, while the other examiner administered the same forms in grades 5 through 9. The correlation coefficients of .82 and .79 must, then, be considered as a measure of intrascorer reliability.

Other Tests

The Letter Knowledge Tests, the Basic Sight Words and Basic Sight Phrases Tests, the Phonics Tests, the Structural Analysis Tests, and the Reading Interests Survey–Elementary were added to the ESRI in the previous edition. Each of these tests was originally developed in the 1970s. They have been refined over more than twenty years and given to thousands of children and adults from diverse backgrounds in urban, rural, and suburban school settings. The Knowledge of Contractions Test, the El Paso Phonics Survey, and the Quick Word List Survey have been a part of the ESRI since its earliest editions.

The Phonemic Awareness Tests and the Concepts about Print Test are new. They were created for this edition of the ESRI using the most common forms of assessment for these abilities. Also new to this edition is the Reading Interests Survey–Adult. Finally, the Quick Check for Basic Sight Words, while new to the ESRI, was carefully developed and its accuracy verified over many years.

Implementation of the Ekwall/Shanker Reading Inventory

Before you can test your student, you will need to prepare materials, learn how to code oral reading errors, and be aware of the importance of testing the student in a proper setting.

Assembling Your Diagnostic Kit

This section provides instructions to help you construct a complete kit for diagnosing students' reading difficulties. Once you have prepared the necessary materials, you will find it much easier to conduct the diagnosis. This kit can also be used any time in the future.

All materials for administering the ESRI are contained in this spiral-bound manual, with the exception of the flash cards needed for testing basic sight words and phrases. In addition to the manual, which contains information on administering, scoring, and interpreting the various tests, you will use several additional materials as part of this inventory. The **Test Sheets** are the items you place in front of the student to test his or her reading abilities. The **Scoring Sheets** are the forms you write on to record the student's performance. In most cases, the Scoring Sheets also provide you with information to use while giving the tests. Three different **Summary** and **Analysis Forms** are provided to assist you in conducting the reading diagnosis. Finally, a **Chart** and a **Crib Sheet** help you give the Reading Passages Tests, which are the only tests in the entire inventory that are somewhat difficult to administer. If you are well prepared, you will find that all of these tests are logical and easy to administer, especially after you have given them a couple of times.

Duplicating the Scoring Sheets and Summary and Analysis Forms

Before you begin testing, you will need to duplicate the Scoring Sheets you will be marking while the student is reading and the Summary Sheet and Analysis Sheet you will be using to complete the diagnosis after the testing is finished. If you will be analyzing the student's phonics skills, you may also want to use the Prescriptive Analysis of Phonics Skills Chart. Duplicate one set of the following for each child you test:

1. The Scoring Sheet for the San Diego Quick Assessment or Graded Word List (GWL) (found on pp. 190–191).
2. One set of Scoring Sheets for the Oral and Silent Reading Passages (A and B passages are found on pp. 194–225, and C and D passages are found on pp. 228–261). These passages are also used for the Listening Comprehension Test.
3. The Scoring Sheets for the Emergent Literacy Tests (found on pp. 262–268). Copy these only if you anticipate that you will be testing a prereader.
4. The Scoring Sheets for the Quick Check for Basic Sight Words and the Basic Sight Words and Basic Sight Word Phrases Tests (found on pp. 269–275).
5. The Scoring Sheets for the Phonics and Structural Analysis Tests (found on pp. 276–282).
6. The Scoring Sheet for the Knowledge of Contractions Test (found on p. 283). (Note: This test is optional.)
7. The Scoring Sheets for the El Paso Phonics Survey (found on pp. 284–285). (Note: This test is also optional.)
8. The Scoring Sheet for the Reading Interest Survey (found on pp. 287–288). Copy either the elementary or adult version, depending on which is appropriate for the individual being tested.
9. The Test Summary Sheet (found on pp. 115–117).
10. Prescriptive Analysis of Phonics Skills Chart (found on pp. 123–126).
11. The Analysis Sheet (found on pp. 118–122).

These materials should then be collated and paper clipped together in the order listed above. Numbers 1 through 8 also reflect the recommended order of administration of the tests. (Remember, you will never give all of these tests to any one student.)

You may find it helpful to copy each of these items on different colored paper. It is also a good idea to use different colors for the oral (A or C) and the silent (B or D) reading passages and the three different basic sight word tests. By color-coding these Scoring Sheets and the Summary and Analysis Sheets, it will be easier to select the appropriate item while you are testing or evaluating your student.

You may also wish to detach and copy (for each student tested) the Reading Passages Tests Administration Chart (found on p. 114). This chart will help you keep a record of the student's progress through the various parts of the Reading Passages Tests (Oral Reading, Silent Reading, and Listening Comprehension).

Preparing the Test Materials

The following Test Sheets will be placed in front of the student:

1. The San Diego Quick Assessment or Graded Word List (GWL) Test Sheet (found on p. 128).
2. The Oral and Silent Reading Passages Test Sheets, either A and B or C and D (found on pp. 130–171). (In a pretest–posttest situation, usually Forms A and B are given for the pretest and Forms C and D are given for the posttest. As indicated earlier, these Test Sheets are also used for the Listening Comprehension Test.)
3. The Emergent Literacy Test Sheets (found on pp. 172–173).

4. The Quick Check for Basic Sight Words Test Sheet (found on p. 174). No Test Sheets are used for the administration of the Basic Sight Words and the Basic Sight Word Phrases Tests. Instead, flash cards are used, as will be described later.

5. The Phonics and Structural Analysis Test Sheets (found on pp. 175–182).

6. The Knowledge of Contractions Test Sheet (found on p. 183). (Optional)

7. The El Paso Phonics Survey Test Sheets (found on pp. 186–187). (Optional)

8. The Quick Word List Survey Test Sheet (found on p. 188). (Optional)

9. No Test Sheet is used for either form of the Reading Interests Survey. The student's responses are recorded on the Scoring Sheet.

Copy and laminate, if possible, the Crib Sheet (found on pp. 112–113). Place the Crib Sheet on top of the San Diego Quick Assessment or Graded Word List (GWL) Test Sheet; it provides a reminder of the instructions for administering Tests 1 and 2.

If you anticipate using these tests with many students in the future, you may want to detach and laminate or cover with clear contact paper some or all of the test sheets to protect them from wear. Although it may not be practical or necessary to laminate or cover all of the reading passages, it might be a good idea to protect the other test sheets. Also, if you separate these sheets now and order them correctly, you will not have to flip through the pages of the manual during testing.

You will also need to prepare flash cards for testing the 220 basic sight words and 143 basic sight word phrases. Specific instructions for doing this appear in this manual on page 43.

If you want to time the silent reading passages, you will need a stopwatch or a watch with a second hand or digital readout of seconds. (Timing is optional.)

Finally, you will need an audiotape recorder to record the entire testing process. The tape recorder will be helpful in verifying your transcriptions of the student's oral reading and other records you make of the testing. It will be essential for your evaluation of the student's performance on the basic sight words and phrases tests.

Coding Students' Oral Reading Errors

You will be transcribing the student's oral reading errors while the student is reading orally on the following tests: Test 2a, the Oral Reading Test; Test 5a, Application of Phonics Skills in Context; and Test 6a, Application of Structural Analysis Skills in Context. To do this, you need to learn the code for marking in oral diagnosis. This code is shown on page 24. If you already know a similar code, it will not be necessary to learn this one; however, you should learn to code the types of errors counted in scoring the ESRI. You should also learn to code self-corrected errors, disregard for punctuation, and pauses, even though these are not counted as word recognition errors in the final computation of the student's reading level. Even novice examiners find that the coding system can be learned quickly with a little practice. It is best to practice with students with reading difficulties, but if they are not readily available, you can improve your coding skills by transcribing the reading of skilled readers who make purposeful errors. Remember that when you administer the ESRI in an actual testing situation, you will be tape-recording the session. This recording will allow you to go back over the oral reading portions later to verify the accuracy of your transcriptions.

Creating an Appropriate Setting for Testing the Student

It is important to test in a setting that allows the student to demonstrate his or her best reading ability. Find a place where the student can read to you without being heard and without bothering the rest of the class. Other students should not be able to hear the questions being asked of the student who is taking the inventory. Likewise, the student taking the tests should not be distracted by noise or activity near the testing area.

The time of day the testing takes place is also important. Do not ask the student to miss recess or some other enjoyable activity in which other students are participating. You want the student to perform at his or her best. Sometimes this can be done before school, during the lunch period, after school, or during a subject-matter activity that the student can make up at another time. Sometimes examiners test students on weekends or vacation days with parental permission.

Make every effort to make the student comfortable during the session. Reassure the student that the results of the inventory will have no detrimental effect. If it is true, you should inform your student that the results will be seen only by you or your course instructor, not by the student's parents. If you are the student's teacher, inform the student that you will be using the results to provide more helpful instruction in the future. If you are evaluating the student for a course assignment or to learn how to administer the inventory, by all means tell the student this. This makes the student feel, appropriately, that *you* are the person on the spot. The student will be glad to assist you in your learning. It may seem like a small point, but it is a good idea to avoid using the words *test* or *testing*. You might instead refer to the instruments as *assessments, inventories, evaluation materials,* or *reading activities.*

Be relaxed and informal. Smile a lot and be friendly. Take your time. If this is your initial administration of the inventory, you may need time between tests to review procedures and keep your notes in order. Most examiners find it helpful to bring a fun book or art or puzzle activity with them to keep the student occupied during pauses in the testing. Certainly you should allow your student to take brief breaks if the testing is taking a long time or the student appears to tire. For some students, the administration of the inventory will take more than an hour. The tests may be given at more than one sitting over a period of days, if you prefer.

Do tell the student that you will be taking notes and tape-recording the session. Do this in a matter-of-fact manner. Again, reassure the student you are doing this to assure that the tests are given properly and to keep accurate records of the student's responses. Most examiners find it most comfortable to use a rectangular table and to place the student kitty-corner to the examiner at the opposite side of the examiner's handedness. For example, if you are right-handed, you should sit at the long side of the table and have the student sit at the short side to your left. This way, when you score the tests and make other notes, you can do this to your right, which will be as far away as possible from the student's eyes. Most students do try to see what you are writing, so you will also unobtrusively need to keep your writing covered.

Finally, inform the student that these activities are designed so that some of the tasks will be easy and some will be quite difficult. Tell the student that no one ever gets everything right and that the student should try to do his or her best even on the hard parts. You know that he or she will miss some items and that is just fine. You should not, however, tell the student the correct answer when he or she misses an item (with the exception of the oral reading passages, when you must pronounce a word for the student if he or she is unable to decode the word after about five seconds). If a student misses an item and is concerned about it, simply offer a neutral response, such as: "You're doing fine," or "That was a hard one, wasn't it?" or "Let's try the next one." It is appropriate to offer enthusiastic praise for the student's effort, such as "Good for you!" "I can see you're trying hard," or "I like working with you."

Many examiners are surprised to discover how much their students enjoy participating in the administration of the ESRI. Most students crave individual attention from adults, and you will have many opportunities to make the student feel good about the experience.

ADMINISTERING THE EKWALL/SHANKER READING INVENTORY

Each of the thirty-eight tests in ten different areas in the ESRI are described in the order you will be likely to follow in giving them. You will learn the purposes of each test, read a brief description of the test, and learn what steps to take in preparation before you give it, the detailed procedures for administration, and the procedures for scoring each test.

Again, the tests that compose the ESRI are:

1. **San Diego Quick Assessment or Graded Word List (GWL)**
2. **Reading Passages Tests**
   2a. Oral Reading
   2b. Silent Reading
   2c. Listening Comprehension
3. **Emergent Literacy Tests**
   3a. Phonemic Awareness
      3a1. Rhyme Production
      3a2. Rhyme Recognition [Alternate Test]
      3a3. Initial Sound Recognition
      3a4. Phoneme Blending
      3a5. Phoneme Segmentation
   3b. Concepts about Print
   3c. Letter Knowledge
      3c1. Auditory Stimulus
      3c2. Visual Stimulus
4. **Basic Sight Vocabulary Tests**
   4a. Quick Check for Basic Sight Words
   4b. Basic Sight Words
   4c. Basic Sight Word Phrases
5. **Phonics Tests**
   5a. Application of Phonics Skills in Context
   5b. Initial Consonants
   5c. Initial Blends and Digraphs
   5d. Ending Sounds
   5e. Vowels
   5f. Phonograms
   5g. Blending
   5h. Substitution
   5i. Vowel Pronunciation

6. **Structural Analysis Tests**
   6a. Application of Structural Analysis Skills in Context
      6a1. Lower Level
      6a2. Higher Level
   6b. Hearing Word Parts
   6c. Inflectional Endings
   6d. Prefixes
   6e. Suffixes
   6f. Compound Words
   6g. Affixes
   6h. Syllabication
7. **Knowledge of Contractions Test**
8. **El Paso Phonics Survey**
9. **Quick Word List Survey**
10. **Reading Interests Survey**
    10a. Elementary
    10b. Adult

The ESRI evaluates students' reading abilities in ten different areas. Many of these areas are composed of a number of different tests. The Reading Passages Tests consist of three tests given together. The Emergent Literacy Tests consist of four tests for Phonemic Awareness, a test for Concepts about Print, and two tests for Letter Knowledge. Three different tests are provided for Basic Sight Vocabulary. The Phonics Tests and the Structural Analysis Tests each contain nine separate tests. Finally, two forms are provided for the Reading Interest Survey.

In no case will you give all sections of all tests to one student. The procedures will clarify when to give a certain test, when to stop administering each test, and when to skip part of a test or an entire test. Tests 7, 8, and 9 are optional for all students. The Reading Passages Tests (Test 2) are the most difficult to administer. After the description of these tests, you will find a step-by-step reminder guide or crib sheet that summarizes the critical administration and scoring procedures for them. You may wish to keep this crib sheet handy when you actually administer Tests 2a, 2b, and 2c. A flow chart is then presented that you can use to track your progress as you administer them. The procedures for administering and scoring the remainder of the tests should be easy to understand and implement.

After all the procedures for administering and scoring the various tests are presented, the next section of the manual explains the interpretation of the test data. You will learn the specific steps to follow for translating your test information into a comprehensive diagnosis of the student's reading strengths and weaknesses. This information can then be used to plan an effective program of remediation for the student.

Test 1: San Diego Quick Assessment or Graded Word List (GWL)

(Test Sheet found on p. 128; Scoring Sheets found on pp. 190–191.)

Purposes

1. To obtain a quick estimate of the student's independent, instructional, and frustration reading levels.

2. To obtain information to determine a starting level for the oral reading passages.

3. To obtain information for an initial diagnosis of basic sight vocabulary, phonics, and structural analysis skills.

Description

This test requires the student to pronounce increasingly difficult words that are listed by the grade levels when they are learned by most students. This test takes approximately five to ten minutes to administer.

The reading levels on the Test Sheet (from which the student reads) for the various lists are designated as follows:

PP	= Preprimer	□	= Fourth grade
P	= Primer	□ I	= Fifth grade
I	= First grade	□ L	= Sixth grade
L	= Second grade	□ U	= Seventh grade
U	= Third grade	□ □	= Eighth grade
		□ □ I	= Ninth grade

You will also note that twenty-nine of the words on the Scoring Sheet of this test are italicized. That is because these words are Dolch basic sight words. Dolch words are the words that appear most often in materials written in English.

Preparation

1. Have your Scoring Sheets copied (from pp. 190–191). You will need one set of the two pages for each child you test. The two pages need not be on separate sheets but may be copied back to back if you wish.

2. Open the manual to the Test Sheet (found on p. 128).

3. Have a pencil ready to take transcriptions on the Scoring Sheet as the student reads from the Test Sheet.

Administration

1. Place the Test Sheet in front of the student and say, "Here are some words I would like you to read aloud. Try to read all of them even if you are not sure what some of the words are. Let's begin by reading the words on this list" (pointing to the list on which the student is to start).

2. The best place to have most students begin reading is at the preprimer list. For the student who is able to read these words with ease, this starting point allows some early success that may build the student's confidence. Because the lists are not long, little time will be wasted having the student read words that may be too easy. If you feel certain that the student can read, say, above third-grade level, then you may begin with a higher list. If the student misses two or more words on the first list you present, drop down to a lower list until the student makes no more than one error on that list. Then credit the student with all words on the list(s) below the list that is read with zero or one error.

3. Record words pronounced correctly with a plus (+) on your answer sheet and write down all incorrect responses. You may wish to use diacritical marks on your answer sheet. For example, *thank* might be read as *think* or *quietly* might be read as *quit'ly.*

4. If it is obvious that a student can read all the words quite rapidly, you may not want to put a plus (+) mark next to each word. Instead, wait until the student has completed that list and then place a plus mark next to the first word and draw a vertical line quickly through the rest of the blanks to indicate that all words were read correctly. See the following example:

PP   +

see _____

play _____

me _____

at _____

run _____

go _____

and _____

look _____

can _____

here _____

5. Have the student continue reading consecutively higher-level lists until the student misses three or more words on any one list.

6. After the student misses three or more words on any list, stop the testing, collect the Test Sheet, and complete the Results of Graded Word List (GWL) section on the Scoring Sheet.

Scoring

At the bottom of the Scoring Sheet is the Results of Graded Word List chart you may use for writing in the student's independent, instructional, and frustration reading levels. Fill in the following information:

1. The highest-level list at which the student misses zero or one words is the independent reading level.

2. The highest list at which the student misses two words is the instructional reading level.

3. The highest list at which the student misses three or more words is the frustration reading level.

If the student scores at the independent, instructional, or frustration level at more than one level, assign the score to the highest level. For example, if a student scores as follows:

List	*Number of Errors*
PP	0
P	1
1	2
2	2
3	5

you should report the results as follows:

> Independent Level = P
> Instructional Level = 2
> Frustration Level =   3

Occasionally, a student's performance will not translate logically into the three levels indicated. It is impossible to designate a specific instructional level for a student who does not miss exactly two words on any one list. For example, a student may miss one word on list PP and three words on list P. In this case, simply mark the space for instructional reading level as ND for Not Determined.

Sometimes a student's error pattern is even more confusing. For example, the number of errors per list may be as follows:

List	*Number of Errors*
PP	0
P	2
1	1
2	4

In this case, the student appears to have independent levels at both PP and 1, an instructional level at P, and a frustration level at 2. In situations such as this, you will have to use your own judgment. It is recommended that you simply ignore the result from the primer level and reasonably conclude that the student performed as follows:

> Independent Level = 1
> Instructional Level = ND (for Not Determined)
> Frustration Level =   2

Test 2: Reading Passages

Tests 2a and 2b: Oral Reading Test and Silent Reading Test

(Test Sheets found on pp. 130–149; Scoring Sheets found on pp. 194–225.)

Purposes

1. To obtain an accurate assessment of the student's independent, instructional, and frustration reading levels in both oral and silent reading.
2. To obtain, through observation and analysis of the student's performance, specific information that you will use to diagnose the student's reading ability in the following areas: letter knowledge, basic sight vocabulary, phonics, structural analysis, context clues, fluency skills, vocabulary, and comprehension.

Description

These tests require the student to read, both orally and silently, passages that are written according to graded levels of difficulty. *Tests 2a and 2b are administered together.*

The oral and silent reading passages can usually be administered to a student in from ten to thirty minutes. The time it takes to administer the reading passages will depend in part on the examiner's ability to administer the test efficiently. Invariably, examiners find they need a bit longer to administer the passages the first few times. Once they are comfortable with the materials and procedures, the administration of the passages is both quicker and smoother. The administration time will also depend on the reading ability of the student, since some students are very slow readers and will require more time to read as well as to answer the questions about each passage. Usually, however, unskilled readers are able to read only a few of the shorter passages, while more able readers read considerably more and longer passages.

The reading levels of the passages are designated on both the Test Sheets and the Scoring Sheets using the same markings as those described for the San Diego Quick Assessment or Graded Word List (GWL).

Preparation

1. Have the Scoring Sheets for either the A and B or the C and D passages copied (from pp. 194–225). You will need a set of these passages for each child you test.

2. Open the manual to the appropriate Test Sheets (found on pp. 130–149).

3. Be sure you have practiced the procedure for coding (or transcribing) oral reading errors.

4. Have a pencil ready to take transcriptions on the Scoring Sheet as the student reads from the Test Sheet. *Be sure the audiotape recorder is on.*

5. If you want to determine the time it takes the student to read the silent reading passages, have a stopwatch or a watch with a second hand or digital readout of seconds.

Administration

1. Select the first passage for the student to read orally. Have the student read the A or C passage one level below the student's independent reading level as determined by the GWL. If you are in doubt, it is better to start lower (on an easier passage) than higher for two reasons: (1) the student is more likely to experience initial success, which will bolster his or her confidence, and (2) it is easier to administer the passages when you can give progressively more difficult passages, rather than having to go back to easier passages.

2. Begin by saying to the student, "I have some passages for you to read. Read the first one out loud. If you find a hard word, try to read it as best you can and continue reading. It is important to remember what you read so you can answer some questions about the passage when you are through."

3. Place the manual (opened to the proper page) in front of the student and say, "Ready, begin."

4. While the student reads out loud, code the errors or miscues on the Scoring Sheet for the same passage. Do not give any further help to the student, such as saying, "Try to sound that word out." However, if a student hesitates on a word, wait five seconds and then simply tell the word to the student.

5. When the student has completed reading the passage, take the manual back and place it where the student will not be able to look at the passage again for assistance when you ask the comprehension questions.

6. Ask the student the comprehension questions as shown on the Scoring Sheet for the passage. Mark correct answers with a plus (+) and incorrect answers with a minus (-). (If you wish, you may write down the student's incorrect answers.) You may repeat the questions if necessary, or if an answer seems incomplete you may question further by saying, "Tell me more," or "Can you tell me a little more about that?" However, do not rephrase the question to make it easier. For example, if a question was, "What color was the pony?" do not ask, "Was it brown and white?"

7. After completing the questions, score the oral reading and the comprehension questions and determine whether this passage is at the student's independent, instructional, or frustration reading level. (Instructions for scoring the passages are presented in the next section of this manual.)

NOTE: At this point, you will have the student make the transition from oral to silent reading.

8. After scoring the first oral reading passage, say, "Here is another passage. Read this one to yourself and try to remember what you read so that you can answer some questions about it. Tell me when you finish."

9. Hand the student the manual opened to the appropriate B passage corresponding to the A passage that the student has just finished reading (or the D passage if the student has just read the corresponding C passage). For example, if the student began with the 1A passage orally, then you would give the student the 1B passage next, regardless of how well the student read the 1A passage. If the student begins to read the second passage out loud, provide a gentle reminder to read this passage silently.

10. If you wish to determine the *rate of reading,*[6] the time it takes the student to read the silent reading passage, you should have a stopwatch or a watch with a second hand or digital readout of seconds. When the student begins reading, start the stopwatch or note the time in seconds. When the student has finished the passage, again note the time in seconds, determine how long it took the student to read the passage, and write that time on the Scoring Sheet where you see *Time:* _____ beside the small table that shows time factors.

11. When the student has finished reading the passage silently, take back the manual and ask the questions based on that passage. Mark the answers with a + or -.

12. Determine whether the passage is at the student's independent, instructional, or frustration level.

13. After giving the first oral and silent reading passages, you will need to determine whether the student has been able to read them at the independent level. If both the oral and silent passages were at the student's independent reading level, you would continue giving the *next higher* oral passage, followed by the corresponding silent passage, and so on, until the student's frustration level is reached. In many cases, a student will reach frustration level on either oral or silent reading but not on both. In these instances, continue giving *only* the (either oral or silent) passages until the student reaches frustration level on *both* oral and silent reading. For example, a student might reach frustration at fifth-grade level on oral reading because of difficulty with decoding skills. However, this student may be successful reading silently at higher levels because of good comprehension. In this case, continue giving silent reading passages only until the student reaches frustration level in silent reading.

14. If, after giving the first oral and silent reading passages, the student is not reading at the independent level on either of the two or both, give the next *easier*

oral and/or silent passages until both oral and silent independent reading levels have been established. Then continue upward, alternating oral and silent reading passages, until both oral and silent frustration levels are reached.

Scoring Oral and Silent Reading Passages

In scoring the oral reading passages in the ESRI or in any informal reading inventory, two main factors are used in determining a student's reading level. These two factors are *word recognition* (or *decoding* ability) and *comprehension*. (In scoring silent reading passages, only comprehension is taken into consideration.) To learn the code for marking word recognition (or decoding) errors in oral reading, see the box below.

CODE FOR MARKING IN ORAL DIAGNOSIS

▶ *Score each instance as* one *error. Errors below noted by underlining.*
Note: Never count more than one *error on any* one *word.*

Examples	Marking Oral Reading Errors
Kathy (had) always	1. Circle <u>omissions</u>.
Soon the ^big^ airplane	2. Mark all <u>insertions</u> with a caret (∧) and write in the inserted word.
Kathy ~~peered~~ peeked out of	3. Draw a line through words for which <u>substitutions</u> or <u>mispronunciations</u> were made and write the substitutions or mispronunciations above the words. (If the student reads too fast for you to write in all these errors, you can transcribe them later after listening to the tape recording of the reading.)
gave Kathy (something)	4. Use parentheses ( ) to enclose words that were <u>pronounced</u> by the examiner, when the student was unable to decode them within about five seconds.
Her mother helped her	5. Underline <u>repetitions</u> with a wavy line.

▶ *Do not score as errors*

✔ down the runway	1. Put a check mark (✔) over words that were <u>self-corrected</u>.
very small. The	2. Use an arched line (⌒) to connect words wherever there was a <u>disregard for punctuation</u>.
airplane‖was	3. Draw two vertical lines (‖) to indicate a <u>pause</u> before words.

Example of a Coded Reading Passage

Jan has a |brag| b̶r̶o̶w̶n̶ and white (kitten) The kitten w̶a̶s̶ saw (very) l̶i̶t̶t̶l̶e̶ big

when she got it. (Now) the kitten is big. It likes t̶o̶ the run and

play. It is ∧not named T̶a̶b̶. Tad

Here is what the examiner heard as the student read the passage above. The words in italics are the actual words the student read.

"Jan has a (pause) *brag and white* (after 5 seconds the examiner pro-nounced "kitten"). *The kitten saw big when she got it. The . . . now the kitten is big. It likes . . . It likes . . . the, to run and play it is not named Tad."*

The student made nine mistakes that are to be scored as errors: (1) *brag* sub-stituted for *brown;* (2) *kitten* pronounced by the examiner; (3) *saw* substituted for *was;* (4) *very* omitted; (5) *big* substituted for *little;* (6) *the* repeated once; (7) *It likes* repeated once; (8) *not* inserted; and (9) *Tad* substituted for *Tab.*

Neither *Now* nor *to* is counted as an error because both were self-corrected. Also, the pause after *a* and the period that was disregarded after *play* are not counted as errors.

Incidentally, this passage is clearly at the frustration level for this student!

Procedure for Scoring Oral Reading Passages

1. Count the total number of scorable errors as outlined in numbers 1 through 5 in the Code for Marking in Oral Diagnosis. Write the total number of errors in the space indicated on the Scoring Sheet for the passage. Note that omissions, insertions, substitutions or mispronunciations, words pronounced by the ex-aminer, and repetitions are all counted as errors at *each* occurrence. Words that are self-corrected, disregard for punctuation, and pauses of less than five sec-onds are not counted as errors.

2. In counting repetitions, use the following guidelines:

   a. Count all repetitions even though they may all be repetitions of the same word.[7]

   b. Consecutively repeated words are counted as *one* repetition. For example, if a student repeats four words in a row the repetitions are considered one error.

   c. If a word is repeated more than one time, it is still only counted as one er-ror. (Remember, you can never count more than one error on any one word.) See *has* in the sentence below:

   Jan has a brown and white kitten.

   Here is what the examiner heard as the student read the sentence above: *"Jan has, has, has, has, a brown and, and, and white, and white kitten."* Even though *has* was repeated three times, it is still scored as one error.

    d. If some words in a series are repeated more than other words, count one repetition for each different *length* of wavy line used to indicate repetitions. In the previous example, there are two repetitions scored as errors in the words *and white kitten.*

    e. A word is not counted as a repetition error unless it is repeated correctly in its entirety more than one time. For example, if a student said *cough* and corrected it and said *caught,* it would simply be a self-correction, which is *not* an error. Or, if a student did not finish a word and then began again and repeated the first part, it would not be counted as a repetition error.

3. If a student mispronounces a proper name, count it as only one error for the entire passage, even if the student mispronounces the same name more than once while reading the passage.

4. On the Scoring Sheet, a table follows the set of questions for each oral reading passage. Across the top of the table is a series of numbers that denote the number of word recognition (decoding) errors. In the column on the left-hand side of the table is a series of numbers that denote the number of questions missed. Locate the number of word recognition errors made by the student in that passage and draw a circle around the appropriate number. Then locate the number of questions missed and draw a circle around that number. Find the point where the two circled numbers intersect. In that space, you will note one of the following symbols: The (+) means the student is reading at an independent level; the (∗) means the student is reading at an instructional level; and the (×) means the student is reading at a frustration level.

    In the following table, for example, if the student had made seven word recognition errors and had missed two questions, you would first go across the top of the table and circle the space marked "6–8." Then circle the number "2" down the left side to account for the two questions that the student missed. These two figures intersect in an area marked with an asterisk (∗). This means that the student is reading at an instructional level.

Number of Questions Missed	Number of Word Recognition Errors						Reading Level		
	0–2	3–5	(6–8)	9–11	12–14	15+			
0	+	∗	∗	∗	∗	×	+	Independent	
1	+	∗	∗	∗	×	×	∗	Instructional	✔
(2)	∗	∗	(∗)	×	×	×	×	Frustration	
3	∗	∗	×	×	×	×			
4	∗	×	×	×	×	×			
5+	×	×	×	×	×	×			

Procedure for Scoring Silent Reading Passages

1. Determine the number of comprehension errors from the ten questions that were asked of the student (except for the preprimer passages, which have only five questions).

2. Below the questions under each silent reading passage you will see a table. Simply look to see which level the student is reading at depending on the number of questions missed. In the following example, the student missed three ques-

tions. This would place the student in the range indicated by 2–4 in the table. This corresponds to the instructional level; thus the box to the right of the instructional level is checked.

Number of Questions Missed	Reading Level	
0–1 = Independent	Independent	
2–4 = Instructional	Instructional	✔
5+ = Frustration	Frustration	

3. Some students will score artificially high on the silent reading passages if you do not take reading speed into account. Directly below each silent reading passage (Forms B and D) is a chart that reflects reading rate. You should ignore the scores of students who take considerably more time than that indicated in the "Slow" box. For example, the 4B paragraph (see p. 204) shows the "Slow" reading rate to be 66+ seconds. If a student takes more than about two minutes (120 seconds) to read this paragraph silently, you should stop the silent reading testing at that point. Consider this paragraph to have been read at the frustration level, even if the student answered enough questions correctly for this paragraph to have been read at the instructional or independent levels. Some students are able to gather enough information to answer questions about passages even though their struggles with decoding cause them to read very slowly. However, because of their very slow reading rate such students should not be judged as able to read material of this difficulty at instructional or independent levels. Obviously, these determinations require a judgment call on the part of the examiner. Further discussion of the importance of examiner judgment follows.

Procedure for Scoring Comprehension Questions

In scoring the comprehension questions on both the oral and silent reading passages, use the following guidelines:

1. The student need not give the exact answer shown on the Scoring Sheet as long as it is a reasonable answer that means the same thing as the written answer; for example, substituting *Dad* for *Father* is perfectly acceptable. If, however, the student gives an answer that is unclear or seems impossible to score, ask a neutral question such as, "Can you tell me a little more about that?" or simply say, "Tell me more." If the answer given then is obviously incorrect, it should be counted as wrong.

2. In some cases, the student must give two answers to a question to receive full credit. For example, the student may be asked what kinds of animals were on the farm. If the answer calls for at least two kinds to be named and the student responds with only one, then you should ask, "Can you tell me more?" If the student cannot tell more but has given one of the two that were asked for, then give one-half credit for the answer. After the student completes the questions about a passage, there may be two questions for which one-half credit was given. In this case, you would of course give the student credit for one complete question. If there is only one question for which one-half credit was given, the student should not be given credit for the question, because giving credit would possibly place the student at a higher level than actual ability warrants.

Examiner Judgment in Scoring Oral and Silent Reading Passages

According to the scoring criteria for the independent, instructional, and frustration levels shown on pages 8–9, the instructional level is determined as follows:

	Word Recognition	*Comprehension*
Instructional Level	95% or more	60% or more

The frustration level is determined using the following criteria:

	Word Recognition	*Comprehension*
Frustration Level	90% or less	50% or less

In examining these percentages, you might logically ask what happens if a student's word recognition level falls between 91 and 94 percent? Or, what happens when the comprehension level falls between 51 and 59 percent? These percentages have not been taken into consideration, because the criteria for the instructional level are word recognition of 95 percent *or more* and comprehension of 60 percent *or more,* whereas the criteria for the frustration level are word recognition of 90 percent *or less* and comprehension of 50 percent *or less.*

These levels were designed this way to give the examiner the opportunity to make a judgment as to whether the student should be placed at the higher of the two levels (instructional) or the lower of the two levels (frustration), based on the student's performance during the testing. For example, a student might score at the 94 percent level on word recognition, which is near the minimum of 95 percent or more for the instructional level. This same student may then score at the 100 percent level on comprehension. If this were the case, the teacher would probably want to look at the types of errors the student made in word recognition. If the majority of the student's word recognition errors were less serious ones, such as repetitions, then the student would probably be given the benefit of the doubt and placed at the higher (instructional) level. On the other hand, if a student scored at the 91 percent level on word recognition and was near the minimum in comprehension for the instructional level (60 percent), the teacher would probably choose to place the student at the lower (frustration) level.

On the Scoring Sheet for each oral reading passage, you will find a table showing the recommended level when both the student's oral reading errors and comprehension are taken into consideration.

Number of Questions Missed	*Number of Word Recognition Errors*							*Reading Level*	
	0–2	3–5	6–8	9–11	12–14	15+			
0	+	⊛	*	*	⊛	⊗	+	Independent	
1	+	⊛	*	⊛	⊗	×	*	Instructional	✔
2	⊛	*	⊛	⊗	×	×	×	Frustration	
3	*	⊛	⊗	×	×	×			
4	⊛	⊗	×	×	×	×			
5+	×	×	×	×	×	×			

This table makes it easy to determine the student's reading level regardless of where the two scores fall with respect to percentages, because the calculations have already been done for you. However, when a student's score falls in an area just bordering another area, such as between the independent and instructional levels or between the instructional and frustration levels, as indicated by the circled asterisks and the circled x's, respectively, then you may want to exercise more judgment in deciding exactly which level would be appropriate for the student. For example, for some students awareness of an error and an effort to go back and correct it can cause them to make repetition errors in the process. The research referred to earlier indicated that repetitions should be counted as errors when the percentages commonly given for scoring informal reading inventories are used. If they are not, the student may physiologically reach the frustration level even though there would not be a high enough percentage of errors to place the student at that level if repetitions were not counted as errors. In using the ESRI, however, the experienced examiner may use some judgment in the scoring procedure. If a student makes one or two repetition errors in a relatively short passage and comprehends it nearly perfectly, for example, this student would probably be placed at the instructional level, not at the independent level. In such a case, you may want to give the student the benefit of the doubt and consider the performance to be at the independent level. Similarly, making a meaningful substitution is not as serious as making a nonmeaningful one. If a single error such as this causes the student to drop from independent to instructional level or from instructional to frustration level, the examiner may want to disregard the error. However, the examiner should keep in mind that this type of judgment should not be overexercised, or the student will ultimately be placed at too difficult a reading level.

A certain amount of teacher judgment should also be used in counting errors that are obviously a result of dialect or syntax. For example, in certain families or in certain parts of the country it may be common for a student to say, as in passage 3A, "Kathy had always wanted to go for a ride *in* an airplane," rather than "Kathy had always wanted to go for a ride *on* an airplane." If the student obviously knows all of the basic sight words and does not continuously make other substitutions that change the meaning of the passage, then you may want to ignore such minor errors.

In recording the student's reading rate on the silent reading passages, remember that a student classified in the *average* category but at the fast end of the *average* rate reads considerably faster than the average student. For this reason, you should keep in mind that the student, in reality, reads at a *high average* rate. The same is of course true for a student who reads on the low end of the average category; that is, the student should, in reality, be considered as reading at a *low average* rate.

One additional problem may require the examiner to exercise judgment in evaluating or reporting the test scores. As noted earlier when discussing the San Diego Quick Assessment, a student's performance may result in confusing levels. These difficulties may occur with the oral or silent reading passages. Occasionally, for example, a student will perform better on a more difficult passage. Such a student might read at the *instructional* level on a third-grade passage and at the *independent* level on a fourth-grade passage. This might occur if the student happened to be especially interested in or knowledgeable about the topic presented in the fourth-grade passage, or if the student happened to become distracted or for some other reason performed below his or her ability on the third-grade passage. When this occurs, you will have to exercise your judgment in determining and reporting the student's performance levels.

If you do not plan to use the C and D passages later with this student, you could administer them to resolve the confusion. However, this is not always necessary. It is important to remember that the results of these tests are merely the best measure of the student's reading ability under the conditions that existed at the time of the testing. These results are not carved in stone. Examiners frequently become overly concerned about identifying the various reading levels precisely. The results of this testing may be used to assist the teacher, tutor, or reading specialist in pairing the student with reading materials of appropriate difficulty and in observing and analyzing the reading behavior to arrive at a diagnosis that is used to plan effective instruction. A paradox does exist here: On the one hand, the examiner wants to be scrupulously accurate in administering and scoring the tests in the inventory; on the other hand, the examiner must be careful about assigning too much significance to the data that are gathered. Ultimately, it may matter little whether the student reads fourth-grade material at an independent or an instructional level. Of far greater importance is the guidance and the direction the student is given in selecting the material to be read and the instruction the student receives to remediate the reading difficulty.

Test 2c: Listening Comprehension

(Uses the same set of passages as oral and silent reading tests.)

Purposes

1. To determine the level at which a student can understand material when it is read to the student by the examiner. This level suggests the student's *capacity* for reading. In other words, if a student's listening comprehension level is, say, fifth grade, this would suggest that the student has the capacity or potential to understand fifth-grade reading material once the student has been taught to decode and comprehend at this level.
2. To obtain an estimate of the student's vocabulary knowledge, which is an important prerequisite for listening comprehension.

Description

This test requires the student to listen and then answer comprehension questions about graded passages that are read out loud by the examiner. The listening comprehension test can usually be administered to a student in five to ten minutes.

Preparation

1. Use the passages on the examiner's Test Sheets to read to the student.
2. Have a pencil ready to mark the Scoring Sheet and indicate the student's listening comprehension level.

Administration

1. After the student's frustration level has been reached on both oral and silent reading, select the first available A or B passage *at* or *just above* the student's *highest frustration* level on oral or silent reading. For example, if the student scored frustration level on the 5A (oral) passage and the 6B (silent) passage, select the 6A passage. (This is the next available passage *at* the student's highest

frustration level. See the following example of student #1.) If, however, the student scored frustration level on the 4A (oral) passage and the 4B (silent) passage, then select the 5A passage to begin this test. (No passage is available *at* the highest frustration level, so you must select the first available passage *just above* the highest frustration level. See the following example of student #2.) If you tested for oral and silent reading using the C and D passages, you would also use the C and D passages for the listening comprehension test.

2. Say to the student, "I am going to read a story to you. I want you to listen very carefully and be ready to answer some questions when I have finished reading. Okay?"

3. Read the passage to the student and ask the questions concerning that passage. Mark the answers on the Scoring Sheet and check the space near the bottom of the sheet that indicates this passage was used for the Listening Comprehension Test.

4. If the student gets 70 percent or more of the questions correct, check the space marked "Passed" on the bottom of the Scoring Sheet and then continue in order with more difficult passages until the student is unable to comprehend at least 70 percent of the questions.

5. It is not necessary to test above the student's grade *placement* level. If the student is a disabled reader, then he or she certainly reads below grade level. If this same student's listening comprehension level is at or above his or her grade placement level, this test result suggests the student has the capacity to read at least at grade level with proper instruction. This test can be time consuming to administer if the examiner must read many passages. If your objective is to determine if the student appears to have the capacity to read above the level at which he or she is currently performing, it is unnecessary to test at levels above the student's grade placement. Also, do not test at levels at or below the student's highest instructional level. The student must have adequate comprehension on a passage to score at the instructional level when actually reading.

6. If the student fails the first passage you read, check the space marked "Failed" and then estimate the student's listening comprehension level. Three examples are listed in the following chart:

	Student #1	Student #2	Student #3
Oral Reading Frustration Level	5A	4A	4A
Silent Reading Frustration Level	6B	4B	7B
First Listening Comprehension Passage	6A	5	7A
Result	Fail	Fail	Fail
Estimated Listening Comprehension Level	5	3 or 4	6

All three of these students failed to answer 70 percent of the questions correctly on the first passage that was read to them by the examiner. Student #1 has an estimated listening comprehension level of grade 5 because she read at the *instructional* level on the fifth-grade silent reading passage. Student #2 has an estimated listening comprehension level of grade 3 or 4 because he read at the *instructional* level on the third-grade oral and silent reading passages. He could not be tested for listening comprehension at the fourth-grade level because both the A and B paragraphs were used during oral and silent reading. Student #3 has an estimated listening comprehension level of grade 6 because she read at the *instructional* level on the sixth-grade silent reading passage.

Below are three examples of students who *passed* the first passage administered to find the listening comprehension level:

	Student #1	Student #2	Student #3
Student's Grade Placement	8	6	7
Oral Reading Frustration Level	5A	4A	3A
Silent Reading Frustration Level	6B	4B	5B
First Listening Comprehension Passage	6A	5A	5A
Result	Pass	Pass	Pass
Second Listening Comprehension Level	7A	6A	6A
Result	Pass	Pass	Fail
Third Listening Comprehension Passage	8A	N/A	N/A
Result	Pass	N/A	N/A
Listening Comprehension Level	8	6	5

Student #1 is an eighth grader who passed the initial (6A) passage. He was then given the 7A passage, which he also passed, then the 8A passage, which he also passed. His listening comprehension level is 8.

Student #2 is a sixth grader who passed the initial (5A) passage. She was then given the 6A passage, which she also passed. At this point, testing was stopped because this student had passed the test at her grade placement level. Her listening comprehension level is 6.

Student #3 is a seventh grader who passed the initial (5A) passage. He was then given the 6A passage, which he failed. At this point, testing was stopped because the student had failed the 6A passage. His listening comprehension level is 5.

The Crib Sheet

The numbers on the instructions that appear on the crib sheet match the numbers on the detailed directions provided earlier in this manual. You may want to detach these pages (also provided on pp. 112–113) and keep them in front of you when you administer the first two tests in the ESRI. The instructions for the remaining tests are considerably easier to master. Once you have learned the procedures for the Basic Sight Vocabulary Tests, you are not likely to forget them. The instructions for the Emergent Literacy Tests, the Phonics Tests, and the Structural Analysis Tests are summarized on their respective Scoring Sheets. Tests 7, 8, and 9 are optional and should be administered to students only if you need the additional information they provide. The instructions for the El Paso Phonics Survey are somewhat more complicated. The other optional tests, however, are quite easy to administer and score. Nonetheless, you may want to wait until you have some experience in giving the tests from the first six areas before giving Tests 7, 8, and 9. Test 10, the Reading Interests Survey, is simple to administer.

You may also use the crib sheet to check your knowledge of the instructions for the first two tests. If you know what to do by reading these steps without having to look back at the detailed instructions, that is a sign you understand the procedures well.

CRIB SHEET INSTRUCTIONS

▶ **Turn on the tape recorder and leave it on for the entire testing session. Turn it off only to change tapes if necessary.**

TEST 1: SAN DIEGO QUICK ASSESSMENT OR GRADED WORD LIST (GWL)

[Test Sheet found on p. 128; Scoring Sheet found on pp. 190–191.]

1. Place the Test Sheet in front of the student and say, "Here are some words I would like you to read out loud. Try to read all of them even if you are not sure what some of the words are. Let's begin by reading the words on this list" (pointing to list PP).

2. Begin at list PP. Mark (+) for correct responses; transcribe incorrect responses.

3. Highest list that student reads with zero or one error is independent level.

4. Have student read harder lists until student makes three or more errors on any one list.

5. After student misses three or more words, stop, collect Test Sheet, and indicate three levels on Scoring Sheet.

6. To establish levels: 0–1 error = independent; 2 errors = instructional; 3 or more errors = frustration.

▶ **Mark the part of the Summary Sheet indicating the student's scores on the GWL.**

TEST 2: READING PASSAGES TESTS

Tests 2a and 2b: Oral and Silent Reading Tests

[Test Sheets found on pp. 130–149; Scoring Sheets found on pp. 194–225.]

1. Start at A or C passage below student's independent level (from GWL).

2. Say to the student, "I have some passages for you to read. Read the first one out loud. If you find a hard word, try to read it as best you can and continue reading. It is important to remember what you read so that you can answer some questions about the passage when you are through."

3. Hand manual to student and say, "Ready, begin."

4. Code student's errors on Scoring Sheet. Say unknown words for student after five-second pause.

5. Take back manual.

6. Ask comprehension questions. Score with + or –.

7. Score oral paragraph (mark chart).

8. Give corresponding silent paragraph and say, "Here is another passage. Read this one to yourself and try to remember what you read so that you can answer some questions about it. Tell me when you finish."

9. Hand manual to student.

10. Optional. Time student's silent reading. Write time on Scoring Sheet.

11. Take back manual. Ask questions. Mark + or –.

12. Determine if passage is at independent, instructional, or frustration level.

▶

13. Go to next *higher* passages if both at independent level until frustration level is reached on both.

14. Go to *lower* passages on oral and/or silent reading until independent level is reached and then go back up, alternating oral and silent until frustration level is reached on both.

15. Use tables on Scoring Sheets; mark independent, instructional, or frustration levels for each passage read.

Test 2c: Listening Comprehension

(Uses the same set of passages as oral and silent reading tests.)

1. Go to first available passage *at* or *just above* frustration level on oral or silent reading.

2. Tell student you will read passage and he or she will answer questions about it when you are finished.

3. Read the passage, then ask questions and mark Scoring Sheet.

4. If student gets 70 percent or higher, go to next higher passage until grade *placement* level is reached.

5. Do not test above the student's grade-placement level.

6. If the student fails the first passage, estimate the listening comprehension level.

▶ **Mark the chart to indicate and check the student's progress through the various passages.**

▶ **Mark the part of the Test Summary Sheet indicating the student's scores on oral and silent reading and listening comprehension.**

▶ **Go on to administer the remaining tests in the battery as needed.**

Chart for Administering the Reading Passages Tests: Tests 2a, 2b, and 2c

(The actual chart appears on page 114.)

The chart is designed to help you keep a record of the student's progress through the various parts of Tests 2a, 2b, and 2c. By marking this chart as you administer the passages to determine the student's oral, silent, and listening comprehension levels, you can guide your progress and be sure you have given the passages in the correct order. When you have become more adept at administering the inventory, the chart can be completed *after* the first three tests are administered and serve as a check of your progress.

Begin by completing the information at the top of the chart. The sample chart on page 36 was completed for a student named Rashonda. The information at the top of the page indicates that Rashonda is a sixth grader whose independent reading level as determined by the San Diego Quick Assessment or Graded Word List (GWL) is at third-grade level. (This was the list on which Rashonda missed zero or one word.) The instructions tell the examiner to have Rashonda begin reading the oral passage at least one year below this level, so the first passage Rashonda read orally was the 2A passage. This is indicated on the sample chart by circling this area. Rashonda scored at instructional level on the 2A passage, so the examiner wrote "instr" inside the circle and proceeded to administer the 2B passage (silently) per instructions. The order of all subsequent passages given for oral and silent reading, and then for listening comprehension, is indicated by the arrows on the chart. Rashonda's performance on each passage is shown by the abbreviated words written on the chart. The chart thus shows that Rashonda performed as follows on the various passages:

Order Given	Passage	Score
1	2A	Instructional
2	2B	Independent
3	1A	Instructional
4	PPA	Independent
5	3A	Frustration
6	3B	Instructional
7	4B	Frustration
8	4A	Listening Comp.—Pass
9	5A	Listening Comp.—Pass
10	6A	Listening Comp.—Fail

The summary section at the bottom of the chart shows the results of testing. This information can be transferred to the ESRI Test Summary Sheet at the conclusion of the testing session.

Tests 3 through 6: Which Should You Administer?

It is not necessary to give all of the decoding tests to any student. Depending on the degree of the student's reading difficulty and the experience of the examiner, administration of the decoding tests will take anywhere from ten to forty minutes.

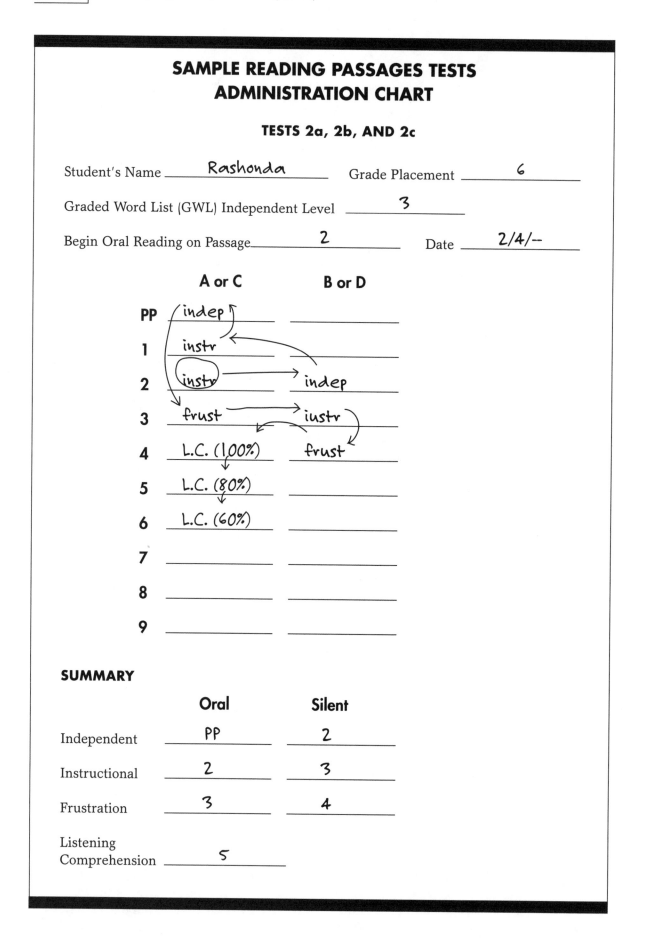

SAMPLE READING PASSAGES TESTS
ADMINISTRATION CHART

TESTS 2a, 2b, AND 2c

Student's Name _____Rashonda_____   Grade Placement _____6_____

Graded Word List (GWL) Independent Level _____3_____

Begin Oral Reading on Passage _____2_____   Date _____2/4/--_____

	A or C	B or D
PP	indep	
1	instr	
2	instr (circled)	indep
3	frust	instr
4	L.C. (100%)	frust
5	L.C. (80%)	
6	L.C. (60%)	
7		
8		
9		

SUMMARY

	Oral	Silent
Independent	PP	2
Instructional	2	3
Frustration	3	4
Listening Comprehension	5	

You must determine where to begin the testing of decoding skills and when to stop testing. Do this by comparing the student's independent level on the San Diego Quick Assessment or Graded Word List (GWL) with the following chart:

San Diego Independent Level GWL	Begin with Test	Continue (as Needed) with Tests	Skip This Test
Below Grade 1	3a	3b, 3c, 4b, 5	6
Grades 1 to 3	4b	4c, 5, and 6?	6?
Grades 4 to 6	4a	6	5?

Generally, with a student whose independent level is below 1.0 on the GWL, you should begin testing with the Emergent Literacy Tests (Tests 3a, 3b, and 3c). This student may be able to read a few of the basic sight words on Test 4b and will likely have only minimal success on Test 5 (phonics). This student will be totally unable to perform on Test 6 (structural analysis).

Generally, a student whose independent level is between 1.0 and 3.0 on the GWL can skip the Emergent Literacy Tests and begin with Test 4b, Basic Sight Words. Most likely this student will correctly pronounce some or all of the basic sight words. If the student's independent level on the GWL is at grade 1, the student is likely to know relatively few basic sight words. However, if the student's independent level on the GWL is at grade 3, the student is likely to know all or nearly all of the basic sight words. If the student correctly pronounces approximately half or more of the basic sight words, administer Test 4c, Basic Sight Word Phrases.

Next, give the student the first phonics test, Test 5a. As with the Basic Sight Words Test, this student's performance on the phonics tests is likely to reflect the achievement on the GWL. The student whose independent level on the GWL is at grade 1 surely will not master Test 5a and may become frustrated on or after the first few tests beginning with Test 5b. However, a student whose independent level on the GWL is grade 3 may well master Test 5a. If the student masters this test, skip the rest of the phonics tests and begin testing structural analysis, Test 6a1.

Do not administer Test 6a1 *unless* the student masters Test 5a. It is unlikely that a student in this category (having an independent level on the GWL between first and third grade) will master Test 6a1. This student may be able to master a few of the tests beginning with 6b but will become frustrated on the more difficult structural analysis tests.

As you will see in the descriptions of the various tests that follow, both Test 5a for phonics and Tests 6a1 and 6a2 for structural analysis were designed to assess the student's ability to apply these decoding skills in the act of reading (in context). Students who master these tests do *not* need to be given the phonics or structural analysis tests respectively that follow them.

Generally, a student whose independent level is between 4.0 and 6.0 on the GWL will master Tests 4, 5, and 6. You may want to administer Test 4a to confirm mastery of basic sight words. This test is both quick and easy to give.

In nearly all cases, you can skip Test 5. It would be most unusual for a student to be able to score at the fourth-grade level or higher and not have mastered phonics. However, if you want to confirm phonics mastery, you could give Test 5a to be sure.

Do give Test 6a. If the student masters both 6a1 and 6a2, you can be sure that any existing reading difficulty does not result from inadequate phonics or structural analysis skills. However, this student may exhibit weaknesses in context usage, efficiency, or comprehension.

Once you establish a starting point, continue administering these tests until the student consistently fails to attain mastery on the tests, *when it is clear that the student is frustrated by the tasks,* or when you are no longer obtaining useful diagnostic information. It is important not to overtest.

Because of the ease of administering Tests 3, 4, 5, and 6, the following instructions will summarize the purpose of each test, give a description of each subtest, and combine the directions for administration and scoring.

Test 3: Emergent Literacy

Test 3a: Phonemic Awareness

(Test and Scoring Sheets found on pages 262–266.)

Purpose

To determine if the student can successfully complete the following phonemic awareness tasks: Rhyme Production, Initial Sound Recognition, Phoneme Blending, Phoneme Segmentation. If the student does not succeed at Rhyme Production, an Alternate Test for Rhyme Recognition is provided.

Generally, the Phonemic Awareness Tests should be given only to students who are nonreaders or who can read only a few words.

Description of the Subtests

Each of the Phonemic Awareness Tests is easy to administer and score, and all follow a similar format. More than a dozen different phonemic awareness skills have been identified and can be tested. The ESRI provides simple tests for the phonemic awareness skills that seem to be most closely related to future reading success.

Emergent literacy tests are generally given to young children who are not test-wise. It is very important that the examiner be especially alert and careful when giving such tests. Children may perform poorly for reasons that may not be obvious. Often children do not fully understand the directions, and their failure may be more a reflection of their confusion than of their inability to succeed at the task being tested. Sometimes youngsters do not understand the meaning of words such as *beginning, rhyming, sound, letter, word, top, bottom,* and others. Frequently, these students will listen for cues in your voice inflection and will try to guess the answer they think will please you, rather than listening carefully to directions being given or the words in the test items.

For each of the Phonemic Awareness Tests, you will use the Scoring Sheet for your instructions to the student and for marking the student's responses to the items tested. There is no Test Sheet because all of the test items are spoken by you. The five Phonemic Awareness Tests all follow a similar format. Refer to the Phonemic Awareness Scoring Sheet on pages 262–266 as you read the directions that follow. In each subtest, you will model the skill being tested, provide one or two practice items, and then give eight test items.

The Rhyme Production test requires the student to say a word that rhymes with two rhyming stimulus words given by the examiner. Some youngsters will not succeed at this task, even after you have modeled the skill and assisted the student with practice items. When this happens, you should cease testing and move to the Alternate Test, Rhyme Recognition, which is a lower-level rhyming task. It is easier for a youngster to recognize two words that rhyme than it is to produce, or say, a new rhyming word after hearing the examiner pronounce two words that rhyme.

The Initial Sound Recognition subtest requires the student to say the beginning sound of words after the examiner pronounces two words with the same beginning sound.

The Phoneme Blending subtest requires the student to pronounce a whole word after the examiner says the word slowly, separating each of the phonemes.

The Phoneme Segmentation subtest is the opposite of the Phoneme Blending subtest. In this case, the examiner pronounces the whole word and the student repeats it by segmenting it into each of its phonemes or sounds.

These tests are not set up in a pretest/posttest format. While the tests may be administered at different times to assess progress, criteria for mastery are not provided. This test is designed to assess students' abilities in these areas so that teachers may use this information to guide instruction.

Administration and Scoring

1. Simply follow the instructions as they are provided on the Scoring Sheet.
2. Determine the number of correct responses after each subtest is completed and write this number in the space provided.

Test 3b: Concepts about Print

(Test Sheet found on p. 172; Scoring Sheet found on p. 267.)

Purpose

To determine if the student has knowledge of critical concepts learned in the early stages of reading.

Generally, the Concepts about Print Test should be given only to students who are nonreaders or who can read only a few words.

Description

The Concepts about Print Test consists of a Test Sheet with a letter, a word, a sentence, and a paragraph on it. The examiner has the student look at the Test Sheet and answer ten questions designed to assess the student's knowledge of critical prereading concepts.

Administration and Scoring

1. Simply follow the instructions as they are provided on the Scoring Sheet.
2. Determine the number of correct responses and write this number in the space provided. Additional space is provided on the Scoring Sheet for anecdotal comments regarding the student's performance.

Test 3c: Letter Knowledge

(Test Sheet found on p. 173; Scoring Sheet found on p. 268.)

Purpose

To determine if the student can associate the letter symbols with the letter names, with both an auditory and a visual stimulus.

Description of the Subtests

The Letter Knowledge Tests are usually given only to young children (ages 4–7), though occasionally an older remedial reader will not know the letter names. The two subtests include all twenty-six lowercase letters. Because lowercase letters are usually more difficult for students to identify, you can safely assume that if mastery is established on these subtests, then the uppercase letters will be known as well.

Subtest 3c1 evaluates the student's ability to visually identify the letters when an auditory stimulus (the letter names) is provided by the examiner. Subtest 3c2 requires the student to recognize and say the letter names when the examiner provides a visual stimulus (points to the letters).

Subtest 3c2 requires a skill that is closer to that required in the act of reading and is more difficult than the skill tested in 3c1. Generally, if a student is having difficulty on these subtests, it will be reflected in a lower score on 3c2 than on 3c1. This generalization will not hold if the student is guessing wildly or does not understand the directions, but this should be apparent to the examiner through observation.

The subtests are constructed so that the most confusable letters tend to appear in the same sets or tests. For example, the letters *t, l,* and *f* appear in Subtest 3c1 and the letters *b, p, d,* and *q* appear in Subtest 3c2. This is done intentionally to ensure that the items are tested in a way that requires maximum discrimination.

Administration and Scoring

SUBTEST 3c1

1. Place the appropriate Test Sheet in front of the student and say, "Point to the letter *t* . . . , the letter *o* . . . ," and so on.

2. As you pronounce the letters, one at a time, from the Scoring Sheet, the student points to them on the Test Sheet. (The letters on the Test Sheet are in a different order than the letters on the Scoring Sheet.)

3. As the student points, indicate which letters the student does not know by circling them on the Scoring Sheet.

4. Determine the number of correct responses (letters that are not circled) and write this number as a fraction (items correct out of a total of thirteen). This fraction can then be compared to the criterion for mastery, which is indicated on the Scoring Sheet.

SUBTEST 3c2

1. Place the appropriate Test Sheet in front of the student and say, "Now you say the letters as I point to them."

2. As you point to the letters, one at a time, on the Test Sheet, the student pronounces them. (The letters on the Test Sheet are in the same order as the letters on the Scoring Sheet.)

3. Indicate which letters the student does not know by circling them on the Scoring Sheet.
4. Determine the number of correct responses, write this number as a fraction, and compare it to the criterion for mastery.

Test 4: Basic Sight Vocabulary

Test 4a: Quick Check for Basic Sight Words

(Test Sheet found on p. 174; Scoring Sheet found on p. 269.)

Purpose

To test quickly students' knowledge of basic sight words.

Description

This test, which takes approximately two minutes to administer, allows you to determine whether a student has mastered the basic sight words. If there is any doubt in your mind as to whether a student should be given an entire basic sight word test, you may give the student this list first. A student who does not miss any words on this test need not take the entire Basic Sight Word Test. However, if a student misses even *one* word on this list, he or she should be given the entire Basic Sight Word Test (Test 4b).

The Quick Check for Basic Sight Words was developed by giving Ekwall's basic sight word list to five hundred students in grades 2 through 6 using a tachistoscopic presentation. One hundred students were tested at each of these five grade levels. Computer analysis then listed, in ascending order of difficulty, the words students most often missed. From this list, thirty-six words were chosen. The first few words are the easier ones; following the first few easier words are the ones students tended to miss more often. The list also includes words commonly confused by many students. When giving this test, make sure the student is exposed to each word briefly (approximately one second). Given more time, the student may use word-attack skills instead of knowledge of basic sight words.

Preparation

Before administering the Quick Check for Basic Sight Words (Test 4a), make multiple copies of the Scoring Sheet to be used in quickly assessing students' knowledge of basic sight words. Also copy or remove the Test Sheet. This page can then be placed on a surface such as tagboard and fastened with rubber cement or transparent tape. After it is cemented in place, you may want to laminate it or place it in a plastic sleeve to keep it from becoming soiled from handling.

Administration and Scoring

1. Place the Test Sheet in front of the student and say, "I want you to read the words on this list out loud. Start here [point to the word *I* in the upper left-hand corner] and read each word as you go DOWN the columns."
2. Provide assistance if the student loses place.

3. As the student reads, mark those words read correctly with a plus (+) and those read incorrectly with a minus (–). If the student pauses more than approximately *one* second before saying a word, count it as wrong.

4. If the student says he or she does not know an answer, mark it with the letters *DK* (for "Don't Know"). If the student skips a word completely, mark it with the letters *NR.* (for "No Response").

5. If the student misses *any* words on this test, he or she should be given Test 4b. If the student pronounces approximately half or more of the words on Test 4b correctly, then also administer Test 4c.

Tests 4b and 4c: Basic Sight Words and Basic Sight Word Phrases Tests

(Flash cards used instead of Test Sheets; Scoring Sheets found on pp. 270–275.)

Purpose

To determine which of the 220 basic sight words and 143 basic sight word phrases can be recognized and pronounced instantly by the student.

Description

These tests require the student to pronounce up to 220 basic sight words and 143 basic sight word phrases as they are flashed on cards by the examiner. The examiner records the student's performance on the student Scoring Sheets while listening to the tape recording of the tests. These tests take approximately five to twelve minutes to administer and score.

The words on these tests are drawn from the Dolch Basic Sight Word Test,[8] the best known and most frequently used test of basic sight words. Subtest 4b consists of the 220 Dolch words reordered according to frequency of occurrence as found in the Durr (1973) list.[9] The 220 basic sight words are divided into eleven sublists of 20 words each for ease of scoring and instruction. Subtest 4c was developed so that each of the basic sight words is presented in a phrase. Only 16 new words are added to complete the phrases. These are nouns, all of which were drawn from the preprimer level of a popular basal series. The 143 basic sight phrases are divided into the same eleven sublists as the basic sight words, with each sublist composed of 10 to 16 phrases.

Preparation

1. Have your student Scoring Sheets copied (from pp. 270–275). You will need one set of the Scoring Sheets for both the basic sight words (Subtest 4b) and the basic sight word phrases (Subtest 4c) for each student you test.

2. You will need a tape recorder to record the student's responses to the cards as they are flashed.

3. Have a pencil ready to record the student's responses on the Scoring Sheet after the tests have been administered. (Usually, this scoring is done after the test session has been completed and the student has departed.)

4. You will need to prepare flash cards for each of the 220 basic sight words and 143 basic sight word phrases. Your flash cards should be arranged in the same order as the words on the Scoring Sheets.

To prepare flash cards, purchase either 3 × 5 inch or 4 × 6 inch index cards (either blank or lined) or heavier stock cards in a similar or slightly smaller size. Most school supply stores sell cards ready-made for this purpose in various colors. Also, they often have rounded corners, which makes them last longer. You will need 363 cards, but you should purchase a few more in case you make mistakes.

Once you have selected your cards, look at the lists of words on the Scoring Sheets (pp. 270–275). Print one word on each flash card, using neat, lowercase manuscript printing. On the back of each card, you can designate each word by indicating the Scoring Sheet list and number for each word. For example, on the back of the first card, write I-1. This indicates List I, word one. The designation IV-16 indicates the word *ride*, List IV, word sixteen. If your cards should become mixed up, you will find it easy to reassemble them in the correct order if you identify each word on the back as described. You also may wish to use different colored cards for each list.

An alternative to hand printing the cards is to use a computer to print out each of the words and phrases in a large, clear font. Space the words so they match standard 8½ × 11 inch label sheets. These pages can be printed and then copied onto self-adhesive label sheets. Then each label can be peeled off and applied to a flash card. Once again, you would hand print the designation for each word on the back of the card.

Administration

SUBTEST 4b

1. Make sure the tape recorder is turned on and the microphone is placed on the table near the student being tested. Say to the student, "I am going to show you some words on flash cards and I want you to say them when you see them. I will be flashing the cards quickly, so if you don't know a word, don't worry about it and go on."

2. Lift off twenty to thirty words from the ordered stack. Flash these to the student at a rate of one-half to one second per card.

3. Your attention should be focused on flashing the cards, not on the student's responses. Do not separate the cards into "right" and "wrong" piles because this may distract you, upset the student, and confuse the order of the flash cards. Instead, you will rely on the tape recording of the tests to determine later exactly which words were missed.

4. Continue flashing the cards until the student does not respond to about ten consecutive words or otherwise indicates an inability to complete the test successfully. If the student appears to be pronouncing most of the words correctly, continue the procedure until all cards are flashed.

SUBTEST 4c

1. Repeat the same procedure for testing the sight word phrases. However, with the phrase test you may allow up to two seconds per phrase when flashing the cards.

Scoring

To score the tests, rewind the audiotape, select the appropriate Scoring Sheet, and indicate, by marking + or –, whether the student correctly or incorrectly pronounced each word or phrase. (As indicated earlier, the scoring is usually completed after the student has left the testing site.) When scoring, only the first response counts. Once a student masters a word, he or she recognizes it instantly. If the student hesitates, the flashed word is not known by sight. It is not necessary to transcribe the student's errors on these tests because basic sight words should be recognized instantly, at sight. So you may simply mark the scoring with pluses for correctly pronounced words and minuses for incorrectly pronounced words. Students should not be taught to sound out these words, especially because many of the basic sight words are phonetically irregular. The number of correct responses for each test is written as a fraction on the Scoring Sheets. For example, a student might score 185/220 on the basic sight words and 95/143 on the basic sight word phrases.

You must use judgment in deciding how quickly to flash the cards. Young children may have difficulty with a speed of one word per second, although ultimately the words must be recognized at this rate. Likewise, for students with speech difficulties the rate of flashing may need to be adjusted.

Format for Tests 5 and 6

Test 5 assesses the student's phonics ability and Test 6 assesses structural analysis skills. Together these tests evaluate the student's ability to use word analysis skills; they are sometimes referred to as the decoding tests. These tests can be administered quickly and easily, and provide considerable information in an easy-to-read format.

The decoding tests use a common format on the Scoring Sheets, which contain the following beginning with Tests 5b and 6b (see pp. 276–282):

- Down the left column, a summary of the directions for administering each subtest, including the spoken instructions you will give to the student
- Down the center, places to mark the student's responses to each test item (Space is provided for both pre- and posttest scores on the Scoring Sheets. You may use different colored ink to distinguish the pretest responses from posttest responses on each subtest.)
- Down the right column, spaces to indicate the student's total score on each subtest (You can determine the student's mastery of each skill on both pre- and posttests by comparing the student's performance to the criterion score for mastery provided for each subtest.)

Test 5: Phonics

(Test Sheets found on pp. 175–178; Scoring Sheets found on pp. 276–278.)

Purpose

To determine if the student has mastered letter-sound associations (phonics) at three levels, with both an auditory and visual stimulus.

Description of the Subtests

The Phonics Tests consist of nine subtests, the first of which evaluates the student's ability to use phonics skills while reading a short passage. This contextual evaluation can be used to determine quickly whether the student has mastered phonics skills. If this is the case, no further phonics testing is necessary.

The next five tests are identical in format and evaluate the student's knowledge of initial consonant sounds, blends and digraphs, ending sounds, vowels, and phonograms. The remaining tests evaluate blending ability, phonic substitution, and vowel digraphs.

Administration and Scoring

SUBTEST 5a

1. Place the appropriate Test Sheet in front of the student and say, "Read this story aloud until I say stop."
2. As the student reads, indicate specific reading errors on the Scoring Sheet, using the same code for marking oral reading errors you used on the oral reading passages.
3. Encourage the student to pronounce as many words as possible. Do not provide assistance by pronouncing words for the student, but rather encourage the student to go on and "do the best you can." Cease testing if the student becomes overly frustrated.
4. Only the words underlined on the Scoring Sheet are considered in scoring. The words that are not underlined are basic sight words, which should be pronounced without phonic analysis, or repetitions of previously underlined words.
5. To score this test, compare the oral reading transcription with the response chart just below the paragraph on the Scoring Sheet. The chart lists seventy-three phonic elements that are tested, with the underlined words from the paragraph. Circle each phonic element on the response chart that the student failed to pronounce correctly. Some of the phonic elements are tested by more than one underlined word from the paragraph. In such cases, circle the phonic element if even one of the underlined words is mispronounced. Mastery of the phonic element requires that it be pronounced correctly in all cases.
6. Circle the phonics element only if the element itself is mispronounced, regardless of the total pronunciation of the underlined word. For example, to determine the student's symbol-sound association for beginning *b*, the underlined words are *barn* and *bird*. Circle the item if *either* beginning *b* is mispronounced. If, however, the student says *bank* for *barn*, the symbol-sound association for the beginning *b* is correct, so the item is not circled.
7. Determine the number of correct responses, write this number as a fraction, and compare it to the criterion for mastery. To achieve mastery, the student must correctly pronounce sixty-five of the seventy-three phonic elements, as indicated on the Scoring Sheet.
8. If the student masters this test (5a), *stop* testing phonics at this point and go on to Test 6a. If the student does not master this test, go on to Test 5b and continue testing phonics skills until the student is unable to complete the tasks successfully or when it is clear that the student is becoming frustrated.

SUBTEST 5b

1. Place the appropriate Test Sheet in front of the student and say, "Look at number one. Point to the letter you hear at the beginning of *water.*"
2. The student must point to the *w* from among the five letter choices. If the student makes an incorrect choice, circle the word *water* on the Scoring Sheet.

Then pronounce the next word, *dog,* and continue marking the Scoring Sheet in the same way. Continue to pronounce words and circle incorrect responses until the ten items are completed. (Of course, you may stop sooner if the student's performance reflects a total inability to succeed at this task.)

3. Determine the number of correct responses, write this number as a fraction, and compare it to the criterion for mastery.

SUBTESTS 5c THROUGH 5f

1. Subtests 5c through 5f follow the same format as Subtest 5b. Subtest 5c assesses initial blends and digraphs, 5d assesses ending sounds, 5e assesses short and long vowel sounds, and 5f assesses common ending phonograms or word elements.

SUBTEST 5g

1. Place the appropriate Test Sheet in front of the student, then check to see that the student can recognize and pronounce the two phonograms *at* and *in.* If the student does not know these, they should be taught, if it is possible to do so in a short time.

2. Complete the sample item for the student, demonstrating how the initial consonant *t* is pronounced /t/, then blended with the phonogram *in,* to arrive at *tin.*

3. Ask the student to do the same with the ten items provided, while you circle the incorrect responses.

4. On this subtest and Subtest 5h, you should not only circle the incorrect responses but also write phonetic transcriptions of the mispronounced words. This will aid in later analysis. Space is provided on the Scoring Sheet for this.

5. Determine the number of correct responses, write this number as a fraction, and compare it to the criterion for mastery.

SUBTEST 5h

1. Place the appropriate Test Sheet in front of the student and say, "Read these words. I will tell you the first one in each column in case you don't know it. Some of these are real words, some are not."

2. The student then reads the other twenty-five words in the five columns, while you follow the same scoring procedure as indicated for Subtest 5g.

SUBTEST 5i

1. Place the appropriate Test Sheet in front of the student and say, "Read as many of these words as you can."

2. Follow the same scoring procedure as for Subtests 5g and 5h.

Test 6: Structural Analysis

(Test Sheets found on pp. 179–182; Scoring Sheets found on pp. 279–282.)

Purpose

To determine of the student can use structural analysis skills to aid in decoding unknown words.

Description of the Subtests

The Structural Analysis Tests consists of eight subtests, the first of which (Test 6a) evaluates the student's ability to use structural analysis skills while reading one or two passages. This contextual evaluation can be used to determine quickly whether the student has mastered structural analysis skills. If this is the case, no further testing is necessary in this area.

Test 6b assesses the student's ability to hear the separate parts (syllables) of words, a prerequisite skill for structural analysis. Subtest 6c assesses the student's ability to combine the various inflectional endings with root words and pronounce the resulting new words. Subtests 6d and 6e assess the student's ability to decode prefixes and suffixes, respectively. Subtest 6f assesses the student's ability to recognize the two separate units of compound words for purposes of pronunciation. Subtest 6g assesses the student's ability to pronounce two-syllable words containing one easy affix (prefix or suffix). Finally, Subtest 6h assesses the student's ability to pronounce regular three-, four-, and five-syllable words.

Administration and Scoring

SUBTEST 6a

This subtest consists of two passages. The first (Test 6a1) is written at approximately the 5.1 grade level, and the second (Test 6a2) is written at the 7.0 grade level, according to the Flesch-Kincaid readability formula. The student may read either or both, depending on the performance level. When in doubt, start the student on the first passage and proceed to the second only if the student attains mastery on the first.

1. Place the appropriate Test Sheet (either 6a1 or 6a2) in front of the student and say, "Read this story aloud until I say stop."
2. As the student reads, follow the procedure for transcribing oral reading errors described earlier. It is essential to determine if the underlined words are pronounced correctly. All of these words require structural analysis skills for decoding, unless of course the student is able to recognize the words by sight. The words that are not underlined are either basic sight words or words that can be decoded using phonic analysis.
3. Encourage the student to pronounce as many words as possible. Do not provide assistance by pronouncing unknown words for the student. Cease testing if the student becomes overly frustrated.
4. To score this test, evaluate the student's oral reading of the underlined words. Each mispronounced word should be circled on the response chart on the Scoring Sheet. The words on this chart are categorized according to the structural analysis skill required.
5. Write the number of correct responses as a fraction on the Scoring Sheet to be compared with the criterion for mastery. If the student meets or exceeds the criterion for the first passage (Test 6a1), administer the second passage (Test 6a2), following the same instructions.

SUBTEST 6b

1. This test requires no Test Sheet. Hold the Scoring Sheet so that you can read from it and say, "How many syllables do you hear in the word *cowboy*?" Circle incorrect responses on the Scoring Sheet.

2. Continue the test with the other four items, circling the incorrect responses.

3. Write the number of correct responses as a fraction on the Scoring Sheet to be compared with the criterion for mastery.

SUBTESTS 6c THROUGH 6e

1. For each subtest, place the appropriate Test Sheet in front of the student and read the first word (the root word) in each column, then ask the student to pronounce the other words in the columns. (You should not read the first word in column two until the student has read all the words in column one, and so on.)

2. As the student reads the words, circle each incorrect response on the Scoring Sheet.

3. Write the number of correct responses as a fraction on the Scoring Sheet to be compared with the criterion for mastery.

SUBTEST 6f

1. Place the appropriate Test Sheet in front of the student and say, "Read as many of these words as you can. Some are not real words."

2. As the student reads the words, circle the errors. On this test, the errors are not determined by imprecise pronunciation but rather by the student's failure to recognize and attempt to decode the two parts of the *compound* word. For example, if a student says *baskethorse* for *baskethouse*, this is considered correct, since it is clear that the student identified the two pronounceable units. However, if the student attempts to pronounce *baskethouse* by sounding the *th* digraph in the middle of the word, this is incorrect. Such an error reflects a lack of recognition of the two obvious word parts.

3. Write the number of correct responses as a fraction on the Scoring Sheet to be compared with the criterion for mastery.

SUBTEST 6g

1. Place the appropriate Test Sheet in front of the student and say, "Read as many of these words as you can. Some are not real words."

2. As the student reads, circle the errors. The determination of errors on this subtest follows the same restrictions described for the previous subtest.

3. Write the number of correct responses as a fraction on the Scoring Sheet to be compared with the criterion for mastery.

SUBTEST 6h

1. Place the appropriate Test Sheet in front of the student and say, "Read as many of these words as you can."

2. As the student reads, circle the errors. Although all of the words on this test are real words, most students will not recognize them as sight words. If the student misplaces the accent, count the item correct as long as each of the syllables is pronounced correctly.

3. Write the number of correct responses as a fraction on the Scoring Sheet to be compared with the criterion for mastery.

Test 7: Knowledge of Contractions

(Test Sheet found on p. 183; Scoring Sheet found on p. 283.)

Purpose

To determine if the student has knowledge of contractions.

Description

Test 7 requires the student to pronounce forty-seven common contractions and tell what two words the contraction stands for. A rather high percentage of students have occasional problems with the pronunciation of contractions; however, you are likely to find a greater percentage who do not know what two words are represented by the various contractions. Although pronunciation is more important for reading purposes, students will not use a contraction in their writing until they know the two words each contraction stands for.

Preparation

1. Copy the Scoring Sheet (from p. 283).
2. Open the manual to the Test Sheet (found on p. 183).

Administration

1. Have your Scoring Sheet ready and give the student the Test Sheet.
2. Read to the student the directions written on the Scoring Sheet.
3. As indicated on the Scoring Sheet, you will put a plus (+) in the first blank if the student can pronounce the contraction correctly and a plus (+) in the second blank if the student can tell you what two words the contraction stands for. You will mark wrong answers with a minus.

Scoring

To score the tests, use the box at the bottom of the Scoring Sheet. Count up the total number of pluses in the left columns to determine the number of contractions pronounced correctly. Count up the total number of pluses in the right columns to determine the number of contractions for which the student knows the words represented. The overall test score is the total of these two scores, with 94 a perfect score.

Test 8: El Paso Phonics Survey

(Directions found on pp. 184–185; Test Sheets found on pp. 186–187; Scoring Sheets found on pp. 284–285.)

Purpose

To determine if the student has the ability to pronounce and blend ninety phonic elements.

Description

Test 8 requires the student to pronounce and blend ninety phonic elements. This test has both advantages and disadvantages. Some of the advantages are:

1. It tests a student in a situation that is analogous to actual reading.
2. It tests a student's high-level phonics and blending ability (see the Interpretation section for a discussion of these levels).
3. The test is comprehensive.
4. Because nonsense words are used, the student cannot get items correct by recognizing the words as sight words.
5. The test has high interscorer reliability.

Some of the disadvantages are:

1. The test can take quite a while to administer.
2. It does not test a student's knowledge of low-level phonics.
3. The test is difficult for some students, and many students can achieve the goals of phonics instruction (to decode unknown one-syllable words) without being able to master all the items on this test.
4. Testing using only nonsense words poses special problems for some students.
5. The phonics skills are not tested in context.

Preparation

1. Copy the two Scoring Sheets (found on pp. 284–285).
2. Place the Test Sheets (found on pp. 186–187) in front of the student.
3. While administering this test, you will need to look at the General Directions and the Special Directions Sheets and write on the copies of the Scoring Sheets. To do this easily, detach the Test Sheets before giving the test. You may want to rubber cement or tape the Test Sheets to pieces of tagboard. You may also laminate these pages to prevent them from becoming soiled with use.

Administration and Scoring

Follow the instructions on the General Directions and Special Directions on pages 184–185.

Test 9: Quick Word List Survey

(Test Sheet found on p. 188; Scoring Sheet found on p. 286.)

Purpose

To determine quickly if the student has mastered phonics and structural analysis. With older, capable readers, this test may be used as a pretest to determine if it is necessary to administer Tests 5 and 6.

Description

Test 9 enables you to determine quickly if a student has the necessary decoding skills to read successfully material written at an adult level. This test may be given to a student at approximately fourth-grade level and above to verify that the student has mastered phonics and structural analysis. Test 9 should not be given to a student who you know has difficulty with phonics or structural analysis, because it will be frustrating for that student and you will not gain useful diagnostic information.

A student who can read these words successfully does not have a decoding problem, although it is possible the student has difficulty with context clues, efficiency, vocabulary, or comprehension skills.

Preparation

Review the Pronunciation of Quick Survey Words on page 286 so that you are aware of the correct pronunciation of the test words. If necessary, you may refer to this sheet while testing the student.

Administration and Scoring

1. Place the Quick Word List Survey Test Sheet in front of the student and ask the student to read the nonsense words out loud.
2. If the student can pronounce each of these words correctly, it will not be necessary to administer any of the decoding tests (Tests 5 and 6).
3. If it becomes apparent after one or two words that the student is not able to pronounce the words on the Quick Word List Survey, it should be discontinued and you should administer the appropriate decoding tests.
4. The correct pronunciations of the words on the Quick Word List Survey are shown on p. 286. Remember, however, that accent rules or generalizations pertaining to the English language are not consistent; therefore, if the words are pronounced correctly except for the accent or stress shown on certain syllables, they should be considered correct.

Test 10: Reading Interests Survey

(No Test Sheet is used; Scoring Sheets are found on pp. 287–288.)

Purpose

To assess the student's attitude toward reading and school, areas of reading interest, reading experiences, and conditions affecting reading in the home.

Description

Test 10 enables you to assess quickly a student's reading attitudes and interests. It consists of two forms: Test 10a, for elementary-age students, and Test 10b, for older students or adults. The test may be given orally to young children or students unable to read the questions. Older students or more able readers may complete the form themselves.

Preparation

Both of the Reading Interests Survey forms consist of a one-page Scoring Sheet. You need only select the appropriate form, copy it, and decide whether to administer it orally or have the student complete it in writing on his or her own.

Administration and Scoring

1. If you are giving this test in a one-to-one situation at the conclusion of your administration of the ESRI, you might want to give it orally regardless of the student's reading ability. This will allow you to discuss with the student his or her responses to some of the questions.

2. Encourage the student to give you candid responses to these items. Reassure the student that there are no right or wrong answers; you want to know how the student honestly feels about these questions.

3. Part I consists of seven open-ended statements. Write down the student's responses as he or she finishes the sentences.

4. Part II assesses the student's reading interests. If necessary, explain to the student what some of the categories are on Test 10a.

5. Part III assesses the student's reading experiences and some of the factors that may affect the student's reading behavior at home or outside of school.

6. After you have recorded the student's responses, you may use this information when you plan the remediation program.

Interpretation of Test Results

The purpose of administering the various diagnostic tests is to gather data about the student's reading behavior. These data are then analyzed or interpreted so the examiner can form conclusions about the student's current reading levels and his or her reading strengths and weaknesses. Once these are determined, a program of remediation may be undertaken to improve the student's reading ability.

COMPLETING THE TEST SUMMARY SHEET

On pages 115–117 you will find the blank Test Summary Sheet for the ESRI. Recording the student's scores from the various tests on this form is the first step in the analysis of the student's reading difficulties. Included in this section are two sample Test Summary Sheets. You may refer to these while reading the following instructions.

1. At the top of the Test Summary Sheet, fill in the following information about the student: name, school, teacher, grade, age, examiner, and test date.

2. Under Test 1, fill in the student's independent, instructional, and frustration reading levels as derived from the GWL. This information may be copied from the bottom of the Scoring Sheet for the GWL, where you indicated these levels after administering this test to the student.

3. Under Tests 2a and 2b, fill in the student's independent, instructional, and frustration reading levels for both oral and silent reading as derived from the Reading Passages Tests.

4. Under Test 2c, fill in the student's listening comprehension level as derived from the Reading Passages Tests. The following guidelines will be helpful in completing steps 3 and 4:

   ■ *Independent Levels.* List the highest-level passage at which the student read on an independent level when reading orally and the highest-level passage at which the student read on an independent level when reading silently. Thus, only one level will appear under each of the Oral and Silent headings at the independent reading level. You may assume that any level below these would also be at the student's independent reading level.

- *Instructional Levels.* List the highest-level passage at which the student read orally at the instructional level. Do the same for the student's silent instructional level. Once again you may assume that any level below these—but above the student's independent level—would also be at the student's instructional reading level. For example, let's say the student's independent level is grade 1, but the instructional level spans grades 2–4. If you simply write 4 in the space next to instructional level, that will mean the same thing as writing 2–4. Of course you may also write in 2–4, if you prefer.

- *Frustration Levels.* List the lowest-level passage at which the student read at a frustration level orally and the lowest-level passage at which the student read at a frustration level silently. As in the case of the independent level, only one level would appear under Oral and only one level under Silent. You may assume that any level above these would also be at the student's frustration reading level.

- *Listening Comprehension Level.* List the highest level at which the student comprehended at least 70 to 75 percent of the questions asked by the examiner. Again you may assume that anything below that level would also be at the student's listening comprehension level. (As indicated earlier in the directions for administering this test, you may want to stop testing at the student's grade-placement level if the student passes the listening comprehension criterion at this level and it is above the student's instructional reading levels. This would indicate that the student has the potential to read above the current performance level and will reduce the time it takes to administer this test.)

5. Fill in the student's scores on all the subtests given for Tests 3 through 6 and the optional Tests 7 through 9.

6. Space is provided on the Test Summary Sheet for you to comment on the student's responses to Test 10.

TEST SUMMARY SHEET

Student __Maya__   School __Douglass Elementary__

Teacher __Kara Locke__   Grade __2__   Age __7__

Examiner __Kara Locke__   Test Dates __2/8-9/0x__ _____

                                               Pretest   Posttest

[* indicates mastery]

TEST 1: SAN DIEGO QUICK ASSESSMENT OR GRADED WORD LIST (GWL)

	Pretest	Posttest
Independent Reading Level:	Grade PP	Grade ___
Instructional Reading Level:	Grade 1	Grade ___
Frustration Reading Level:	Grade 2	Grade ___

TESTS 2a, 2b, AND 2c: READING PASSAGES TESTS

Oral

	Pretest	Posttest
Independent Reading Level:	Grade Below PP	Grade ___
Instructional Reading Level:	Grade 1	Grade ___
Frustration Reading Level:	Grade 2	Grade ___

Silent

	Pretest	Posttest
Independent Reading Level:	Grade Below PP	Grade ___
Instructional Reading Level:	Grade 2	Grade ___
Frustration Reading Level:	Grade 3	Grade ___
Listening Comprehension Level:	Grade 2	Grade ___

TEST 3: EMERGENT LITERACY TESTS

	1st	2nd
3a. Phonemic Awareness		
3a1. Rhyme Production	NA /8	___/8
3a2. Rhyme Recognition [Alternate]	NA /8	___/8
3a3. Initial Sound Recognition	NA /8	___/8
3a4. Phoneme Blending	NA /8	___/8
3a5. Phoneme Segmentation	NA /8	___/8
3b. Concepts about Print	NA /10	___/10
3c. Letter Knowledge		
3c1. Auditory Stimulus	*13 /13	___/13
3c2. Visual Stimulus	*13 /13	___/13

▶ ## TEST 4: BASIC SIGHT WORDS AND PHRASES

	Mastery	Pretest	Posttest
4a. Quick Check for Basic Sight Words	36	NA /36	___/36
4b. Basic Sight Words	200	47 /220	___/220
4c. Basic Sight Word Phrases	125	NA /143	___/143

TEST 5: PHONICS

	Mastery	Pretest	Posttest
5a. Application in Context	65	54 /73	___/73
5b. Initial Consonants	9	*10 /10	___/10
5c. Initial Blends and Digraphs	9	*10 /10	___/10
5d. Ending Sounds	8	*8 /10	___/10
5e. Vowels	9	*10 /10	___/10
5f. Phonograms	9	*9 /10	___/10
5g. Blending	9	*10 /10	___/10
5h. Substitution	22	*22 /25	___/25
5i. Vowel Pronunciation	13	3 /15	___/15

TEST 6: STRUCTURAL ANALYSIS

	Mastery	Pretest	Posttest
6a. Application in Context			
6a1. Lower Level	24	NA /27	___/27
6a2. Higher Level	48	NA /53	___/53
Total	72	NA /80	___/80
6b. Hearing Word Parts	4	NA /5	___/5
6c. Inflectional Endings	9	NA /10	___/10
6d. Prefixes	18	NA /20	___/20
6e. Suffixes	9	NA /10	___/10
6f. Compound Words	4	NA /5	___/5
6g. Affixes	9	NA /10	___/10
6h. Syllabication	9	NA /10	___/10

TEST 7: KNOWLEDGE OF CONTRACTIONS

	Pretest	Posttest
Number of Words Pronounced (from left columns)	NA /47	___/47
Number of Words Known (from right columns)	+ NA /47	___/47
Total Score	NA /94	___/94

▶

▶ ## TEST 8: EL PASO PHONICS SURVEY

	Pretest	*Posttest*
Initial Consonant Sounds	NA /22	___/22
Ending Consonant X	NA /1	___/1
Initial Consonant Clusters	NA /35	___/35
Vowels, Vowel Teams, and Special Letter Combinations	NA /32	___/32

TEST 9: QUICK WORD LIST SURVEY

Comments __NA_____

_____
_____
_____
_____

TEST 10: READING INTERESTS SURVEY

Comments __NA_____

_____
_____
_____
_____
_____

Information Gained from Maya's Test Summary Sheet

Maya's Test Summary Sheet provides considerable information about her reading abilities. She is a seven-year-old second grader whose independent, instructional, and frustration levels on the GWL are PP, 1, and 2 respectively. When reading passages, Maya has no independent level. She has an instructional level of first grade when reading orally and second grade when reading silently. Her frustration levels are second grade when reading orally and third grade when reading silently.

This indicates that although Maya has mastered some beginning reading skills, she is unable to read comfortably at her grade-placement level. Her listening comprehension level of second grade suggests that Maya has the potential to read better.

As would be expected of a student who reads at these levels, Maya knows some but not all of the basic sight words, has mastered letter knowledge, and has mastered some but not all of her phonics skills. She is not yet able to use structural analysis skills for decoding, so these tests were not administered.

Maya's examiner chose not to give her the Phonemic Awareness and Concepts about Print Tests. Maya's performance on the oral passages persuaded the examiner that Maya had mastered these skills. This was later confirmed by Maya's performance on the Phonics Tests.

Next we will look at the Test Summary Sheet for another student, David. As you will see, David reads at a higher level than Maya. After presenting David's test scores and briefly summarizing some of the information that can be derived from them, we will take you through the entire diagnosis process step by step. We will use the actual performances of Maya and David to illustrate how the analysis is conducted. Then we will provide you with the written reports that were completed for Maya and David by their examiners.

TEST SUMMARY SHEET

Student __David__   School __Miller__

Teacher __Paula Schaufler__   Grade __4__   Age __9__

Examiner __Paula Schaufler__   Test Dates __3/7-8/0X__
                                       Pretest   Posttest

[* indicates mastery]

TEST 1: SAN DIEGO QUICK ASSESSMENT OR GRADED WORD LIST (GWL)

	Pretest	*Posttest*
Independent Reading Level:	Grade __2__	Grade _____
Instructional Reading Level:	Grade __3__	Grade _____
Frustration Reading Level:	Grade __4__	Grade _____

TESTS 2a, 2b, AND 2c: READING PASSAGES TESTS
Oral

	Pretest	*Posttest*
Independent Reading Level:	Grade __2__	Grade _____
Instructional Reading Level:	Grade __3__	Grade _____
Frustration Reading Level:	Grade __4__	Grade _____

Silent

	Pretest	*Posttest*
Independent Reading Level:	Grade __2__	Grade _____
Instructional Reading Level:	Grade __3__	Grade _____
Frustration Reading Level:	Grade __4__	Grade _____
Listening Comprehension Level:	Grade __4__	Grade _____

TEST 3: EMERGENT LITERACY TESTS

	1st	*2nd*
3a. Phonemic Awareness		
3a1. Rhyme Production	NA /8	___/8
3a2. Rhyme Recognition [*Alternate*]	NA /8	___/8
3a3. Initial Sound Recognition	NA /8	___/8
3a4. Phoneme Blending	NA /8	___/8
3a5. Phoneme Segmentation	NA /8	___/8
3b. Concepts about Print	NA /10	___/10
3c. Letter Knowledge		
3c1. Auditory Stimulus	NA /13	___/13
3c2. Visual Stimulus	NA /13	___/13

TEST 4: BASIC SIGHT WORDS AND PHRASES

	Mastery	Pretest	Posttest
4a. Quick Check for Basic Sight Words	36	NA /36	___/36
4b. Basic Sight Words	200	*205/220	___/220
4c. Basic Sight Word Phrases	125	116/143	___/143

TEST 5: PHONICS

	Mastery	Pretest	Posttest
5a. Application in Context	65	*67/73	___/73
5b. Initial Consonants	9	NA /10	___/10
5c. Initial Blends and Digraphs	9	NA /10	___/10
5d. Ending Sounds	8	NA /10	___/10
5e. Vowels	9	NA /10	___/10
5f. Phonograms	9	NA /10	___/10
5g. Blending	9	NA /10	___/10
5h. Substitution	22	NA /25	___/25
5i. Vowel Pronunciation	13	NA /15	___/15

TEST 6: STRUCTURAL ANALYSIS

	Mastery	Pretest	Posttest
6a. Application in Context			
6a1. Lower Level	24	*25/27	___/27
6a2. Higher Level	48	35 /53	___/53
Total	72	60 /80	___/80
6b. Hearing Word Parts	4	*5 /5	___/5
6c. Inflectional Endings	9	*10/10	___/10
6d. Prefixes	18	17 /20	___/20
6e. Suffixes	9	8 /10	___/10
6f. Compound Words	4	*4 /5	___/5
6g. Affixes	9	7 /10	___/10
6h. Syllabication	9	3 /10	___/10

TEST 7: KNOWLEDGE OF CONTRACTIONS

	Pretest	Posttest
Number of Words Pronounced (from left columns)	46 /47	___/47
Number of Words Known (from right columns)	+ 44 /47	___/47
Total Score	90 /94	___/94

► ## TEST 8: EL PASO PHONICS SURVEY

	Pretest	Posttest
Initial Consonant Sounds	NA /22	___/22
Ending Consonant X	NA /1	___/1
Initial Consonant Clusters	NA /35	___/35
Vowels, Vowel Teams, and Special Letter Combinations	NA /32	___/32

TEST 9: QUICK WORD LIST SURVEY

Comments ___NA_____

_____

_____

_____

_____

TEST 10: READING INTERESTS SURVEY

Comments _David does not enjoy reading books very much at this
point. He would rather watch TV, play computer games, or
participate in sports. He says he enjoys reading about sports,
riddles, & mysteries. He can't name the last book he read
or list his three favorite books._

Information Gained from David's Test Summary Sheet

The sample Test Summary Sheet also tells us a lot about David's reading abilities. He is a nine-year-old fourth grader whose independent, instructional, and frustration levels are 2, 3, and 4 respectively on the GWL. When reading passages, David's performance levels are the same both orally and silently and happen to mirror his performance on the GWL. His independent levels are second grade, his instructional levels are third grade, and his frustration levels are fourth grade.

These scores indicate that David reads about one year below his grade-placement level. His listening comprehension level of fourth grade suggests that David has the potential to read at his grade-placement level.

David's reading strengths and weaknesses are also typical of a student who reads at these levels. He has mastered basic sight words in isolation and is near mastery of these words in phrases. He has mastered letter knowledge and phonics but needs to improve his structural analysis skills.

To learn more about Maya's and David's strengths and weaknesses as readers so that instruction can be tailored to their specific needs, a more thorough analysis must be done. This analysis will require some additional time and a more complete understanding of the reading process. Before conducting this analysis, it may be useful to review the skills or abilities that affect reading success.

The Eight Major Skills or Abilities That Affect Reading Success

The various tests in the ESRI enable you to examine the following areas:

1. Emergent Literacy Skills
2. Basic Sight Vocabulary
3. Phonics
4. Structural Analysis
5. Context Clues
6. Fluency Skills
7. Vocabulary (Meaning)/Capacity
8. Comprehension

Which Tests Evaluate Which Skills?

Each of these eight skills or abilities is evaluated in more than one of the tests in the battery. A chart summarizing which tests evaluate which skills follows, along with a brief description of each of the eight areas. This description is followed by information about how to analyze a student's performance on the tests to determine his or her strengths or weaknesses in the eight areas.

Which Tests Evaluate Which Skills?

	Skill or Ability	*Test or Subtest (see List of Tests)*
1	Emergent Literacy Skills	1, 2a, 3a, 3b, 3c
2	Basic Sight Vocabulary	1, 2a, 4a, 4b, 4c, 5a
3	Phonics	
	Low Level	5b, 5c, 5d, 5e, 5f
	High Level and Blending	1, 2a, 5a, 5g, 5h, 5i, 8
4	Structural Analysis	1, 2a, 6a, 6b, 6c, 6d, 6e, 6f, 6g, 6h, 7
5	Context Clues	2a, 2b, 5a, 6a
6	Fluency	2a, 2b, 4c, 5a, 6a
7	Vocabulary (Meaning)/Capacity	1, 2a, 2b, 2c
8	Comprehension	2a, 2b (2c—Listening Comp. Only)

List of Tests

1. **San Diego Quick Assessment or Graded Word List (GWL)**
2. **Reading Passages Tests**
   2a. Oral Reading
   2b. Silent Reading
   2c. Listening Comprehension
3. **Emergent Literacy Tests**
   3a. Phonemic Awareness
      3a1. Rhyme Production
      3a2. Rhyme Recognition [Alternative Test]
      3a3. Initial Sound Recognition
      3a4. Phoneme Blending
      3a5. Phoneme Segmentation
   3b. Concepts about Print
   3c. Letter Knowledge
      3c1. Auditory Stimulus
      3c2. Visual Stimulus
4. **Basic Sight Vocabulary Tests**
   4a. Quick Check for Basic Sight Words
   4b. Basic Sight Words
   4c. Basic Sight Word Phrases
5. **Phonics Tests**
   5a. Application of Phonics Skills in Context
   5b. Initial Consonants
   5c. Initial Blends and Digraphs
   5d. Ending Sounds
   5e. Vowels
   5f. Phonograms
   5g. Blending
   5h. Substitution
   5i. Vowel Pronunciation
6. **Structural Analysis Tests**
   6a. Application of Structural Analysis Skills in Context
      6a1. Lower Level
      6a2. Higher Level
   6b. Hearing Word Parts
   6c. Inflectional Endings
   6d. Prefixes
   6e. Suffixes
   6f. Compound Words
   6g. Affixes
   6h. Syllabication
7. **Knowledge of Contractions Test**
8. **El Paso Phonics Survey**
9. **Quick Word List Survey**
10. **Reading Interests Survey**
    10a. Elementary
    10b. Adult

Using the Analysis Sheet

On pages 118–122 you will find the ESRI Analysis Sheet. To analyze the student's performance in each of the eight areas listed previously, first transfer the information from the Scoring Sheets for the individual tests or the Test Summary Sheet to the Analysis Sheet. (No student will require analysis in all eight of these areas. Thus, one or more of the areas will not be applicable for each student you test.) Then examine the student's performance in each area using the following guidelines to arrive at the initial diagnosis. Because reading performance is not static, your diagnosis must be somewhat tentative and subject to change as you continue to work with the student and observe his or her behavior over time.

After you have gained some experience with the inventory, you may find that you can transfer information directly from the Scoring Sheets to the Analysis Sheet. If so it will be unnecessary for you to use the Test Summary Sheet, saving you some time.

Included in this section are parts of the sample Analysis Sheets for Maya and David. Maya's performance will provide an example for the analysis of letter knowledge, basic sight vocabulary, and phonics, while David's testing will be used to illustrate the evaluation of structural analysis, context clues, fluency skills, vocabulary, and comprehension. Refer to these examples for help in understanding the following instructions.

Emergent Literacy

Phonemic Awareness

The phonemic awareness skills tested in this battery include Rhyme Production, Initial Sound Recognition, Phoneme Blending, and Phoneme Segmentation. If the student does not succeed at Rhyme Production, an Alternate Test for Rhyme Recognition is provided.

Research has shown a strong correlation between youngsters' phonemic awareness abilities and future reading success. Students who are able to recognize or produce rhyming words, recognize initial sounds, and blend and segment phonemes are much more likely to be successful in learning phonics and becoming skilled readers. Therefore, students who perform poorly on these tests should receive instruction and practice in these critical prereading skills.

Concepts about Print

The Concepts about Print Test assesses a student's metalinguistic skills, or the student's awareness of critical concepts learned in the early stages of reading. Specifically, the ESRI tests ten items in the area as follows: (1) recognition of the top of the page, (2) recognition of the bottom of the page, (3) recognition of an individual letter, (4) recognition of an individual word, (5) recognition of a sentence, (6) knowing where to begin reading a paragraph, (7) knowing that reading tracks from left to right along a line of print, (8) knowing the return sweep goes from the end of a line of print to the first word of the next line of print, (9) knowing where a paragraph ends, and (10) ability to read any of the words in the paragraph presented.

Most children learn these skills easily, often without direct instruction. Students who have been read to in early childhood may have learned these skills by seeing them modeled. Teachers can assist children who have not mastered these skills by providing instruction in each of these areas.

Letter Knowledge

Letter knowledge refers to a student's ability to recognize and name the twenty-six letters of the alphabet. Although students can learn to read without knowing letter names, letter names are not difficult to teach, and research has shown a high correlation between letter knowledge and future reading ability. If a student lacks letter knowledge, this will likely be reflected in the student's performance on Test 1 (GWL) and Test 2a (Oral Reading Test). Letter knowledge is tested directly on Tests 3c1 and 3c2.

Evaluating Performance

A student whose independent level is below 1.0 on the GWL (Test 1) may not have mastered emergent literacy skills. Generally, the more words a student is able to read, the more likely the student will have mastered the various prereading skills. If in doubt, these skills can be assessed in a reasonably short amount of time.

Generally, the Phonemic Awareness and Concepts about Print Tests should be given only to students who are nonreaders or who can read only a few words.

If the student scores at the instructional or frustration level on the PP passage during oral reading (Test 2a), the student *may not* have mastered letter knowledge. You should administer Tests 3c1 and 3c2 to a student whose *independent* level is below 1.0 on Test 1 or who reads orally at the instructional or frustration level on the PP passage of Test 2.

Tests 3c1 and 3c2 enable you to determine specifically which letters the student knows or does not know. Test 3c1 is easier than Test 3c2. If one or more letter names are unknown, these should be taught as part of the remedial program.

Using the Analysis Sheet for Emergent Literacy

The scores for the various tests may be copied from the Test Summary Sheet or from the Scoring Sheets for the tests administered. On the Analysis Sheet, spaces are provided to check whether the student has shown mastery of the various emergent literacy skills. Spaces are also provided for listing the student's weaknesses on each of the Phonemic Awareness, Concepts about Print, and Letter Knowledge skills tested.

Analysis of Maya's Emergent Literacy Skills

Maya's instructional level on the GWL (Test 1) was below 1.0, suggesting she may not have mastered *all* emergent literacy skills. Her ability to actually read up to the first- or second-grade level and the examiner's observation during the administration of Tests 1 and 2 persuaded the examiner that Maya had definitely mastered the prereading skills of phonemic awareness and concepts about print. However, the examiner was not certain that Maya had mastered letter knowledge. Her oral reading independent level on the Reading Passages (Test 2) was below PP, which also suggests she may not know all the letters. Therefore, the examiner administered Tests 3c1 and 3c2. On these tests, Maya correctly identified all the letters, indicating that she had indeed mastered letter knowledge. This information is helpful to the teacher or reading specialist. Even though Maya is a beginning reader, it will not be necessary to spend time teaching her phonemic awareness skills or concepts about print, or to recognize and name the letters of the alphabet.

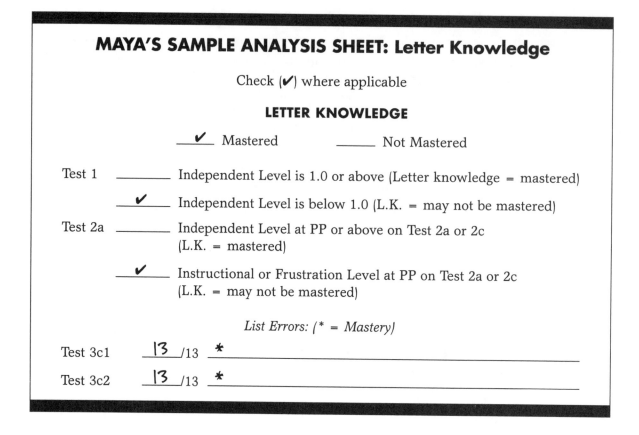

MAYA'S SAMPLE ANALYSIS SHEET: Letter Knowledge

Check (✔) where applicable

LETTER KNOWLEDGE

__✔__ Mastered   _____ Not Mastered

Test 1   _____ Independent Level is 1.0 or above (Letter knowledge = mastered)

     __✔__ Independent Level is below 1.0 (L.K. = may not be mastered)

Test 2a   _____ Independent Level at PP or above on Test 2a or 2c
(L.K. = mastered)

     __✔__ Instructional or Frustration Level at PP on Test 2a or 2c
(L.K. = may not be mastered)

List Errors: (* = Mastery)

Test 3c1   __13__ /13   *_____

Test 3c2   __13__ /13   *_____

Basic Sight Vocabulary

By definition basic sight words are those words that occur most frequently in written materials. The ESRI tests the student's knowledge of the Dolch Basic Sight Words with Tests 4a and 4b. This is the most widely used list of basic sight words. Test 4c evaluates the student's ability to read these words when combined to form phrases. The student's knowledge of basic sight vocabulary is also evaluated in Test 1 (GWL), Test 2a (Oral Reading Test), and Test 5a (Application of Phonics Skills in Context).

Evaluating Performance

Test 4a, the Quick Check for Basic Sight Words, can confirm that the student has mastered basic sight words *if* the student correctly pronounces all the words on this test. If the student misses even one word on Test 4a, Test 4b should be administered. If the student pronounces approximately 150 of the 220 Dolch words correctly on Test 4b, Test 4c should be given.

By examining the results of Tests 4b and 4c, you can determine specifically which basic sight words and phrases the student has not mastered. These can then be taught without having to use instructional time teaching words or phrases that are already known. The student's knowledge of basic sight words is also reflected in his or her performance on the GWL (Test 1). Listed on the following chart are the twenty-nine words on the GWL that are Dolch Basic Sight Words. (These words are printed in italics on the Scoring Sheet for the GWL.) The chart also shows where the words on the GWL appear on the Scoring Sheets for Tests 4b and 4c. At the bottom of the chart, the words are listed in alphabetical order. After you score the GWL, note whether any of these twenty-nine words were mispronounced. Then

BASIC SIGHT WORDS APPEARING ON THE GRADED WORD LIST

Listed below are the 29 words that appear on both the Graded Word List (GWL) and the Dolch Basic Sight Word List. Next to each word is its location on the Dolch Word List.

List PP	*List P*	*List 1*	*List 2*
see III–8	you I–7	live XI–6	our IX–11
play VII–7	come IV–4	thank XI–16	please XI–15
me III–18	not III–9	when III–4	myself VII–19
at II–1	with II–3	how V–8	
run IX–3	jump V–18	always VIII–18	
go II–15	help VI–13	today VII–17	
and I–3	is II–7		
look II–6	work VIII–5		
can III–2	are IV–3		
here VI–5	this III–15		

In alphabetical order, these words are:

always	here	myself	thank
and	how	not	this
are	is	our	today
at	jump	play	when
can	live	please	with
come	look	run	work
go	me	see	you
help			

check to see if these same words were mispronounced in isolation on Test 4b or in the phrases on Test 4c.

The student's knowledge of basic sight words will also be reflected in the student's performance on Test 2a (Oral Reading Test) and Test 5a (Application of Phonics in Context). The passages for both of these tests contain a number of basic sight words, which are printed in italics on the Scoring Sheets of the Oral Reading Passages, levels PP through fourth grade. They are also the nonunderlined words on Test 5a. When you examine your transcriptions of the student's oral reading of these passages, note which, if any, of the basic sight words were omitted, repeated, or mispronounced. (Actually, it matters little which type of error—omission, repetition, or mispronunciation—was made on the basic sight words. Each of these types of errors indicates that the student was unable to recognize and pronounce these words instantly at sight, as required of a capable reader.) Once again you can compare the basic sight words missed on Tests 2a or 5a with the words missed on the GWL and Tests 4b and 4c.

More Information on Basic Sight Words

Adequate knowledge of the letters is considered prerequisite to learning basic sight vocabulary. Usually, formal, systematic instruction on basic sight vocabulary does not begin until the student has completed a primer-level reader. Instant recognition of basic sight words is *essential* for fluent reading and adequate comprehension. By the end of third grade, a student should have mastered the lists of basic sight words and phrases. Unfortunately, remedial readers seldom attain that goal, which makes the testing and teaching of basic sight vocabulary a critical component of the diagnostic–remedial process.

Because your purpose is to test instant sight word recognition, it is imperative that the words be flashed quickly enough (on Tests 4b and 4c) to prevent the student from sounding them out. Likewise, with the exception of Test 4a the student should not read the words from lists because it is difficult to control exposure time. If you pronounce the words while the student merely circles the pronounced words from a group of words on a list, the results are invalid because such a task requires only visual recognition, not pronunciation of the words by the student.

Many students learn the sight words only in isolation and are unable to pronounce these same words when reading a passage orally. This is the major reason for testing, and later teaching, the sight word phrases. The phrases seem to build a bridge between isolated pronunciation and contextual reading. It is also essential for students to have frequent practice reading sentences or teacher-created stories that contain the words being learned, in addition to generous exposure to easy trade books.

If the student persistently misses most or all of the basic sight words, this student may need instruction on all of these words. However, if the student misses only a few words repeatedly, he or she may need instruction on only the specific words missed.

Using the Analysis Sheet for Basic Sight Words

On the Analysis Sheet, spaces are provided to check whether the student has shown mastery of basic sight words on each of the six tests described earlier. Before checking these boxes, copy the scores for Tests 4a, 4b, or 4c from the Test Summary Sheet or from the Scoring Sheets for these tests. The basic sight words that appear on Tests 1 and 5a are indicated on the Scoring Sheets for those tests. Count the number of basic sight words on these tests that the student read correctly and indicate that number on the Analysis Sheet. Likewise, examine the student's pronunciation of the basic sight words on the Oral Reading Tests through grade level 4 (these words are denoted by the use of italics on the Scoring Sheets) and indicate the number of basic sight words missed on the Oral Reading Tests in the appropriate box on the Analysis Sheet. After reviewing the student's performance on all of these tests, go back and check the appropriate spaces at the top of the Basic Sight Vocabulary section of the Analysis Sheet. You may simply check one or more of the boxes to indicate that the words were mastered in isolation, the phrases were mastered in isolation, or the words were mastered in context. Or you may use words to describe the student's performance, such as *near mastery* or *mostly*. If you wish, you may also list the words that were missed on each of the tests on a separate sheet.

The criterion for mastery of the total lists on Tests 4b and 4c is 90 percent. To make matters simple, the figures of 200 correct responses on Test 4b and 125 correct responses on Test 4c are given as mastery levels. If the student attains these levels, you should not feel it necessary to teach the few words that may have been missed unless the same words are missed repeatedly on the other tests. It is reasonable to expect that a few words may be mispronounced due to the speed of Tests 4b and 4c.

MAYA'S SAMPLE ANALYSIS SHEET: Basic Sight Words

Check (✔) where applicable

BASIC SIGHT VOCABULARY

_____No_____ Words Mastered in Isolation

_____N/A_____ Phrases Mastered in Isolation

_____No_____ Words Mastered in Context

Number of Basic Sight Words Pronounced
(See Scoring Sheets for errors)

Text 1 ___23___/29 _____

Test 2a _All ok on PP & I_ |_____

Test 4a ___NA___/36 _____

Test 4b ___47___/220 _____

Test 4c ___NA___/143 _____

Test 5a ___18___/21 _____

Analysis of Maya's Basic Sight Vocabulary

Maya's errors on basic sight words are typical of a reader who has no independent reading level on the oral and silent reading passages and whose instructional level is second grade. She pronounced 47 (or approximately 20 percent) of the 220 Dolch words correctly when these were tested in isolation on Test 4b. Because this was such a low score, the examiner correctly chose not to administer the Dolch phrases (Test 4c). Maya did not miss any of the Dolch words that appeared on the PP or first-grade level oral reading passages. She correctly pronounced 23 of the 29 Dolch words that appear on the GWL. Of the 21 basic sight words that appear on Test 5a, Maya correctly pronounced 18.

Maya has difficulty with many Dolch words, particularly when she must pronounce them quickly. Maya will need direct instruction on basic sight words. Because she knows relatively few of them, the teacher or reading specialist may choose to teach Maya all of the basic sight words and phrases.

Phonics

Phonics is an approach to the teaching of reading that emphasizes symbol–sound relationships. The ESRI tests phonics directly in Tests 5a through 5i and Test 8. In addition, phonics skills can be evaluated indirectly by examining the student's responses on Tests 1 and 2a. Before you can accurately assess a student's phonics abilities, it is important to understand the levels or stages of phonics ability.

Three Levels of Phonics Testing

Testing for phonics ability, like the teaching of phonics skills, occurs in three stages. Mastery of *low-level* skills requires the student to recognize the letter or letters when the sound is provided. In this case, the student is going from sound to symbol, as evaluated in Tests 5b through 5i.

To utilize phonics as an aid in decoding, however, the student must do precisely the opposite—go from symbol to sound. When reading, the student first sees the letter(s) or symbol(s) and then must think of the associated sound. This stage is identified as *high-level* phonics. In addition, for phonics to be effective the student must *blend* the sounds or phonemes together. The high-level phonics and blending skills are evaluated in Tests 5a, 5g–5i, 1, 2a, and 8.

Frequently, phonics tests do not enable the examiner to evaluate the higher-level phonics skills, and this may lead to a faulty diagnosis because many students possess only the low-level skills. Adequate analysis requires individual testing because it is impossible to test higher-level skills in a group situation.

Description of the Tests

TEST 5a

Test 5a evaluates the student's ability to apply phonics skills in a carefully constructed passage. Phonics skills are of most benefit to a student when used in conjunction with context clues. For some students, context ability is sufficiently developed for them to decode successfully with only minimal phonics ability.

On Test 5a, the student is asked to read aloud a short passage. When he or she completes it, you will be able to evaluate the student's application of seventy-three phonics elements in context.

This test should be given prior to Tests 5b through 5i. If the student performs at mastery level on this test, you should skip the other phonics tests and go directly to the structural analysis tests.

The 5a passage consists of 105 one-syllable words, based on the assumption that only one-syllable words should be used in evaluating phonics abilities. (Words of more than one syllable usually require structural analysis, which is a separate decoding skill.) Only 44 of the words in the passage (those that are underlined) are used to evaluate phonics skills. The 61 words that are not underlined include 19 basic sight words a student should recognize instantly without phonic analysis. (Some of these words are also phonetically irregular.) These 19 basic sight words appear a total of fifty-two times in the passage. In addition, 4 of the underlined words are repeated a total of nine times, and these nine repetitions are not counted in the analysis. A few of the words that are counted do appear on lists of basic sight words. However, they tend to appear with less frequency than most basic sight words and are phonetically regular.

The 44 underlined words allow for evaluation of 73 phonics elements as follows: 16 beginning single consonant sounds, 13 ending single consonant sounds, 7 beginning consonant blends, 8 ending consonant blends, 4 beginning consonant digraphs, 1 ending consonant digraph, 5 short vowels, 5 long vowels, 5 *r*-controlled vowels, and 9 vowel digraphs, diphthongs, and other vowel combinations.

Some or all of the words may be in the student's sight vocabulary, depending on the student's reading ability. For those students reading at or below a third-grade level, however, Test 5a provides an opportunity to evaluate the student's ability to use phonic analysis in the act of reading. In addition, if a careful transcription is made you will be able to observe the student's use of context clues and fluency skills. You should not attempt to evaluate the student's comprehension on this test.

TESTS 5b THROUGH 5f

Test 5b evaluates the student's ability to identify the single consonant letter (from a choice of five) that represents the beginning sound in a word pronounced by the examiner. Tests 5c through 5f provide for similar evaluation of initial blends and digraphs, ending sounds, short and long vowels, and common phonograms, respectively.

Tests 5b through 5f each consists of ten items. The mastery level for each test is nine correct of ten, except for Test 5d (ending sounds), for which eight of ten is considered mastery. This is because ending sounds are both more difficult and less important factors in the student's phonics instruction program.

The items and choices in Tests 5b through 5f were carefully selected to reflect a sampling of the most critical phonics elements and to require of the student maximum discrimination (minimal guess factor). Although guessing alone should account for two correct answers on the ten items of each test, the mastery level requires sufficient knowledge on the student's part. You will observe that students who have mastered the items tested will work quickly and easily.

It is important to remember that these are *low-level* phonics tests. Failure on these tests *does indicate* that the student lacks sufficient phonics skill, but mastery *does not prove* that the student possesses adequate phonics ability in the act of reading.

TEST 5g

Test 5g evaluates the student's ability to blend a beginning sound with one of two common phonograms. High-level phonics skill is required to pronounce the beginning sound, and blending skill is required to complete the item. Two factors in this test may be disconcerting to the student and should be considered when analyzing the results.

First, the appearance of the test items may confuse some students. This is unfortunate but unavoidable because it is necessary to separate the word parts. Second, some students may balk at pronouncing nonsense words, especially older students. The use of nonsense words (they also appear in Test 5h) is necessary to ensure that the student is not relying solely on sight recognition to pronounce the words. The test is designed with three nonsense words and a fourth word (*din*), which is not likely to be in the student's meaning vocabulary. Note whether the error pattern consists of only these words.

Because Test 5g evaluates two different skills (high-level phonics and blending), note which skill is lacking when errors are made. If the student lacks high-level phonics ability, the beginning sounds will be mispronounced. Blending will go awry if the student lacks blending ability or is confused by the format of the test or the pronunciation of the two phonograms.

The student should be discouraged from reading the words too quickly, as this will also cause errors. Correct pronunciation for each item may occur in either of two ways. For example, for the item *m* + *at*, the student may pronounce the /m/ then the /at/ separately, then blend them together to pronounce the word /mat/, or the student may simply pronounce the whole word, /mat/. If the student is unable to pronounce the word correctly, the item is scored as failed, even if the separate parts were pronounced correctly. (Some students may say the letter name or names for the beginning sound, then pronounce the phonogram and blend the word. This is acceptable, as long as the whole word is pronounced correctly.)

TEST 5h

Test 5h evaluates the student's ability to substitute a new phonics element and blend it with the rest of the word. The examiner pronounces the first word in each column. Then the student reads each word below the first word as a whole word. The first column requires the student to substitute and blend seven beginning single consonants. Subsequent columns require the student to substitute and blend beginning blends and digraphs, short vowels, long vowels, and ending consonants. Most students will find the columns increasingly difficult. The last column (ending consonants) may be particularly difficult if the student attempts to read the words too quickly.

TEST 5i

Test 5i evaluates the student's ability to pronounce fifteen real words that represent the more difficult vowel patterns: selected digraphs, diphthongs, and *r*-controlled vowels. Because of the variable pronunciation of these vowel patterns, nonsense words could not be used. Accordingly, it is possible for students to pronounce these words by relying on sight recognition. However, most of the words are not usually in the meaning vocabularies of remedial readers. This is a difficult test for a student who has any difficulty with phonics.

Evaluating Performance

Once the data have been gathered, you must analyze the various test results before planning specific instruction for the student. If the student performs well on the phonics tests, you may simply scan the Scoring Sheet to identify the few areas, if any, that warrant instruction. These specific phonics elements may be recorded on the Analysis Sheet. (Note: If the student masters Test 5a, you may consider the student's phonics knowledge to be sufficient and ignore the errors that appear on this and the other phonics tests.)

If the student misses a great many items on the phonics tests, an exacting analysis may also be unnecessary. Students who are unable to master Tests 5b through 5f may be so deficient in phonics ability that thorough reteaching of all skills is required.

For many students, however, only a portion of the phonics skills need to be taught. In such cases, the accuracy and efficiency of the diagnosis will have a significant impact on the quality of the instruction. Various tests identify as many as 100 different phonic elements. As noted previously, Test 5a evaluates the student's ability to apply 73 phonic elements, and Test 8, the El Paso Phonics Survey, evaluates 90 phonic elements.

More Information on Phonics

There is no infallible method for determining precisely which phonics skills a student has mastered. It is often the nature of remedial readers to "know" certain phonics elements one day and not the next. Some tests that purport to be diagnostic provide such a cursory evaluation of phonics skills as to be useless for instructional purposes. Others may allow for thorough testing but are impractical because they require so much time to administer and score.

The phonics tests in the ESRI provide for the analysis of every *critical* phonics element. Testing occurs at all three levels of phonics knowledge, and total administration and scoring time for all the phonics tests should not exceed thirty minutes.

Two other factors should be considered when diagnosing students' phonics abilities. These are the utility of phonics skills in the act of reading and the scope of phonics instruction.

The Utility of Phonics Skills

Phonics is only one of the tools students may use to decode. Millions of people have learned to read without ever receiving direct instruction in phonics. Many people learn to read by relying on a substantial sight vocabulary combined with skill in using context clues. Indeed, too much emphasis on phonics may hamper reading progress, particularly if emphasis is placed on the least important aspects of phonics instruction.

On the other hand, it is clear that for most students effective instruction in phonics can be a crucial aid in unlocking the puzzle of reading. The following principles are important and should help you understand the advantages and limitations of phonics abilities:

1. *Phonics instruction tends to be most helpful to students reading at or below a second-grade reading level.* Students who can read at or above a third-grade reading level rarely profit from an emphasis on letter-sound associations.

2. *Phonics is a useful tool for unlocking one-syllable words that are phonetically regular.* Unphonetic words (such as many of those on basic sight vocabulary lists) must be learned as sight words. Words of more than one syllable are most efficiently decoded through the combined use of structural analysis and context. (It would be a hopelessly inefficient approach for a reader to decode a word such as *disagreement* by sounding and blending each of the nine phonemes.) To read at a third-grade level, a student must be able to decode most one-syllable words. Those missed will likely be unphonetic sight words or words of more than one syllable.

The Scope of Phonics Instruction

For the student who is unable to decode regular one-syllable words, some phonics skills are more helpful than others. Research has shown that beginning letter sounds are most useful. Generalizations about ending sounds and vowel sounds are less helpful and much less reliable. This is not to suggest that such phonics skills not be taught; rather, you must make careful judgments about the scope and intensity of phonics instruction.

Older students may have particular difficulty with phonics for two reasons. In some cases, these students may fail to achieve mastery on some phonics tests because they have supplanted these skills with more advanced and efficient decoding techniques. Because phonics skills are a temporary crutch for beginning decoding, you should not be surprised or disappointed when older students fail to remember certain generalizations. Indeed, there are few literate adults, outside the field of reading, who can accurately demonstrate the short vowel sounds. Thus, a student's failure on some phonics tests should not be interpreted as proof that these skills require instruction. The phonics tests in the ESRI are designed to minimize this problem by focusing on the application of phonics skills rather than the recitation of rules.

In addition, many older students who have never mastered some of the phonics skills will fail to profit from intensive instruction on ending sounds or vowel sounds. These remedial readers may have consistently failed to master phonics skills over time in spite of substantial direct instruction. More repetition of the same failure is unlikely to improve reading performance. If you are certain the student has mastered beginning single consonants, consonant blends, and consonant digraphs, it may be most effective to minimize additional phonics teaching in favor of instruction in other decoding skills and more time engaged in the act of reading.

Using the Prescriptive Analysis of Phonics Skills Chart

On pages 123–126 you will find the Prescriptive Analysis of Phonics Skills Chart. This chart is designed with a grid format for use in evaluating the student's ability on ninety-six specific phonics elements. An x is noted for each phonic element that is tested on the various tests. You may transfer the data from the Scoring Sheets to the Prescriptive Analysis Chart by circling the appropriate x's on the grid, thus identifying not only which elements were missed but also the number of times the errors occurred. This enables you to determine whether each phonics error was an isolated mistake or whether there is a pattern of such errors. Because many possible phonics errors may be made on Test 1 (GWL) and Test 2a (Oral Reading Test), you must first identify the phonics errors made, then mark the x's in the appropriate spaces in the grid, and then circle them. After the grid is completed, you may then identify the student's phonics strengths and weaknesses and transfer this information to the spaces on the Analysis Sheet.

These steps were followed to assess Maya's phonics skills. First, the information from the Scoring Sheets was transferred to the Prescriptive Analysis Chart (where the errors were indicated by circling the x's), and then this information was transferred to the Analysis Sheet. Each of these steps is illustrated and described below.

Prescriptive Analysis of Maya's Phonics Skills

An examination of Maya's phonics errors as they appear on the Prescriptive Analysis Chart reveals a considerable number of errors on the vowel combinations and a few other errors on long vowels, ending consonant blends, and ending single consonants. Overall, Maya has made relatively few phonics errors; her weaknesses are in the less important areas of phonics.

Using the Analysis Sheet for Phonics

The information from Maya's Scoring Sheets and the Prescriptive Analysis of Phonics Skills Chart is summarized on the Analysis Sheet. The Analysis Sheet provides write-on lines to allow you to indicate the student's mastery of individual tests or to summarize the weaknesses revealed. After evaluating the student's performance on the various phonics tests, you may indicate on the Analysis Sheet whether the student has achieved mastery of phonics at each of the three levels.

MAYA'S SAMPLE PRESCRIPTIVE ANALYSIS OF PHONICS SKILLS

Phonic Element ↓	5a	5b	5c	5d	5e	5f	5g	5h	5i	8	1	2a
Beginning Single Consonants	↓	↓	↓	↓	↓	↓	↓	↓	↓	↓	↓	↓
b	×	×						×		×		
hard c	×							×		×		
d	×	×					×			×		
f	×	×					×			×		
hard g	×	×								×		
h	×	×					×			×		
j	×							×		×		
k										×		
l	×							×		×		
m	×						×			×		
n	×	×								×		
p	×	×								×		
r	×							×		×		
s	×	×								×		
t	×							×		×		
v								×		×		
w	×	×								×		
z	×									×		

↓	5a	5b	5c	5d	5e	5f	5g	5h	5i	8	1	2a
Ending Single Consonants	↓	↓	↓	↓	↓	↓	↓	↓	↓	↓	↓	↓
b	×			×				×				
soft c	×											
d	×			×				×				
f								×				
hard g	×							×				
soft g	(×)											
k	×											
l	×			×								
m								×				
n	×											
p	×			×								
r	×											
s	×											
t	×			×								
x	×									×		

Phonic Element ↓		Test											
	5a	5b	5c	5d	5e	5f	5g	5h	5i	8	1	2a
Beginning Consonant Digraphs	↓	↓	↓	↓	↓	↓	↓	↓	↓	↓	↓	↓
ch	×		×				×	×		×		
sh	×		×					×		×		
th	×		××				×			×		
wh	×							×		×		

	5a	5b	5c	5d	5e	5f	5g	5h	5i	8	1	2a
Ending Consonant Digraph	↓	↓	↓	↓	↓	↓	↓	↓	↓	↓	↓	↓
sh	×			×								

	5a	5b	5c	5d	5e	5f	5g	5h	5i	8	1	2a
Beginning Consonants Blends	↓	↓	↓	↓	↓	↓	↓	↓	↓	↓	↓	↓
bl			×				×			×		
cl	×									×		
pl	×		×					×		×		
br	×		×							×		
fr								×		×		
gr	(×)		×							×		
tr	×						×			×		
sm	×		×							×		
sp			×					×		×		
st								×		×		
str	×						×			×		

	5a	5b	5c	5d	5e	5f	5g	5h	5i	8	1	2a
Ending Consonants Blends	↓	↓	↓	↓	↓	↓	↓	↓	↓	↓	↓	↓
nd	(×)											
ng	×			×								
nt				×								
rd	×			×								
rk	(×)											
rl	×											
rn	(×)											
rt	(×)											
sk				×								
st	×											

Phonic Element / Test

Short Vowels

Short Vowels	5a	5b	5c	5d	5e	5f	5g	5h	5i	8	1	2a
a	×				×					×		
e	×				×			×		×		
i	×				×			×		×		
o	×				×			×		×		
u	×				×			×		×		

Long Vowels

Long Vowels	5a	5b	5c	5d	5e	5f	5g	5h	5i	8	1	2a
a	⊗				×					×		
e	×				×					×		
i	⊗				×			×		×		⊗
o	×				×			×		×		
u	⊗				×			×		×		

Vowel Combinations

Vowel Combinations	5a	5b	5c	5d	5e	5f	5g	5h	5i	8	1	2a
ar	⊗								×	×		
er	⊗								⊗	×		
ir	⊗								⊗	×		
or	×								×			
long or									⊗	×		
ur	⊗								⊗	×		
ai	⊗								⊗	×		⊗
au									⊗	×		
aw	⊗								⊗	×		
ay	×									×		
ea	⊗									×	⊗	⊗
oa									×	×		
oi	⊗								⊗	×		
oo	×									×		
ou	⊗								⊗	×		
diph ow	⊗								⊗	×		
long ow									⊗	×		
oy	×								⊗	×		

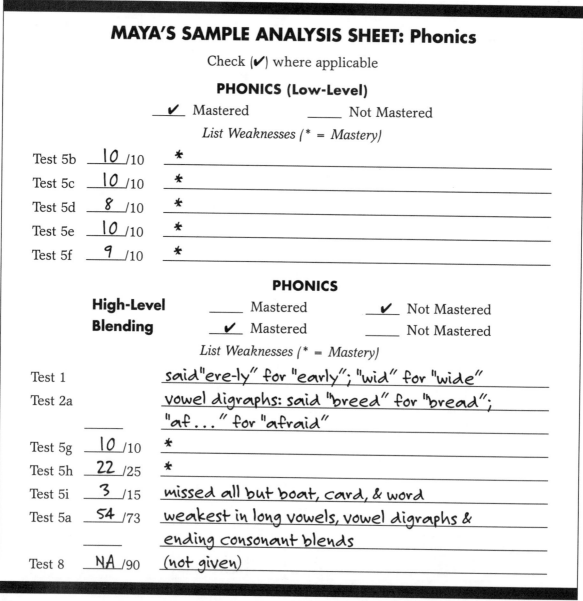

Phonic Element ↓	Test											
Phonograms	5a ↓	5b ↓	5c ↓	5d ↓	5e ↓	5f ↓	5g ↓	5h ↓	5i ↓	8 ↓	1 ↓	2a ↓
ame						×						
ime						×						
ike						×						
ock						(×)						
eep						×						
ight						×						
ing						×						
ade						×						
ang						×						
ill						×						

MAYA'S SAMPLE ANALYSIS SHEET: Phonics

Check (✔) where applicable

PHONICS (Low-Level)

__✔__ Mastered   _____ Not Mastered

List Weaknesses (* = Mastery)

Test 5b __10__/10   * _____
Test 5c __10__/10   * _____
Test 5d __8__/10   * _____
Test 5e __10__/10   * _____
Test 5f __9__/10   * _____

PHONICS

High-Level   _____ Mastered   __✔__ Not Mastered
Blending   __✔__ Mastered   _____ Not Mastered

List Weaknesses (* = Mastery)

Test 1   said "ere-ly" for "early"; "wid" for "wide"
Test 2a   vowel digraphs: said "breed" for "bread";
_____   "af..." for "afraid"
Test 5g __10__/10   *
Test 5h __22__/25   *
Test 5i __3__/15   missed all but boat, card, & word
Test 5a __54__/73   weakest in long vowels, vowel digraphs &
_____   ending consonant blends
Test 8 __NA__/90   (not given)

Analysis of Maya's Phonics Skills

Maya's performance on the tests of low-level phonics skills was excellent overall. She achieved mastery on all five of the low-level tests. Maya made two errors on the GWL (Test 1) that might be attributed to phonics weaknesses: She mispronounced *wide* and *early*. On the Oral Reading Test (Test 2a), Maya's mispronunciation of two words (*bread* and *afraid*) may have resulted from her inability to recognize and decode vowel digraphs. Maya's weakness in this area appeared again on Tests 5a and 5i. She also missed three long vowels and four ending consonant blends on Test 5a. Maya did master Tests 5g and 5h, indicating that her blending skills are satisfactory.

Maya has many more strengths than weaknesses in phonics, and she has mastered phonics skills in the most important areas: beginning consonants, beginning consonant blends, beginning consonant digraphs, and short vowels. She has mastered most but not all of the high-level phonics skills and has mastered blending ability. Maya's weaknesses in phonics are in the areas of vowel combinations, long vowels, and ending consonant blends.

Structural Analysis

Structural Analysis is a decoding skill analogous to phonics. It is often referred to as *morphology,* which is concerned with the study of meaning-bearing units such as root words, prefixes, suffixes, possessives, plurals, accent rules, and syllables. To use structural analysis to decode a multisyllable word, the reader first identifies the separate units in the word, then pronounces the units, then blends them together. (In using phonics, the reader goes through the same process with phonemes, or individual sounds.) The ESRI tests structural analysis directly in Tests 6a through 6h. In addition, a student's structural analysis skills can be evaluated indirectly by examining the student's responses on Tests 1 and 2a.

Description of the Tests

TEST 6a (CONSISTING OF 6a1 AND 6a2)

This test evaluates the student's ability to apply the various structural analysis skills during contextual reading. The two passages, 6a1 and 6a2, contain a total of eighty words that require the application of structural analysis. Because of the disproportionate number of long words, the readability of these passages is high. Subtest 6a1, according to the Flesch-Kincaid readability formula, is written at the 5.1 grade level. Using the Fry formula, this passage is judged to be at approximately the low fifth-grade level. Subtest 6a2 is written at the 7.0 grade level according to the Flesch-Kincaid formula and at approximately the mid-seventh-grade level according to the Fry formula. You should not assume, however, that students who successfully read these passages can comfortably read other materials at these levels.

Test 6a should be given before Tests 6b through 6h. Give Test 6a1 first and determine whether the student mastered this passage. If so, have the student read the second passage out loud (6a2). If the student performs at mastery level on Test 6a2, you may skip the other structural analysis tests. A student who masters this test probably is not lacking in structural analysis skills. If the student fails to master both of the passages, continue on to Test 6b.

TEST 6b

Tests 6b through 6h vary in difficulty. Generally, the initial tests are much easier than the later tests. Test 6b evaluates the student's ability to hear the separate parts (syllables) of words. If the student is unable to do this, instruction should focus on this area prior to other structural analysis skills. You should not be concerned about the student's ability to identify the *specific points* in words where syllable division takes place. Although this skill, often called *end-of-line division,* is frequently tested, it is not useful for decoding purposes. (Indeed, the only time it is useful is when an individual is engaged in formal writing and there is no dictionary at hand. To further complicate matters, dictionaries do not always agree on where words are divided. Even so, the need for this skill has been virtually eliminated by the development of word-processing programs that automatically determine where to divide words at the end of a line of print.)

TESTS 6c THROUGH 6e

These tests evaluate the student's ability to combine various inflectional endings, prefixes, and suffixes with root words, and to pronounce the resulting new words. Test 6c presents the six most common inflectional endings; Test 6d presents ten of the most common and easily teachable prefixes; and Test 6e presents eight of the most common suffixes. In every case, you begin by pronouncing the root word for the student so that the task is easier than that required in actual reading. The student, however, must pronounce the whole word correctly to receive credit for the item. If the student fails on any of these items, your task is to determine whether the failure results from the student's inability to pronounce the structural part, blend the part with the root, or both.

TEST 6f

This test evaluates the student's ability to recognize that many long words are the combination of two shorter, whole words. The five compound words presented consist of one real word and four nonsense words. Because it is more important for the student to *recognize* the two separate units of the compound words, perfect pronunciation is not required as long as the student demonstrates recognition of the compound characteristic. Nonsense words must be used to ensure that the student is not recognizing the whole words merely by sight.

TEST 6g

This test evaluates the student's ability to pronounce two-syllable words containing common affixes. On this test, you do not pronounce the root word, so the task is significantly more difficult for the student than Tests 6c through 6e. In this case, the student must go through all three steps of decoding through structural analysis: (1) separating the parts; (2) pronouncing the word parts; and (3) blending the separate parts to pronounce the whole word. As with Test 6f, most of the items on this test are nonsense words.

TEST 6h

This test evaluates the student's ability to pronounce ten multisyllable words. Accurate pronunciation of these words requires the student to use the structural analysis skills previously tested as well as the ability to divide words into parts when obvious affixes are not present. Because they are especially difficult and not likely to be recognized by sight, these words are all real words.

Evaluating Performance

First, examine the student's error pattern on Test 1 (GWL). A few of the words on lists 2 and 3 of the GWL require the student to apply structural analysis if he or she does not recognize these words by sight. All of the words on lists 4 and above are multisyllable words requiring structural analysis ability for decoding. This test, then, gives you a quick assessment of the student's structural analysis ability.

Next, review the student's performance on Test 2a, the Oral Reading Test. Again, look to see if the student fails to pronounce multisyllable words correctly. As you might imagine, minimal structural analysis skills are required for the passages written at the second- and third-grade levels. But beginning at the fourth-grade level, these skills are essential for the student to read at the instructional or independent level.

Then examine the student's performance on Tests 6b through 6h. With these tests, you may determine whether the student is having difficulty with structural analysis and identify the *types* of structural analysis weaknesses the reader exhibits. This then directs you to the specific instruction needed to remedy the difficulty. Finally, a rather minor part of structural analysis is evaluated in Test 7, Knowledge of Contractions. This test tells you not only which contractions the student can or cannot pronounce but also whether the student knows the words from which the contractions were formed.

It is important to remember that the various decoding skills work interdependently. Test 6a, like the phonics Test 5a, reveals the extent to which the student relies on context clues along with structural analysis. Some students may perform significantly better on Test 6a2, for instance, than on Test 6h due to the contextual presentation. Likewise, Test 6a enables you to evaluate the student's fluency skills. The procedures for evaluating context usage and fluency skills are presented in the sections following the evaluation of David's structural analysis skills.

Using the Analysis Sheet for Structural Analysis

On the Analysis Sheet, spaces are provided to list the student's scores on the various tests that evaluate structural analysis abilities. These scores may be copied from the Test Summary Sheet or from the Scoring Sheets for Tests 6a through 6h and Test 7. Spaces are provided to indicate the types of errors the student has made on each test. You may also indicate in these spaces if the skill tested was mastered. Mastery levels for each of the Tests 6a through 6h are indicated on the Analysis Sheet.

Analysis of David's Structural Analysis Skills

David mastered the lower-level tests and understands the concept of structural analysis. When a word is at all familiar to him, he pronounces part of the word correctly. He recognizes that the length of a word is indicative of more than one syllable and tries to say a familiar word. This strategy enabled David to achieve mastery on Subtest 6a1, because the multisyllable words were familiar to him. However, in Subtest 6a2 the words were not sufficiently familiar and David lacks the more advanced structural analysis skills needed to help him separate the word parts, pronounce them, and then blend them together to make the whole word. David's structural analysis skills are inadequate both in and out of context.

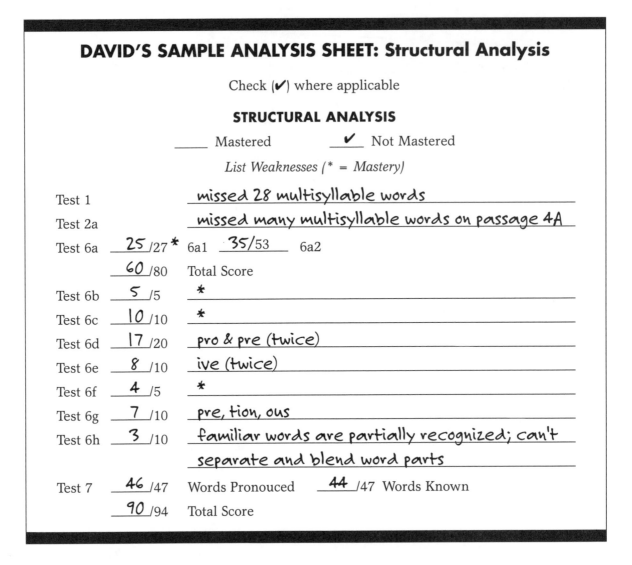

DAVID'S SAMPLE ANALYSIS SHEET: Structural Analysis

Check (✔) where applicable

STRUCTURAL ANALYSIS

_____ Mastered   ✔ Not Mastered

List Weaknesses (* = Mastery)

Test 1	missed 28 multisyllable words
Test 2a	missed many multisyllable words on passage 4A
Test 6a _25_/27 * 6a1 _35_/53 6a2	
_60_/80 Total Score	
Test 6b _5_/5 *	
Test 6c _10_/10 *	
Test 6d _17_/20 pro & pre (twice)	
Test 6e _8_/10 ive (twice)	
Test 6f _4_/5 *	
Test 6g _7_/10 pre, tion, ous	
Test 6h _3_/10 familiar words are partially recognized; can't separate and blend word parts	
Test 7 _46_/47 Words Pronouced _44_/47 Words Known	
_90_/94 Total Score	

Context Clues

Context clues (sometimes called *contextual analysis*) are clues to the pronunciation and meaning of an unknown word derived from the words or sentences preceding or following that word. For example, one can use context clues to determine that the missing word in the following sentence is *dog:* "The _____ was barking all night and kept me awake." Context clues are an extremely important part of decoding skills. Research has shown that readers decode most effectively when they use phonics or structural analysis in conjunction with context clues.

Because context clues are used along with other decoding skills, it is somewhat difficult to test the student's ability to use context alone. However, it is usually not difficult to evaluate the student's strengths and weaknesses in this area by examining the student's performance during contextual reading.

Evaluating Performance

A student's ability to use context clues can be determined by examining the performance on Test 2a, the Oral Reading Test. Look at each error made (a word may be mispronounced, omitted, inserted, or repeated) and try to ascertain if the error was related to the student's use of context. Sometimes students make errors by overrelying on the graphic features of a word. Suppose a passage contains the following sentence: "The boy went into the house." A student might read this sentence as follows: "The boy went into the *horse*." It would be logical to conclude that this student has not relied on context (the sense of the sentence) to help in decoding the word *house*. Instead, the student substituted the word *horse*, which is quite similar in appearance. Another student might read the same sentence as follows: "The boy went into the *building*." This student may have overrelied on context and substituted a word that was similar in meaning but quite dissimilar in appearance. Most reading experts would agree that both students have a problem, though they might disagree about which student has the more serious problem. A student may have difficulty in the area of context clues by either underrelying or overrelying on context.

You may examine the student's performance on Tests 5a or 6a in a similar way. Did the student's errors on these passages reflect either under- or over-reliance on context clues? One other test *may* give you information about a student's ability to use context clues. The student's answers to questions asked after reading the Silent Reading Passages (Test 2b) may reveal an inability to comprehend what was read as a result of poor use of context clues.

Using the Analysis Sheet for Context Clues

Space is provided on the Analysis Sheet for you to write brief comments or give examples regarding the student's use of context clues. Corrective procedures exist for helping students who either under- or overrely on context clues.

DAVID'S SAMPLE ANALYSIS SHEET: Context Clues

Check (✔) where applicable

CONTEXT CLUES
(Most of the time)

✔	Uses Context Clues Effectively
_____	Underrelies on Context
_____	Overrelies on Context

Comments

Test 2a	most substitutions were logical
Test 5a and/or 6a	substitutions not logical on these tests, esp. as decoding became difficult
Other Tests	not given

Analysis of David's Use of Context Clues

Most students can use context clues as long as they are reading at their independent or instructional levels. When they read passages at their frustration level, most students are no longer able to use context clues effectively as an aid to decoding.

David's use of context clues is inefficient, which is not unusual for students with reading difficulties. On the Oral Reading Passages, David tended to use context effectively to assist in pronouncing unknown words up through the fourth-grade level passage. His substitutions were logical both semantically (word meaning) and syntactically (word arrangement in sentences); for example, *purpose* for *process*. However, on Tests 5a, 6a1, and 6a2, David used context less effectively. This is not unusual. These passages are designed to test directly for knowledge of phonics and structural analysis and present context clues to the reader that will be less helpful if the reader has difficulty with the other decoding skills.

Fluency Skills

Fluency skills, sometimes called efficiency skills, refer to a student's ability to read smoothly. Some students have adequate decoding skills but may have difficulty with speed, accuracy, or both. Some try to read too fast and so stumble on words they can attack and pronounce in isolation. On the other hand, some students are slow to use the word-attack skills they have, and as a result, they read word by word and/or they phrase improperly. Many students who lack fluency skills have picked up faulty reading habits that persist long after they should.

Evaluating Performance

Fluency skills may be evaluated by examining the student's performance on Test 2a, the Oral Reading Test. You should examine at least two different passages, if possible, one at the student's independent level and a second at the instructional level. You may examine the transcriptions of the student's oral reading of both of these passages to evaluate fluency skills. Until you have gained some experience in doing this, however, you will find it helpful to listen to the tape recording of the student's reading while you evaluate performance in the following areas:

1. *Speed.* Did the student read too fast, causing unnecessary word recognition errors, or was the reading speed too slow for acceptable comprehension and adequate rate of learning?
2. *Phrasing.* Was the phrasing appropriate, or did the student read word by word, or with other inappropriate phrasing?
3. *Accuracy.* Did the student correctly pronounce the words in the passage, or were the words miscalled due to excessive speed or poor phrasing? If omissions, repetitions, insertions, or substitutions occurred, were these the result of poor decoding skills, fluency problems, or both?
4. *Punctuation.* Were punctuation cues followed, or did the student ignore or misinterpret punctuation marks?

Similar observations may be made by listening to, or examining the transcriptions of, the student's reading of the passages on Tests 5a and 6a.

The student's *rate of reading* may be determined on Test 2b, the Silent Reading Test. While the student is reading these passages, you may also observe the following fluency skill problems: lip movements, finger pointing, or head movements.

Finally, a significant discrepancy in the student's performance on Test 4b, Basic Sight Words, versus Test 4c, Basic Sight Word Phrases, is often an indicator of poor fluency skills. Students who do significantly better on Test 4b, which tests the words in isolation, than on Test 4c, which tests the words in phrases, are likely to have difficulty with fluency skills.

Using the Analysis Sheet for Fluency Skills

Space is provided on the Analysis Sheet for you to write brief comments about the student's fluency skills as they were revealed on each of the aforementioned tests. You may use a check mark to indicate whether the rate of reading was slow, medium, or fast, according to the charts provided on the B and D passages of Test 2b. After the data have been gathered and evaluated, check the appropriate boxes on the Analysis Sheet at the top of the Fluency Skills section.

Analysis of David's Use of Fluency Skills

As indicated on the Analysis Sheet, David has no difficulty with fluency skills when reading up to his current instructional level, grade 3. However, when he

---

DAVID'S SAMPLE ANALYSIS SHEET: Fluency Skills

Check (✔) where applicable

FLUENCY SKILLS

___✔___ Reads Fluently (at Instructional Level)

Difficulty with:
(at Frustration Level)

___✔___ Speed

___✔___ Phrasing

___✔___ Accuracy

___✔___ Punctuation

_____ Other _____

Comments

Test 2a   no problems through 3rd grade level; poor efficiency skills at 4th grade level

Test 2b   no lip movements, finger-pointing, or head movements

Rate of Reading: ___✔___ Slow   _____ Medium   _____ Fast

Test 4c   weakness in basic sight word phrases

Test 5a and/or 6a   Poor efficiency on 6a, Part II

attempts to read more difficult material, such as the 4A passage or the passage on Test 6a2, his fluency skills deteriorate quickly, with his speed, phrasing, attention to punctuation, and accuracy all affected. His relatively poor performance on the sight word phrases contributes to the difficulty. He tends to mispronounce basic sight words when reading orally in context as well as when reading the phrases flashed in isolation.

Vocabulary (Meaning)/Capacity

Vocabulary refers to the student's knowledge of the *meaning* of words encountered in reading. It is strongly related to comprehension. If a student is unaware of the meaning of certain words, the student's ability to pronounce the words will be affected, regardless of the student's skill in decoding. More important, when the student does not know the meaning of certain words, his or her comprehension of the material being read will be diminished. The term *capacity* is used to indicate the student's potential for improvement in reading. This is, of course, related to intelligence. If the student's capacity is significantly limited, it is unlikely that the student will be able to read as well as his or her peers even after receiving special instruction. Meaning vocabulary is also related to capacity. Usually, students with large meaning vocabularies have greater potential for reading improvement.

Unfortunately, capacity is difficult to measure precisely. Intelligence tests can be given; students with higher IQs generally have better potential for reading achievement, whereas those with lower IQs probably have lower reading achievement potential. However, exceptions do exist. Some students with very high IQs have serious reading difficulties and other students with low IQs achieve an adequate level of literacy. So you must regard estimates of capacity with caution.

Evaluating Performance

Test 2c measures the student's *listening comprehension*. This provides an estimate of the student's capacity and, as you might expect, is strongly influenced by the student's meaning vocabulary. As you recall, the test is administered by the examiner reading to the student passages of increasing difficulty. After each passage is read, ask the student questions about the material, then score the responses to determine whether the student's listening comprehension is acceptable on material at each grade level. If the student's listening comprehension is adequate on material written at his or her grade-placement level, that indicates the student has the capacity or potential to read at least up to grade level. Because most students tested with an informal reading inventory read below grade level, it is usually not necessary to test for listening comprehension above the student's grade-placement level.

On each passage at third-grade level or above, one question is a vocabulary question specifically asking the student about the meaning of one word in the passage. If a student frequently misses the vocabulary questions when reading orally, silently, or during listening comprehension, that would indicate the student may have difficulty with meaning vocabulary.

Vocabulary knowledge may also be inferred from the student's answers to many of the other questions in the inventory. Vocabulary knowledge may also be indicated by the student's performance on Test 1 (GWL). Students must be able to at least recognize the correct pronunciation of difficult words to decode them properly. For example, the word *apparatus* (list 6, word 5 on the GWL) may be mispronounced in many ways if the student is unfamiliar with the word. This is true for many of the words on the higher-level lists of the GWL. Even with good decoding skills, the student must have at least low-level vocabulary knowledge of the words to pronounce them correctly.

Finally, you can often gain information about the student's vocabulary knowledge simply by engaging in conversation with the student. This normally occurs during testing; however, if the examiner is also the student's teacher, this individual is likely to have more information about both the student's vocabulary knowledge and learning potential.

Although it will not be possible to obtain a precise assessment of the student's meaning vocabulary or capacity from the tests in the ESRI, you can usually compare the student in these areas with other students you have tested and, in doing so, arrive at an estimate of the student's vocabulary knowledge and capacity.

Using the Analysis Sheet for Vocabulary/Capacity

Space is provided on the Analysis Sheet for you to write brief comments about the student's meaning vocabulary and capacity as they were revealed on each of the tests indicated.

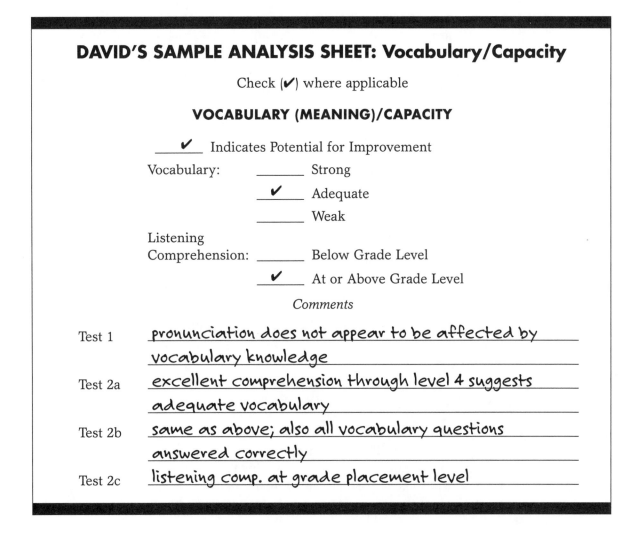

DAVID'S SAMPLE ANALYSIS SHEET: Vocabulary/Capacity

Check (✔) where applicable

VOCABULARY (MEANING)/CAPACITY

_____✔_____ Indicates Potential for Improvement

Vocabulary: _____ Strong

        __✔__ Adequate

        _____ Weak

Listening
Comprehension: _____ Below Grade Level

        __✔__ At or Above Grade Level

Comments

Test 1 pronunciation does not appear to be affected by vocabulary knowledge

Test 2a excellent comprehension through level 4 suggests adequate vocabulary

Test 2b same as above; also all vocabulary questions answered correctly

Test 2c listening comp. at grade placement level

Analysis of David's Vocabulary/Capacity

David is relatively strong in these areas. His vocabulary appears to be at least adequate. It did not limit his ability to pronounce words in isolation on the GWL, he answered all specific vocabulary questions correctly, and his comprehension remained strong up through the fourth-grade passages, both orally and silently. He also demonstrated adequate listening comprehension on the fourth-grade passage, which is above his present reading level. It appears from these tests that David has the capacity to read at least up to grade level. At present, it is his weak decoding skills that prevent this.

Comprehension

Comprehension refers to the meaning gained from what is written on a page when read. This is, of course, the ultimate objective of reading. Instruction provided to students, including that in the area of decoding, is designed to help students understand what they read. Although comprehension is vitally important, it too is difficult to measure precisely.

Comprehension is affected by many factors. Reading comprehension is dependent on decoding ability. Thus, students who cannot decode material fluently simply cannot be expected to understand it. Vocabulary knowledge is also a critical component of reading comprehension. In addition, each student's ability to comprehend a particular passage will also be affected by that student's prior knowledge of the subject, interest in the subject, and purpose for reading.

Research has shown that comprehension is not an automatic consequence of fluent decoding. Many students must be taught *how* to comprehend what they read. Fortunately, there are many effective strategies teachers can employ to accomplish this goal.

Evaluating Performance

The ESRI provides questions for evaluating three aspects of comprehension: factual, inferential, and vocabulary. The preprimer-level passages contain five comprehension questions. All other passages contain ten questions. At grade 3 and above, eight questions evaluate the student's understanding of factual information in the passage, and one each evaluates inferential understanding and vocabulary. One reason for emphasizing factual questions is to enhance the validity of the tests. For a test to be valid, it must have a high degree of interscorer reliability. That means that different individuals who administer a test must agree on what constitutes correct or incorrect answers. It is considerably easier for different scorers to agree about answers to factual questions. With inferential and other higher-level questions, many answers may be considered acceptable by different test administrators.

The ESRI enables you to determine the student's comprehension level in conjunction with the student's word-recognition level when using Test 2a, the Oral Reading Test. By examining the student's error pattern, you can determine whether a student's failure to read a passage successfully was a result of poor word-attack skills, poor comprehension, or both. Once a student has reached frustration level, it is normal for comprehension to drop considerably. To determine whether poor comprehension is causing the reading difficulty, examine the student's performance on the passage or passages at the instructional level and the first passage at the frustration level.

Test 2b, the Silent Reading Test, probably provides the best overall estimate of the student's reading comprehension. Most readers comprehend better when reading silently rather than orally. (Exceptions are most beginning and some remedial readers whose comprehension may benefit from hearing the words as they read them.) If the student attains higher independent and/or instructional levels on the silent reading passages than on the oral reading passages, this suggests the student's comprehension is strong relative to word-attack skills. Test 2c, the Listening Comprehension Test, evaluates the student's listening comprehension level, which is related to, but not the same as, the student's reading comprehension level.

Using the Analysis Sheet for Comprehension Ability

Space is provided on the Analysis Sheet for you to write brief comments about the student's comprehension when reading orally and silently or when listening to material being read by the examiner.

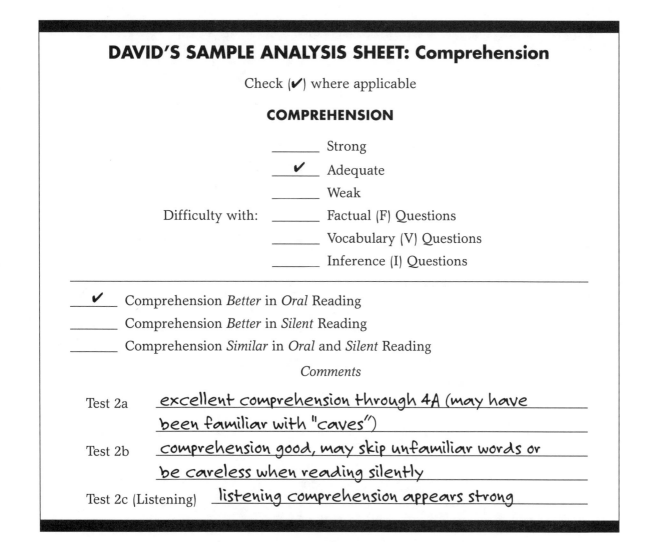

DAVID'S SAMPLE ANALYSIS SHEET: Comprehension

Check (✔) where applicable

COMPREHENSION

	Strong
✔	Adequate
	Weak

Difficulty with:

	Factual (F) Questions
	Vocabulary (V) Questions
	Inference (I) Questions

✔ Comprehension *Better* in *Oral* Reading
____ Comprehension *Better* in *Silent* Reading
____ Comprehension *Similar* in *Oral* and *Silent* Reading

Comments

Test 2a — excellent comprehension through 4A (may have been familiar with "caves")

Test 2b — comprehension good, may skip unfamiliar words or be careless when reading silently

Test 2c (Listening) — listening comprehension appears strong

Analysis of David's Comprehension Ability

Comprehension appears to be another of David's strengths. His familiarity with the topic covered on Test 2a, passage 4A may have enhanced his comprehension of that selection. Although still good, his comprehension was less impressive on the silent reading passages. It may be that David skips unfamiliar words or reads carelessly when reading silently.

Reading Interests

Test 10, the Reading Interests Survey, can provide you with additional information you may use in planning a remedial program for a student. The survey includes a number of open-ended questions that may provide a clue about the student's attitude toward reading and school, a section for the student to indicate areas of reading interest, and a section about the student's reading experiences, television-watching habits, and so forth. The survey may be completed by the student if he or she has sufficient reading and writing skills to respond to the questions, or it may be given orally with the examiner writing in the student's responses.

David's responses to the Reading Interests Survey are summarized on the following Analysis Sheet.

DAVID'S SAMPLE ANALYSIS SHEET:
READING INTERESTS SURVEY

Comments   David does not enjoy reading books very much at this point. He would much rather watch TV, play computer games, or participate in sports. He says he enjoys reading about sports, riddles, and mysteries. He can't name the last book he read or list his three favorite books.

Using the Analysis Sheet for Reading Interests

David's responses to the Reading Interests Survey suggest that motivating his interest in reading and books will be an important part of his remedial program. Like most remedial readers, David does not like to read and spends a considerable amount of his free time watching television, playing video games, and participating in sports or other activities.

Certainly, David needs instruction on the reading skills in which he is weak. Such instruction should include ample amounts of contextual reading that provide him with an opportunity to apply these skills in the act of reading. Although some skill instruction is essential, David's reading abilities simply will not improve dramatically unless he spends considerable time practicing reading. David may need to give up some of the time he now spends watching television or playing computer games. Perhaps his teacher can find books about sports, riddles, or mysteries that will be at David's independent reading level.

REMEDIATION OF READING DIFFICULTIES

Now that you have identified the student's reading difficulties, the most important task lies ahead—correcting the student's reading problems. Although this is not always an easy task, our reading of the research and the many years we have spent as classroom teachers, reading specialists, and directors of university reading clinics have convinced us that all students can improve their reading abilities if provided with proper instruction.

A number of books have been written on this subject. The one we are most familiar with is:

James L. Shanker and Eldon E. Ekwall. *Locating and Correcting Reading Difficulties,* 7th ed. Columbus, OH: Merrill/Prentice Hall, 1998. [ISBN 0-13-862962-5]

This text, a handbook for diagnosing and remediating reading difficulties, emphasizes practical procedures for immediate use by the teacher, tutor, reading specialist, or other educator.

Preparation of Diagnostic Reports

The writing of diagnostic reports can be time consuming. If you are a student learning how to use reading assessment instruments, such reports can be helpful because—in writing them—you will be synthesizing the information you have gathered in the testing process. If you are a teacher or reading specialist, there will be times when you want to prepare diagnostic reports to communicate your findings about a student's reading abilities. You will want to include all pertinent information and exclude information of little value. Listed below are general suggestions to help you accomplish that goal. Following this list is a form you may want to follow in preparing diagnostic reports. This section concludes with sample reports for two students.

General Suggestions for Preparing Diagnostic Reports

1. Use an outline form that will make sections and subsections clearly visible.
2. Include important information but be clear and concise in your presentation.
3. Where impressions are stated, they should be identified as such.
4. Use a first-name pseudonym for the student if the testing was done for your training and not for the student's records or placement.
5. Give dates of the administration of each test.
6. List specific test scores and the source for each score.
7. Summarize significant strengths and weaknesses.
8. List specific skills needing remediation.
9. Use care with the mechanics of the report. Correct spelling and diligent proofreading are essential.
10. Be sure that the report has a professional appearance. Number the pages and provide adequate margins.

Form for Diagnostic Reports

Presented on the next page is a sample format for preparing diagnostic reports. A description is provided of the contents of each of the six common sections of a diagnostic report.

Name of Student:	John
Age:	12
Date of Birth:	January 10, 1988
Grade:	6
School:	Lincoln Elementary, Metropolitan School District
Examiner:	Pat Smith
Date of Testing:	April 22, 2000

I. PREVIOUS EDUCATIONAL HISTORY

Include such information as number of schools attended, tardiness, absence, grades repeated, when difficulty was first observed, what remedial help or special placements have been given previously. Note behavior history and previous test scores, if pertinent. When reporting previous scores, omit raw scores and other unimportant data. You may include comments from current or former teachers, but exercise judgment when quoting others and be sure to provide sources for all information reported. The student's cumulative records are often helpful but frequently incomplete. Limit this section to two or three paragraphs.

II. HEALTH RECORD

Report general medical examinations and specialized exams such as vision and hearing, including dates. Omit technical or esoteric information. Limit this section to one paragraph.

III. GENERAL OBSERVATIONS

Describe the test setting; number of sittings; the child's attitude, behavior, and appearance, if significant. You may want to provide direct quotes or anecdotes to describe the student's attitude toward reading, school, or self. Does the student possess a sense of humor, for example, or exhibit persistence, or frustration?

IV. TESTS ADMINISTERED AND RESULTS

Test 1: San Diego Quick Assessment or Graded Word List (GWL)

Independent Reading Level:	Grade _____
Instructional Reading Level:	Grade _____
Frustration Reading Level:	Grade _____

Tests 2a, 2b, and 2c: Reading Passages Tests

	Oral	Silent
Independent Reading Level:	Grade _____	Grade _____
Instructional Reading Level:	Grade _____	Grade _____
Frustration Reading Level:	Grade _____	Grade _____
Listening Comprehension Level:	Grade _____	

Test 3: Emergent Literacy Tests

	Score
3a. Phonemic Awareness	
3a1. Rhyme Production	____/8
3a2. Rhyme Recognition [Alternate]	____/8
3a3. Initial Sound Recognition	____/8
3a4. Phoneme Blending	____/8
3a5. Phoneme Segmentation	____/8

3b. Concepts about Print ____/10

3c. Letter Knowledge

    3c1. Auditory Stimulus ____/13

    3c2. Visual Stimulus ____/13

Test 4: Basic Sight Words and Phrases

	Mastery	Score
4a. Quick Check for Basic Sight Words	36	____/36
4b. Basic Sight Words	200	____/220
4c. Basic Sight Word Phrases	125	____/143

Test 5: Phonics

	Mastery	Score
5a. Application in Context	65	____/73
5b. Initial Consonants	9	____/10
5c. Initial Blends and Digraphs	9	____/10
5d. Ending Sounds	8	____/10
5e. Vowels	9	____/10
5f. Phonograms	9	____/10
5g. Blending	9	____/10
5h. Substitution	22	____/25
5i. Vowel Pronunciation	13	____/15

Test 6: Structural Analysis

	Mastery	Score
6a. Application in Context		
6a1. Lower Level	24	____/27
6a2. Higher Level	48	____/53
Total	72	____/80
6b. Hearing Word Parts	4	____/5
6c. Inflectional Endings	9	____/10
6d. Prefixes	18	____/20
6e. Suffixes	9	____/10
6f. Compound Words	4	____/5
6g. Affixes	9	____/10
6h. Syllabication	9	____/10

Test 7: Knowledge of Contractions

	Score
Number of Words Pronounced (from left columns)	____/47
Number of Words Known (from right columns)	____/47
Total Score	____/94

▶ *Test 8: El Paso Phonics Survey*

	Score
Initial Consonant Sounds	____/22
Ending Consonant X	____/1
Initial Consonant Clusters	____/35
Vowels, Vowel Teams, and Special Letter Combinations	____/32

Test 9: Quick Word List Survey

Comments _____

_____

_____

Test 10: Reading Interests Survey

Comments _____

_____

_____

Section IV is for tests you have administered as part of this diagnosis. You may want to include additional tests if you gave them. The format under Section IV lists all the tests in the Ekwall/Shanker Reading Inventory. You would never administer all these tests to any one student. When preparing your report, you may list only those tests you actually gave, or you may list all the tests and indicate those that were not given with the abbreviation NA (for Not Applicable).

V. ANALYSIS

In this section, you interpret the student's performance in each of the nine areas evaluated. You may present this information by describing the student's strengths and weaknesses, then providing a summary in an extended outline form (see Maya's report on pp. 96–100). Or you may present this information by summarizing the student's performance on the various tests that evaluate each of the nine areas (see David's report on pp. 101–106). In either case, look for reading strengths and weaknesses as revealed in the tests. You should not report each error; rather, give specific examples where appropriate. In some cases, short lists are helpful in discerning patterns of errors.

VI. SUMMARY AND RECOMMENDATIONS

In this section, you may want to state the reading strengths and weaknesses of the student. A list form is often easier for the reader to follow. Usually, the strengths and weaknesses are reported sequentially, following the order of the nine areas evaluated in the preceding section. Where possible, you should also provide a list of recommendations for areas of remediation. (Often when new examiners write diagnostic reports, they are not sufficiently experienced to suggest specific procedures or materials for remediating identified reading difficulties. If this is true for you, just identify the *specific areas* in which instruction is needed.) The list of recommendations is usually presented in priority order, with the most important areas listed first. Sometimes it is useful to provide two sets of recommendations: one for general approaches or considerations in working with this student, and the other for areas of specific instruction. It is a good practice to provide a kind word or two about the student before closing.

SAMPLE REPORTS

Maya's Diagnostic Report

Name of Student:	Maya
Age:	7
Date of Birth:	October 1, 1992
Grade:	2
School:	Frederick Douglass Elementary, Central School Distict
Examiner:	Kara Locke
Date of Testing:	February 8 and 9, 200x

I. PREVIOUS EDUCATIONAL HISTORY

Maya has attended Frederick Douglass Elementary School since kindergarten. She moved her residence after kindergarten but continued to attend Douglass. Neither tardiness nor absence has been a problem. She has not been retained, nor recommended for retention. A kindergarten speech test showed she had developmental errors in speech and a problem with irregular verbs. Maya's kindergarten teacher reported that she had strong readiness skills. Her first-grade teacher reported that she was low in reading. This year she has the same teacher in second grade. The teacher reports that Maya continues to have difficulty in reading and is getting extra help through the Title I program.

II. HEALTH RECORD

Unfortunately, no records of vision or hearing tests or any other medical examinations were available in Maya's cumulative folder. If she is unable to locate this information, her teacher plans to see to it that vision and hearing examinations are conducted.

III. GENERAL OBSERVATIONS

I tested Maya in two sittings. The first was approximately 30 minutes long and we covered Tests 1, 2a, 2b, and 2c. During the second sitting, which took approximately 35 minutes, we covered Tests 3c, 4b, 4c, and 5a through 5i. Maya was very quiet and reserved. She agreed to help me willingly enough, but I felt unable to help her relax. She did not smile or talk much. She seemed to tire easily and would begin sighing. She also became frustrated. She would keep going but her heart did not seem to be in it.

IV. TESTS ADMINISTERED AND RESULTS

Test 1: San Diego Quick Assessment or Graded Word List (GWL)

Independent Reading Level:	Grade	PP
Instructional Reading Level:	Grade	1
Frustration Reading Level:	Grade	2

▶

▶ *Tests 2a, 2b, and 2c: Reading Passages Tests*

	Oral	Silent
Independent Reading Level:	Grade Below PP	Grade Below PP
Instructional Reading Level:	Grade 1	Grade 2
Frustration Reading Level:	Grade 2	Grade 3
Listening Comprehension Level:	Grade 2	

Test 3: Emergent Literacy Tests

	Score
3c. Letter Knowledge	
3c1. Auditory Stimulus	*13/13
3c2. Visual Stimulus	*13/13

Test 4: Basic Sight Words and Phrases

	Mastery	Score
4b. Basic Sight Words	200	47/220
4c. Basic Sight Word Phrases	125	NA/143

Test 5: Phonics

	Mastery	Score
5a. Application in Context	65	54/73
5b. Initial Consonants	9	*10/10
5c. Initial Blends and Digraphs	9	*10/10
5d. Ending Sounds	8	*8/10
5e. Vowels	9	*10/10
5f. Phonograms	9	*9/10
5g. Blending	9	*10/10
5h. Substitution	22	*22/25
5i. Vowel Pronunciation	13	3/15

* Indicates Mastery

V. ANALYSIS

A. Letter Knowledge

Strengths: Maya's performance on Test 1 (GWL) and Test 2a, Oral Reading, indicates that she may not have mastered letter knowledge. However, she got perfect scores on both Tests 3c1 and 3c2. By listening to her oral reading on Test 2a, I concluded that she has also mastered her metalinguistic and segmentation skills. Therefore, the other Emergent Literacy Tests were not given.

Weaknesses: None

Summary: Maya has mastered letter knowledge and other readiness skills.

B. Basic Sight Vocabulary

Strengths: Maya correctly pronounced 47 of the 220 basic sight words. On the GWL (Test 1), she knew 23 of the 29 basic sight words. She did read the sight words she knew in context on the PP and first-grade level passages during oral reading.

Weaknesses: Maya did not know approximately 80 percent of the basic sight words, so I did not attempt the basic sight word phrases. She also did not know 6 of the 29 sight words on the GWL (Test 1) and missed 3 words in context (on Test 5a) that she had pronounced correctly in isolation.

Summary: Maya needs instruction on basic sight words. She will probably need to be taught all of the words rather than just a portion because her knowledge covers so few of the words and because of her inability to consistently pronounce known words in context.

C. Phonics

Strengths: Maya has mastered low-level phonics skills as reflected in her performance on Tests 5b through 5f. These include initial consonants, initial blends and digraphs, ending sounds, vowels, and phonograms. In listening to her oral reading on Tests 1 and 2a, it became clear that Maya is trying to use beginning sounds to read words. Maya has also mastered most of the high-level phonics skills as well as phonic blending and substitution.

Weaknesses: Maya's weaknesses in phonics are in the areas of ending consonant blends, long vowels, and vowel combinations. On the GWL, Maya mispronounced *wide* and *early*. On the Oral Reading Test, she mispronounced *bread* and *afraid*. These errors reflect Maya's difficulty with long vowels and vowel digraphs. Her weaknesses in these areas appeared again on Tests 5a and 5i.

Summary: Maya has many strengths in the area of phonics but needs to improve her ability to use ending consonant blends, long vowels, and vowel combinations when decoding unknown words.

D. Structural Analysis

Maya does not yet read at a level where structural analysis could be used or tested. The only example I found was the word *sometimes* (Test 2a, Passage 2A), which she pronounced *somethings*. This indicates that perhaps Maya understands the concept of compound words.

E. Context Clues

Strengths: On the easiest passages of the Oral Reading Test, Maya's occasional self-corrections indicated that she was using context to try to make sense of what she was reading.

Weaknesses: On the Silent Reading Passage 1B (Test 2b), Maya did not try to use context to decipher words she did not know. For example, when asked: "What was on the cake?" she did not guess frosting or candles. Instead she just said she didn't know. She was apparently frustrated by the level of the reading, which, although shown to be at an instructional level, appeared in fact to be too difficult for her. Maya also was unable to use context to assist her with the decoding of words on Test 5a.

Summary: Maya has some difficulty using context. She uses it effectively at the lower levels but loses her ability to use context when she gets frustrated. It appears that context clues remain useful to Maya only when she reads at a comfort level.

F. Fluency Skills

Strengths: On the Oral Reading passage PPA, Maya's fluency was fair.

Weaknesses: Maya is a slow and choppy reader. She reads most material orally with great difficulty.

Summary: Maya's decoding skills are so weak that it is not surprising she lacks fluency. Most written materials are too frustrating for her.

G. Vocabulary/Capacity

Strengths: Maya scored at second-grade level on Test 2b (Silent Reading Passages) and Test 2c (Listening Comprehension). This suggests she has the capacity to read at second-grade level.

Weaknesses: While it is difficult to judge at this point, it does appear that meaning vocabulary is not a particular strength of Maya's. Her oral vocabulary seems somewhat limited for her age.

Summary: Maya appears capable of reading up to grade level with appropriate instruction.

H. Comprehension

Strengths: Maya remembers most of what she reads. At the level she can decode, her comprehension is excellent. On Test 2a, Oral Reading Test, it was Maya's decoding difficulties that prevented her from reaching a higher instructional level.

Weaknesses: None apparent.

Summary: Maya's comprehension is satisfactory. Her comprehension abilities appear to be similar in oral and silent reading.

VI. SUMMARY AND RECOMMENDATIONS

A. Summary

Maya's major reading problems are her limited sight vocabulary and phonics weaknesses in the areas of ending consonant blends, long vowels, and vowel combinations. Her use of context clues and her fluency skills will improve when these other skills are mastered and she gets enough practice in the act of reading. Specifically, Maya:

- has mastered letter knowledge and other readiness skills
- needs instruction on all of the basic sight words
- has strong phonics skills, except in the areas of ending consonant blends, long vowels, and vowel combinations
- has mastered the skill of phonic blending
- is not yet at the stage where she should have mastered structural analysis
- uses context clues effectively only with low-level materials
- has poor fluency skills due to her limited decoding skills
- appears to have the capacity to read at a second-grade level
- has adequate comprehension of the material she can decode at this time

B. Recommendations

Hearing and vision abilities should be tested if recent results are unavailable. The following *general approaches* are recommended:

1. Find books at the preprimer level for Maya to read on her own and encourage her to do this beginning with at least 15 minutes per day.
2. Provide opportunities for Maya to be successful; give her praise whenever it is warranted.

3. Use language experience activities to help build up Maya's sight vocabulary, and provide materials for her to read and to motivate her to read.

4. Perhaps pair Maya with a reading buddy so she will have another student to read with.

The following *specific approaches* are recommended:

1. Teach the basic sight words in isolation, phrases, sentence, and story contexts.

2. Teach the ending consonant blends, long vowels, and vowel combinations and provide Maya with many opportunities to use these skills in contextual reading.

3. Teach Maya how to use context clues to aid her in decoding difficult reading material.

4. Provide instruction on vocabulary to increase the number of words for which Maya has meaning.

5. Provide instruction designed to increase Maya's reading fluency.

6. As Maya's basic sight word knowledge and phonics skills improve, begin teaching her structural analysis skills.

Maya is a pleasant and cooperative girl who, when provided with proper instruction, should be able to increase her reading ability, her confidence, and her reading pleasure.

David's Diagnostic Report

Name of Student:	David
Age:	9
Date of Birth:	July 16, 1990
Grade:	4
School:	George P. Miller, Alameda Unified School District
Examiner:	Paula Schaufler
Date of Testing:	March 7 and 8, 2000

I. PREVIOUS EDUCATIONAL HISTORY

David attended kindergarten and part of first grade in Mountain View. His family moved to Bakersfield for the second half of first grade. David's family moved again in November of his second-grade year, and he attended Woodstock School in Alameda. David then entered third grade at George P. Miller School. He now attends fourth grade at Miller School. Upon entering Woodstock School, David was virtually a nonreader, according to his teacher. Although he made progress that year, David remained well below grade level in reading. Two years ago, David was tested for the Resource Specialist Program but did not qualify. The examiner reported that a significant discrepancy existed between David's performance score (which was high average) and his verbal score (which was low average). This, according to the examiner, was indicative of poor language processing and weak listening abilities. No serious disabilities were seen, and therefore David did not meet eligibility criteria for the program. The examiner recommended small group instruction in reading, summer school, oral reading at home, and tutorial help. According to previous teachers, David relates well to others and wants to please, but his attention is inconsistent and he often daydreams.

II. HEALTH RECORD

As a toddler, David suffered frequent ear infections and at age two he had tubes inserted in his ears. Subsequent to this operation, he began to speak. Vision and hearing records are up to date and report normal functioning.

III. GENERAL OBSERVATIONS

David was tested on two afternoons. The first session lasted approximately 45 minutes, the second about one hour. David was cooperative and eager to please. He was initially quiet and reserved. His voice cracked, he coughed a lot, and he made apologies for mistakes. However, he gained confidence quickly and became quite talkative and animated. As he became more comfortable, he began to relate personal anecdotes. David did seem to tire at the end of the second session, but it could have been the hour (4 p.m.) as well as the length of the session.

IV. TESTS ADMINISTERED AND RESULTS

Test 1: San Diego Quick Assessment or Graded Word List (GWL)

Independent Reading Level:	Grade ___2___
Instructional Reading Level:	Grade ___3___
Frustration Reading Level:	Grade ___4___

▶

Tests 2a, 2b, and 2c: Reading Passages Tests

	Oral	Silent
Independent Reading Level:	Grade 2	Grade 2
Instructional Reading Level:	Grade 3	Grade 3
Frustration Reading Level:	Grade 4	Grade 4
Listening Comprehension Level:	Grade 4	

Test 4: Basic Sight Words and Phrases

	Mastery	Score
4b. Basic Sight Words	200	*205/220
4c. Basic Sight Word Phrases	125	116/143

Test 5: Phonics

	Mastery	Score
5a. Application in Context	65	*69/73

Test 6: Structural Analysis

	Mastery	Score
6a. Application in Context		
6a1. Lower Level	24	*25/27
6a2. Higher Level	48	35/53
Total	72	60/80
6b. Hearing Word Parts	4	*5/5
6c. Inflectional Endings	9	*10/10
6d. Prefixes	18	17/20
6e. Suffixes	9	8/10
6f. Compound Words	4	*4/5
6g. Affixes	9	7/10
6h. Syllabication	9	3/10

Test 7: Knowledge of Contractions

	Score
Number of Words Pronounced (from left columns)	46/47
Number of Words Known (from right columns)	44/47
Total Score	90/94

Test 10: Reading Interests Survey
Results of this survey will be reported in the Analysis section.

*Indicates Mastery

V. ANALYSIS

Letter Knowledge
David's test scores demonstrate that he has mastered phonemic awareness, concepts about print, letter knowledge, and other emergent literacy skills.

Basic Sight Vocabulary
David correctly pronounced 93 percent of the basic sight words (Test 4b) when these words were tested on flash cards in isolation. (Ninety percent or better is considered mastery in isolation.) He correctly pronounced all 29 basic sight words

that appear in isolation on the Graded Word List (Test 1), further verifying that David has attained mastery of basic sight words in isolation. David correctly pronounced 81 percent of the basic sight word phrases (Test 4c). This figure is below mastery and indicates that David still needs to learn 27 sight word phrases. Occasionally, David does miscall basic sight words in context. For example, on the Oral Reading Test (Test 2a), he miscalled or omitted the following nine basic sight words: *there, an, the, very, is, take, may, be,* and *who.* Of these words, the only one that David missed on Test 4a was *may.* This word was also missed on Test 5a. All other basic sight words (20 of them) were read correctly in context on Test 5a.

Phonics
Because David established an instructional level of third grade on Tests 1, 2a, and 2b, I went directly to Test 5a to assess phonics ability. David's score on this test indicated that he has achieved mastery of phonics skills. Also, David has no difficulty with phonic blending. Therefore, Tests 5b through 5i were not administered. David's oral reading errors on Test 2a did not result from phonic weaknesses. Rather, they reflected weakness in some aspect of structural analysis or miscalling basic sight words.

Structural Analysis
On the Graded Word List (Test 1), David missed 28 multisyllabic words. Most of the errors occurred on lists 4 and 5. (The test was halted at this point.) On the words that were miscalled, David tended to pronounce the correct (or nearly correct) number of syllables. However, he lacked the ability to combine the inflectional endings and affixes with the root words when decoding out of context. A similar pattern of errors occurred on the Oral Reading Test (Test 2a), even when David had the benefit of context. David mastered Hearing Word Parts (Test 6b), Inflectional Endings (Test 6c), and Compound Words (Test 6f). He missed several items on each of the other tests of structural analysis until he got to Syllabication (Test 6h). Here he had great difficulty, getting only 3 of 10 items correct. When required to decode a multisyllabic word, David almost always gets part of the word correct if he is at all familiar with the word. For example, *imperfection* was pronounced as *imperfect.* However, if the word is totally unknown to David, he will sometimes pronounce the correct number of syllables but substitute a word that is familiar to him. For example, *impeachable* was pronounced as *imbleachabale.* David does recognize that the length of such a word indicates more than one syllable. David's syllabication strategy was effective for him in Test 6a1. In this passage, the words were sufficiently familiar for David to decode them and achieve mastery. However, in Test 6a2 the words were not familiar and David lacked the more advanced structural analysis skills he needed to separate the word parts, pronounce them, and blend them together to make the whole word.

Context Clues
David has some ability to use context clues to assist him with decoding. In the Oral Reading Test (Test 2a), David's substitutions tended to be logical, both syntactically and semantically. For example, he substituted *purpose* for *process.* However, on Test 5a David's substitutions were frequently illogical. He mastered the test because he had few errors, but the substitutions made were not appropriate replacements, either syntactically or semantically. For example, David read *park* for *perk, far* for *fur,* and *china* for *chain.* David seemed to be overrelying on the graphic features of the words. His performance on Test 6a1 was similar. He again mastered the passage because he made few errors, but the substitutions made

were not logical; for example, *attraction* for *active* and *positions* for *poisonous*. On Test 6a2, the passage was so difficult for David that he made too many errors for context to be of help. He either made no attempt to use context or couldn't use it because the words were just too difficult. He even substituted nonsense words in some cases; for example, *disamart* for *disappearance* and *displution* for *disqualification.* It appears that David uses context clues on material up to his present instructional reading level but is unable to benefit from context clues on material at his frustration level.

Fluency Skills

David is a fluent reader when reading material up to his instructional reading level. When reading at the fourth-grade level or on Test 6a1, David demonstrates inefficient reading behavior. David also has not mastered the basic sight word phrases, which would improve his fluency. Up to his instructional level, David's speed, phrasing, accuracy, and attention to punctuation are all adequate. When he reads material at the fourth-grade level or higher, he slows down, often repeats words, inserts words that are not printed, and substitutes words. Because the words are not making sense, David's phrasing is inappropriate, he begins to read word by word, and he ignores punctuation. He also misses basic sight words occasionally when reading in context. These difficulties will likely decrease as David's decoding ability improves.

Vocabulary/Capacity

This is an area of relative strength for David. His vocabulary is adequate for his present reading level, and his performance on the Listening Comprehension Test (Test 2c) suggests that David has the capacity to read above his present level. His ability to pronounce words in isolation on the Graded Word List (Test 1) was not limited by his vocabulary knowledge. Also, he had no difficulty with vocabulary questions on the Silent Reading Test (Test 2b).

Comprehension

David understands what he reads. This is true even when he makes a considerable number of word recognition errors. On Oral Reading Passage 4A, David made 15 word recognition errors, yet he still was able to remember enough and deduce enough information to answer the comprehension questions correctly. It is also possible that David had prior knowledge of the topic presented in this passage. David's comprehension is somewhat better in oral reading than silent reading. It is possible that during silent reading David omits unfamiliar words or reads carelessly. David's listening comprehension is at or above his grade placement level.

Reading Interests

David's current interest in reading and books is not high. As would be expected of a student with reading difficulties, he would rather watch television, play computer games, or participate in outdoor activities. David's responses on the Reading Interests Survey suggest he might enjoy reading about sports, riddles, and mysteries. Unfortunately, David was unable to name the last book he had read or list his three favorite books.

VI. SUMMARY AND RECOMMENDATIONS

Reading Strengths

David:

1. knows letter names and has mastered other emergent literacy skills

2. knows 93 percent of the basic sight words

3. knows 81 percent of the basic sight word phrases

4. has mastered phonics skills

5. has mastered the following structural analysis skills:

   a. recognition of word parts

   b. inflectional endings

   c. compound words

6. uses context clues in passages up to his current instructional reading level (third grade)

7. reads with fluency in passages up to his current instructional reading level (third grade)

8. has sufficient understanding of vocabulary up to his present reading level and has the capacity to read at grade-placement level or higher

9. comprehends when reading passages up to his current instructional reading level and has satisfactory listening comprehension at grade-placement level or higher.

Reading Weaknesses

David:

1. needs to master 27 sight word phrases and improve in his ability to correctly pronounce basic sight words in context

2. needs to master the following inflectional ending and affixes: *-ed, pro-, pre-, -ive, -tion, -ous*

3. needs to master the structural analysis process of separating, pronouncing, and blending word parts in isolation and in context

4. needs to improve his ability to use context clues when reading material that is difficult for him

5. needs to improve his reading fluency when reading material that is difficult for him

General Recommendations

Keep instructional sessions short and not too late in the day. Make an extra effort to make David feel comfortable and boost his confidence. To improve his reading ability, David will need substantial practice in the act of reading material at his independent level. Provide books for David to read on his own at the second-grade level or lower. If the material is of particular interest to David (perhaps books about sports, riddles, or mysteries), he may be able to read more difficult selections. It may be necessary to set up scheduled times for David to practice reading outside of school, then hold him accountable for this activity.

▶

Specific Areas for Instruction

1. Teach to mastery the 27 sight word phrases not known and provide instruction and practice to help David improve in his ability to correctly pronounce basic sight words in context.

2. Teach to mastery the following inflectional ending and affixes: *-ed, pro-, pre-, -ive, -tion, -ous.*

3. Teach David the structural analysis process of separating, pronouncing, and blending word parts in isolation and in context.

4. Provide instruction and practice to help David improve his ability to use context clues when reading material that is difficult for him.

5. Provide instruction and practice to help David improve his reading fluency when reading material that is difficult for him.

David was a pleasure to test. He tries hard to please and likes to chat and relate personal anecdotes. He always tried to do his best. I am confident that David's reading ability will improve if he receives appropriate instruction and spends a sufficient amount of time practicing the act of reading.

Notes

1. This figure differs some from the 75 percent often used as the minimum for comprehension at the instructional level. However, research done by Eldon E. Ekwall and Judy English indicates that in most cases students do not show signs of frustration until they fall below 60 percent if their word recognition errors are not excessive. This research may be found in Eldon E. Ekwall and Judy English, "Use of the Polygraph to Determine Elementary School Students' Frustration Level" (Final Report, United States Department of Health, Education, and Welfare, Project no. 0G078, 1971).

2. Marjorie S. Johnson and Roy A. Kress, *Informal Reading Inventories* (Newark, DE: International Reading Association, 1965).

3. The Harris-Jacobson Readability Formula appears in Albert A. Harris and Edward R. Sipay, *How to Increase Reading Ability,* 7th ed. (New York: David McKay, 1981, Appendix D).

4. R. B. Powers, W. A. Sumner, and B. E. Kearl, "A Recalculation of Readability Formulas," *Journal of Educational Psychology 49* (1958), pp. 99–105.

5. Edgar Dale and Jeanne Chall, "A Formula for Predicting Readability," *Educational Research Bulletin* (January 1948), pp. 11–20, 28.

6. It is not essential to measure the student's speed of silent reading to complete your diagnosis. Novice examiners may want to skip this step until they have had some experience administering these tests. There are several reasons you may want to note a student's reading speed for the silent reading passages. One is to determine if the student is an extremely slow reader. Such a student would be likely to do poorly on group standardized reading achievement tests regardless of his or her ability to decode or comprehend because these tests are also timed. Another reason you may want to check a student's silent reading speed is to compare that student's speed with those of other students of a comparable grade level. A student's silent reading speed provides a clue to his or her reading fluency or reading efficiency. The role that fluency plays will be discussed in the section on interpreting the results of your testing, which will be presented later in this manual.

7. Research shows that if all repetitions are not counted as errors, students will become physiologically frustrated before their scores reach frustration level. See E. E. Ekwall, "Should Repetitions Be Counted as Errors?" *Reading Teacher 27* (1974), pp. 365–367.

8. E. W. Dolch, *Basic Sight Word Test* (Champaign, IL: Garrard Press, 1942).

9. W. K. Durr, "Computer Study of High Frequency Words in Popular Trade Juveniles," *Reading Teacher 27* (1973), pp. 37–42. Durr listed the basic sight words in descending order of frequency based on the results of his computer study of the occurrence of these words in popular children's library books.

PART II

Tools of the Ekwall/Shanker Reading Inventory

Forms for Use in Conducting the Diagnosis

CRIB SHEET INSTRUCTIONS

▶ **Turn on the tape recorder and leave it on for the entire testing session. Turn it off only to change tapes if necessary.**

TEST 1: SAN DIEGO QUICK ASSESSMENT OR GRADED WORD LIST (GWL)

(Test Sheet found on p. 128; Scoring Sheet found on pp. 190–191.)

1. Place the Test Sheet in front of the student and say, "Here are some words I would like you to read out loud. Try to read all of them even if you are not sure what some of the words are. Let's begin by reading the words on this list" (pointing to list PP).

2. Begin at list PP. Mark (+) for correct responses; transcribe incorrect responses.

3. Highest list that student reads with zero or one error is independent level.

4. Have student read harder lists until student makes three or more errors on any one list.

5. After student misses three or more words, stop, collect Test Sheet, and indicate three levels on Scoring Sheet.

6. To establish levels: 0–1 error = independent; 2 errors = instructional; 3 or more errors = frustration.

▶ **Mark the part of the Summary Sheet indicating the student's scores on the GWL.**

TEST 2: READING PASSAGES TESTS

Tests 2a and 2b: Oral and Silent Reading Tests

(Test Sheets found on pp. 130–149; Scoring Sheets found on pp. 194–225.)

1. Start at A or C passage below student's independent level (from GWL).

2. Say to the student, "I have some passages for you to read. Read the first one out loud. If you find a hard word, try to read it as best you can and continue reading. It is important to remember what you read so that you can answer some questions about the passage when you are through."

3. Hand manual to student and say, "Ready, begin."

4. Code student's errors on Scoring Sheet. Say unknown words for student after five-second pause.

5. Take back manual.

6. Ask comprehension questions. Score with + or –.

7. Score oral paragraph (mark chart).

8. Give corresponding silent paragraph and say, "Here is another passage. Read this one to yourself and try to remember what you read so that you can answer some questions about it. Tell me when you finish."

9. Hand manual to student.

10. Optional. Time student's silent reading. Write time on Scoring Sheet.

11. Take back manual. Ask questions. Mark + or –.

12. Determine if passage is at independent, instructional, or frustration level.

▶ 13. Go to next *higher* passages if both at independent level until frustration level is reached on both.

14. Go to *lower* passages on oral and/or silent reading until independent level is reached and then go back up, alternating oral and silent until frustration level is reached on both.

15. Use tables on Scoring Sheets; mark independent, instructional, or frustration levels for each passage read.

Test 2c: Listening Comprehension

(Uses the same set of passages as oral and silent reading tests.)

1. Go to first available passage *at* or *just above* frustration level on oral or silent reading.

2. Tell student you will read passage and he or she will answer questions about it when you are finished.

3. Read the passage, then ask questions and mark Scoring Sheet.

4. If student gets 70 percent or higher, go to next higher passage until grade *placement* level is reached.

5. Do not test above the student's grade-placement level.

6. If the student fails the first passage, estimate the listening comprehension level.

▶ **Mark the chart to indicate and check the student's progress through the various passages.**

▶ **Mark the part of the Test Summary Sheet indicating the student's scores on oral and silent reading and listening comprehension.**

▶ **Go on to administer the remaining tests in the battery as needed.**

READING PASSAGES TESTS ADMINISTRATION CHART

TESTS 2a, 2b, AND 2c

Student's Name _____   Grade Placement _____

Graded Word List (GWL) Independent Level _____

Begin Oral Reading on Passage_____   Date _____

	A or C	B or D
PP	_____	_____
1	_____	_____
2	_____	_____
3	_____	_____
4	_____	_____
5	_____	_____
6	_____	_____
7	_____	_____
8	_____	_____
9	_____	_____

SUMMARY

	Oral	Silent
Independent	_____	_____
Instructional	_____	_____
Frustration	_____	_____
Listening Comprehension	_____	

TEST SUMMARY SHEET

Student _____   School _____

Teacher _____   Grade _____ Age _____

Examiner _____   Test Dates _____ _____

Pretest   Posttest

[* indicates mastery]

TEST 1: SAN DIEGO QUICK ASSESSMENT OR GRADED WORD LIST (GWL)

	Pretest	Posttest
Independent Reading Level:	Grade _____	Grade _____
Instructional Reading Level:	Grade _____	Grade _____
Frustration Reading Level:	Grade _____	Grade _____

TESTS 2a, 2b, AND 2c: READING PASSAGES TESTS

Oral

	Pretest	Posttest
Independent Reading Level:	Grade _____	Grade _____
Instructional Reading Level:	Grade _____	Grade _____
Frustration Reading Level:	Grade _____	Grade _____

Silent

	Pretest	Posttest
Independent Reading Level:	Grade _____	Grade _____
Instructional Reading Level:	Grade _____	Grade _____
Frustration Reading Level:	Grade _____	Grade _____
Listening Comprehension Level:	Grade _____	Grade _____

TEST 3: EMERGENT LITERACY TESTS

	1st	2nd
3a. Phonemic Awareness		
3a1. Rhyme Production	___/8	___/8
3a2. Rhyme Recognition [*Alternate*]	___/8	___/8
3a3. Initial Sound Recognition	___/8	___/8
3a4. Phoneme Blending	___/8	___/8
3a5. Phoneme Segmentation	___/8	___/8
3b. Concepts about Print	___/10	___/10
3c. Letter Knowledge		
3c1. Auditory Stimulus	___/13	___/13
3c2. Visual Stimulus	___/13	___/13

TEST 4: BASIC SIGHT WORDS AND PHRASES

	Mastery	*Pretest*	*Posttest*
4a. Quick Check for Basic Sight Words	36	____/36	____/36
4b. Basic Sight Words	200	____/220	____/220
4c. Basic Sight Word Phrases	125	____/143	____/143

TEST 5: PHONICS

	Mastery	*Pretest*	*Posttest*
5a. Application in Context	65	____/73	____/73
5b. Initial Consonants	9	____/10	____/10
5c. Initial Blends and Digraphs	9	____/10	____/10
5d. Ending Sounds	8	____/10	____/10
5e. Vowels	9	____/10	____/10
5f. Phonograms	9	____/10	____/10
5g. Blending	9	____/10	____/10
5h. Substitution	22	____/25	____/25
5i. Vowel Pronunciation	13	____/15	____/15

TEST 6: STRUCTURAL ANALYSIS

	Mastery	*Pretest*	*Posttest*
6a. Application in Context			
6a1. Lower Level	24	____/27	____/27
6a2. Higher Level	48	____/53	____/53
Total	72	____/80	____/80
6b. Hearing Word Parts	4	____/5	____/5
6c. Inflectional Endings	9	____/10	____/10
6d. Prefixes	18	____/20	____/20
6e. Suffixes	9	____/10	____/10
6f. Compound Words	4	____/5	____/5
6g. Affixes	9	____/10	____/10
6h. Syllabication	9	____/10	____/10

TEST 7: KNOWLEDGE OF CONTRACTIONS

	Pretest	*Posttest*
Number of Words Pronounced (from left columns)	____/47	____/47
Number of Words Known (from right columns)	____/47	____/47
Total Score	____/94	____/94

TEST 8: EL PASO PHONICS SURVEY

	Pretest	*Posttest*
Initial Consonant Sounds	___/22	___/22
Ending Consonant X	___/1	___/1
Initial Consonant Clusters	___/35	___/35
Vowels, Vowel Teams, and Special Letter Combinations	___/32	___/32

TEST 9: QUICK WORD LIST SURVEY

Comments _____

_____

_____

TEST 10: READING INTERESTS SURVEY

Comments _____

_____

_____

ANALYSIS SHEET

Check (✔) where applicable

PHONEMIC AWARENESS

_____ Mastered   _____ Not Mastered

List Weaknesses (= Mastery)*

Test 3a1   _____/8 _____

Test 3a2 [Alt.] _____/8 _____

Test 3a3   _____/8 _____

Test 3a4   _____/8 _____

Test 3a5   _____/8 _____

CONCEPTS ABOUT PRINT

_____ Mastered   _____ Not Mastered

List Weaknesses (= Mastery)*

Test 3b   _____/10 _____

LETTER KNOWLEDGE

_____ Mastered   _____ Not Mastered

Test 1   _____ Independent Level is 1.0 or above (Letter knowledge = mastered)

           _____ Independent Level is below 1.0 (L.K. may not be mastered)

Test 2a   _____ Independent Level at PP or above on Test 2a or 2c
           (L.K. = mastered)

           _____ Instructional or Frustration Level at PP on Test 2a or 2c
           (L.K. may not be mastered)

List Errors (= Mastery)*

Test 3c1   _____/13 _____

Test 3c2   _____/13 _____

BASIC SIGHT VOCABULARY

_____ Words Mastered in Isolation

_____ Phrases Mastered in Isolation

_____ Words Mastered in Context

Number of Basic Sight Words Pronounced
(See Scoring Sheets for errors)

Text 1   _____/29   _____

Test 2a   _____   _____

Test 4a   _____/36   _____

Test 4b   _____/220 _____

Test 4c   _____/143 _____

Test 5a   _____/21   _____

PHONICS (Low-Level)

_____ Mastered   _____ Not Mastered

List Weaknesses (= Mastery)*

Test 5b   _____/10   _____

Test 5c   _____/10   _____

Test 5d   _____/10   _____

Test 5e   _____/10   _____

Test 5f   _____/10   _____

PHONICS

High-Level   _____ Mastered   _____ Not Mastered
Blending   _____ Mastered   _____ Not Mastered

List Weaknesses (= Mastery)*

Test 1   _____

Test 2a   _____

                          _____

Test 5a   _____/73   _____

                          _____

Test 5g   _____/10   _____

Test 5h   _____/25   _____

Test 5i   _____/15   _____

Test 8   _____/90   _____

Form 4

FORMS

STRUCTURAL ANALYSIS

_____ Mastered   _____ Not Mastered

List Weaknesses (* = Mastery)

Test 1   _____

Test 2a   _____

Test 6a   _____/27 6a1 _____/53 6a2

           _____/80 Total Score

Test 6b   _____/5   _____

Test 6c   _____/10 _____

Test 6d   _____/20 _____

Test 6e   _____/10 _____

Test 6f   _____/5   _____

Test 6g   _____/10 _____

Test 6h   _____/10 _____

Test 7   _____/47 Words Pronouced   _____/47   Words Known

           _____/94 Total Score

CONTEXT CLUES

_____ Uses Context Clues Effectively

_____ Underrelies on Context

_____ Overrelies on Context

Comments

Test 2a   _____

Tests 5a and/or 6a   _____

Other Tests   _____

FLUENCY SKILLS

_____ Reads Fluently

Difficulty with:

_____ Speed

_____ Phrasing

_____ Accuracy

_____ Punctuation

_____ Other _____

Comments

Test 2a   _____

_____

Test 2b   _____

_____

Rate of Reading: ____ Slow   ____ Medium   ____ Fast

Test 4c   _____

Tests 5a and/or 6a _____

VOCABULARY (MEANING)/CAPACITY

_____ Indicates Potential for Improvement

Vocabulary: _____ Strong

_____ Adequate

_____ Weak

Listening
Comprehension: _____ Below Grade Level

_____ At or Above Grade Level

Comments

Test 1   _____

_____

Test 2a   _____

_____

Test 2b   _____

_____

Test 2c   _____

Form 4

FORMS

COMPREHENSION

_____ Strong

_____ Adequate

_____ Weak

Difficulty with: _____ Factual (F) Questions

_____ Vocabulary (V) Questions

_____ Inference (I) Questions

_____ Comprehension *Better* in *Oral* Reading

_____ Comprehension *Better* in *Silent* Reading

_____ Comprehension *Similar* in *Oral* and *Silent* Reading

Comments

Test 2a   _____

_____

Test 2b   _____

_____

Test 2c (Listening)   _____

READING INTERESTS SURVEY

Comments   _____

_____

_____

_____

_____

ADDITIONAL COMMENTS

_____

_____

_____

_____

_____

_____

_____

_____

_____

PRESCRIPTIVE ANALYSIS OF PHONICS SKILLS CHART

Phonic Element ↓	Test 5a	5b	5c	5d	5e	5f	5g	5h	5i	8	1	2a
Beginning Single Consonants	↓	↓	↓	↓	↓	↓	↓	↓	↓	↓	↓	↓
b	×	×						×		×		
hard c	×							×		×		
d	×	×					×			×		
f	×	×					×			×		
hard g	×	×								×		
h	×	×					×			×		
j	×							×		×		
k										×		
l	×							×		×		
m	×						×			×		
n	×	×								×		
p	×	×								×		
r	×							×		×		
s	×	×								×		
t	×							×		×		
v								×		×		
w	×	×								×		
z	×									×		

↓	5a	5b	5c	5d	5e	5f	5g	5h	5i	8	1	2a
Ending Single Consonants	↓	↓	↓	↓	↓	↓	↓	↓	↓	↓	↓	↓
b	×			×				×				
soft c	×											
d	×			×				×				
f	×							×				
hard g	×							×				
soft g	×											
k	×											
l	×			×								
m								×				
n	×											
p	×			×								
r	×											
s	×											
t	×			×								
x	×									×		

Form 5

FORMS

Phonic Element

Test

Phonic Element ↓	5a	5b	5c	5d	5e	5f	5g	5h	5i	8	1	2a
Beginning Consonant Digraphs	↓	↓	↓	↓	↓	↓	↓	↓	↓	↓	↓	↓
ch	×		×				×	×		×		
sh	×		×					×		×		
th	×		× ×				×			×		
wh	×							×		×		

↓	5a	5b	5c	5d	5e	5f	5g	5h	5i	8	1	2a
Ending Consonant Digraph	↓	↓	↓	↓	↓	↓	↓	↓	↓	↓	↓	↓
sh	×			×								

↓	5a	5b	5c	5d	5e	5f	5g	5h	5i	8	1	2a
Beginning Consonants Blends	↓	↓	↓	↓	↓	↓	↓	↓	↓	↓	↓	↓
bl			×				×			×		
cl	×									×		
pl	×		×					×		×		
br	×		×							×		
fr								×		×		
gr	×		×							×		
tr	×						×			×		
sm	×		×							×		
sp			×					×		×		
st								×		×		
str	×						×			×		

Form 5

Phonic Element ↓

Test

Ending Consonants Blends	5a ↓	5b ↓	5c ↓	5d ↓	5e ↓	5f ↓	5g ↓	5h ↓	5i ↓	8 ↓	1 ↓	2a ↓
nd	×											
ng	×			×								
nt				×								
rd	×			×								
rk	×											
rl	×											
rn	×											
rt	×											
sk				×								
st	×											

Short Vowels	5a ↓	5b ↓	5c ↓	5d ↓	5e ↓	5f ↓	5g ↓	5h ↓	5i ↓	8 ↓	1 ↓	2a ↓
a	×				×					×		
e	×				×			×		×		
i	×				×			×		×		
o	×				×			×		×		
u	×				×			×		×		

Long Vowels	5a ↓	5b ↓	5c ↓	5d ↓	5e ↓	5f ↓	5g ↓	5h ↓	5i ↓	8 ↓	1 ↓	2a ↓
a	×				×					×		
e	×				×					×		
i	×				×			×		×		
o	×				×			×		×		
u	×				×			×		×		

Form 5

FORMS

Phonic Element → / Test

Vowel Combinations ↓	5a ↓	5b ↓	5c ↓	5d ↓	5e ↓	5f ↓	5g ↓	5h ↓	5i ↓	8 ↓	1 ↓	2a ↓
ar	×								×	×		
er	×								×	×		
ir	×								×	×		
or	×								×			
long or									×	×		
ur	×								×	×		
ai	×								×	×		
au									×	×		
aw	×								×	×		
ay	×									×		
ea	×									×		
oa									×	×		
oi	×								×	×		
oo	×									×		
ou	×								×	×		
diph ow	×								×	×		
long ow									×	×		
oy	×								×	×		

↓	5a	5b	5c	5d	5e	5f	5g	5h	5i	8	1	2a
Phonograms ↓	↓	↓	↓	↓	↓	↓	↓	↓	↓	↓	↓	↓
ame						×						
ime						×						
ike						×						
ock						×						
eep						×						
ight						×						
ing						×						
ade						×						
ang						×						
ill						×						

Test Sheets

TEST 1: SAN DIEGO QUICK ASSESSMENT
OR GRADED WORD LIST (GWL)

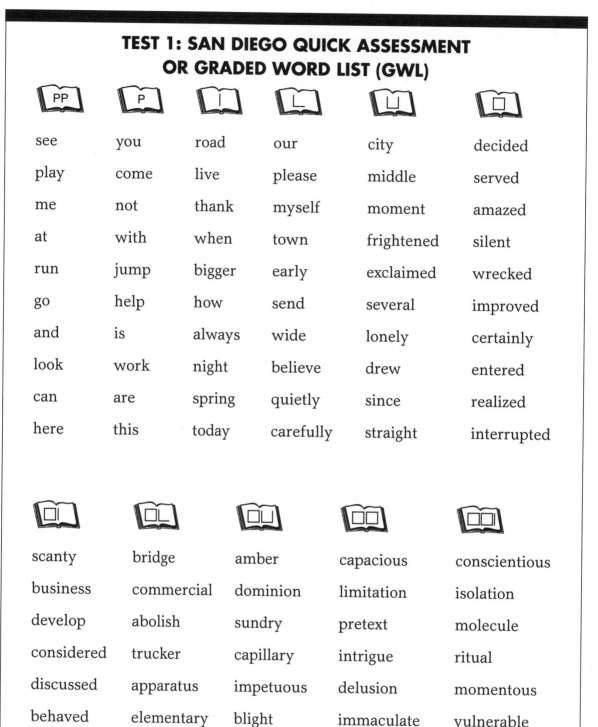

PP	P	I	L	U	
see	you	road	our	city	decided
play	come	live	please	middle	served
me	not	thank	myself	moment	amazed
at	with	when	town	frightened	silent
run	jump	bigger	early	exclaimed	wrecked
go	help	how	send	several	improved
and	is	always	wide	lonely	certainly
look	work	night	believe	drew	entered
can	are	spring	quietly	since	realized
here	this	today	carefully	straight	interrupted

scanty	bridge	amber	capacious	conscientious
business	commercial	dominion	limitation	isolation
develop	abolish	sundry	pretext	molecule
considered	trucker	capillary	intrigue	ritual
discussed	apparatus	impetuous	delusion	momentous
behaved	elementary	blight	immaculate	vulnerable
splendid	comment	wrest	ascent	kinship
acquainted	necessity	enumerate	acrid	conservatism
escaped	gallery	daunted	binocular	jaunty
grim	relativity	condescend	embankment	inventive

Test 2: Reading Passages
Forms A and B

Oral Reading Passages

Silent Reading Passages

PP

A
ORAL

2/Form A

(Scoring Sheet on p. 194)

TESTS

Jan has a dog.

The dog's name is Pat.

He can run fast.

One day Pat ran away.

Jan looked for him.

The dog wanted to eat.

Soon he came home.

Bob likes to play ball.

He plays with Sam.

They play at school.

It is far away.

The boys ride a bus.

It takes them to school.

It also takes them home.

(Scoring Sheet on p. 195)

2/Form B

TESTS

Tuff was a big brown bear. He lived in a big park. He liked to eat honey best of all. He also liked to eat bread.

Some people were in the park having a picnic. They were sitting by a big table. Tuff went to the picnic too. When the people saw him they were afraid. They all jumped up and ran away. Then the bear ate all of their food.

Steve was going to have a birthday party. He asked all of his good friends to come. His mother made a big cake for him. She put eight candles on it.

Steve's dog was in the house that day. Soon Steve's friends were at the door. The dog began to bark. He was afraid of all of Steve's friends. Steve told his dog to go to his room. Then the children began playing some games.

(Scoring Sheet on p. 197)

2/Form B

Bob and his father like to work on old cars. His father has five old cars that belong to him. One of them is black with a white top.

Bob is very young, so none of the cars belong to him. He would like to have his own car when he gets big.

Sometimes Bob and his father go to a car show. At the car show there are many old cars.

One time Bob's father took his black and white car to the car show. One of the men looked at the cars to see which one was best. He gave Bob's father a prize because his car was so pretty.

Kay was waiting by the door for the mail to come. Her father had promised to write her a letter. He told Kay the letter would have a blue stamp on it.

Kay saw the woman walking toward the house. She was carrying a big bag on her side. She reached in her bag and gave Kay some letters. One of the letters had Kay's name on it. When Kay read the letter she was very happy. She was so happy when she read it that she began to jump up and down. In the letter Father told Kay he was going to buy her a pony.

(Scoring Sheet on p. 199)

2/Form B

Kathy had always wanted to go for a ride on an airplane. One day her father told her that she could ride on an airplane to visit her grandmother and grandfather. She was very happy and could hardly wait to get started.

When the time came to go, her father went to the ticket counter and paid for the airplane ticket. Her mother helped her get on the airplane. Then a lady told her to buckle her seat belt and she even helped her with it.

Soon the airplane was going very fast down the runway. Kathy was afraid at first but soon the airplane was in the air. Kathy peered out of the window at the ground below, where the houses and cars looked very small. The lady gave Kathy something to drink and a sandwich to eat.

B
SILENT

Dick and his father liked to go camping. Dick asked his father if they could go camping in the woods. His father told him they would go the next Saturday.

When Saturday came they got up early and rode in the car until they found an excellent place to camp. Father decided that they would put up their tent by a small river. They put up their tent and then gathered some wood to start a fire. After the fire was burning, Father got some food ready and Dick helped him cook it over the fire.

After they finished eating they watched the fire until it was time to go to sleep. When Dick and Father had gone to sleep, something made a terribly loud noise and woke them up. Dick was afraid but Father laughed because it was only an airplane flying over them.

(Scoring Sheet on p. 201)

2/Form B

TESTS

Some people enjoy exploring the many caves in this country. This can be a lot of fun but it can also be dangerous because you might get lost. Many people have been lost in caves because they did not know what to do to find their way out.

One thing that people who explore caves often take with them is a ball of string. The string serves an important purpose in keeping them from getting lost. They tie one end of the string to a stake outside the cave and unroll the string as they walk along. This way, when they want to leave the cave, all they have to do to find their way out is to follow the string.

Some caves may appear small at the opening, but when you get inside there may be many giant rooms or caverns in them. One of the largest known caves in the world is Mammoth Cave in Kentucky. It contains enormous caverns and underground rivers, and may take up as much space as 78 square miles.

One of people's best friends in North America is the bird. Birds are valuable to the farmer and gardener because they eat insects and weed seeds. Birds are also important to the hunter because they provide meat for his table.

When people first came to this country, there were many game birds. However, when the settlers started hunting birds for sport some kinds of birds were nearly all killed off. We now have much smaller numbers of wild turkey than we had in the past. In fact, some birds such as the passenger pigeon had all been killed or died by 1914.

In England a man might have been put in prison for taking wild birds' eggs from land owned by another man. A man might have even been hanged for killing a deer on someone else's land. The Indians in North America only killed wild game to eat.

The elephant is the largest animal in the world that lives on land. A full-grown elephant may have a weight of about four tons and may be nine feet tall. Because elephants are so large, they have no natural enemies other than man. Since elephants have so few enemies, they are usually easy to get along with and almost always act friendly.

Elephants usually live in herds with around thirty members of all ages. A female, or lady elephant, is called a cow. The herd usually has a cow as its leader, who is in charge of all the other elephants. During the hottest part of the day, the herd will huddle together and attempt to find shade. Near sundown the entire herd usually goes to a nearby river or lake for a drink. Elephants normally continue to stay together in a herd for most of their lives.

The first aircraft that man invented was the balloon. The first balloon was sent into the air by experimenters in France in 1783. It was a large bag made of paper and went about 6,000 feet into the air. It had been filled with hot air and smoke from a fire made by burning straw. A balloon rises into the air because it is filled with a gas that is lighter than the air outside.

Some balloons carry engines that turn a propeller, which drives them through the air. This type of balloon can be driven by a pilot and is called a dirigible or an airship.

For quite a long period of time airships were used to carry passengers. Because airships are rather slow and often dangerous, they are now used very little for transportation. Many people still enjoy riding in balloons as a sport because it is so thrilling.

(Scoring Sheet on pp. 208–209)

2/Form B

The beaver is the largest rodent in North America. The weight of an adult may range from 35 to 70 pounds. The hair or coat of the beaver is dense and waterproof, which allows it to swim in cold water without getting cold.

A beaver has sharp teeth that wear away as it uses them to cut down trees. These teeth keep growing as long as the animal lives. The back feet of a beaver are webbed, which help make it a good swimmer. Because of its large lungs that carry oxygen, it can stay submerged in water for as long as 15 minutes. The tail of a beaver is wide and flat and is covered with a scaly skin. When danger approaches, a beaver will warn the others by slapping the surface of the water with its tail.

The dams and canals made by beavers are useful in conserving both water and soil.

One of the most useful insects that can be made to work for man is the bee. Two of the most important ways in which the bee benefits us are in the making of honey and the growing of fruit and flowers.

The three types of bees in each hive are the workers, the queen, and the drones. Probably the most interesting members of the bee colony are the workers. The workers do several interesting jobs such as cleaning the hive, acting as nurses, and protecting the hive from enemies. When the worker bees are about ten days old, they begin to make short excursions away from the hive. When they first leave they learn to find their way back by becoming familiar with landmarks such as trees and houses. During these trips from the hive the bees learn to gather nectar from flowers. The nectar from the flowers is then made into honey.

One man discovered that bees do a certain kind of dance to inform other bees where flowers with nectar are located.

(Scoring Sheet on pp. 212–213)

2/Form B

TESTS

A
ORAL

2/Form A

(Scoring Sheet on pp. 214–215)

TESTS

There are four types of poisonous snakes in North America. One of these is the rattlesnake, which belongs to a family that is often called pit viper. This family of snakes has a deep pit between the eye and nostril on each side of its face. Inside the pit there is a membrane that is sensitive to heat. This membrane enables the snake to locate and strike at any animal with warm blood.

A rattlesnake coils itself into a loop and then strikes with lightning speed. It kills by sinking its poison fangs into its prey.

A rattlesnake gets its name from a series of loosely fitted rings at the end of its tail. A new ring or rattle is formed each time a snake sheds its skin. After the snake sheds its skin the first time, a rattle is formed, which is called a button.

One of the most useful animals in the world is the camel. The camel has helped men living in deserts for thousands of years. One advantage of using camels is that they can travel for great distances without needing water. Because the camel can carry heavy loads of freight, it is sometimes referred to as the "ship of the desert."

The camel is ugly and stupid and has a bad temper. When a camel is loaded for work, it will often show its disapproval by bellowing loudly and by kicking and biting.

There are two kinds of camels; these are the single-humped and the two-humped. The hump contains a great deal of fat and does not have any bone in it. When a camel is required to go without food, the fat in its hump can furnish it with energy for several days.

The main reason camels can go without water for so long is that they do not sweat.

(Scoring Sheet on pp. 216–217)   *2/Form B*

The most prominent feature in the sky at night is the moon, which is the earth's natural satellite. Astronomers, however, might think our moon is small and insignificant. They would be likely to feel our moon is small because the moons of other planets are so much larger.

People began to study lunar geography when the telescope was invented. One of the earliest of these astronomers was Galileo, who began looking at the moon in 1609. Later researchers found large craters, mountains, plains, and long valleys on the surface of the moon.

Manned vehicle landings were made on the moon in 1969. These were attempted because people were not satisfied with the information they had obtained by looking through telescopes. Rock samples taken from these explorations of the moon's surface have provided us with a great deal of knowledge about the age of the moon.

Because of our natural curiosity, few people would be willing to predict what we may accomplish in space.

No substance has been more eagerly sought after than gold. Because it is rare and durable, gold has been widely accepted as money. In past years gold coins were circulated, but this practice ceased in 1934. Gold is still kept by many nations because they know it will retain its value.

Another important use of gold is in the making of jewelry and metalwork. When gold is made into jewelry it is usually mixed with another metal to form an alloy. Alloys of gold are used because in its pure form gold is too soft to withstand the wear caused from regular usage.

Tiny quantities of gold occur in most soils and rocks throughout the world. However, in most cases the amount of gold is so small that it is not worth extracting. Gold is often found in association with metals such as copper.

(Scoring Sheet on pp. 220–221)

2/Form B

TESTS

2/Form A
(Scoring Sheet on pp. 222–223)
TESTS

There are approximately 3,000 types of lizards, which vary considerably in such characteristics as size, color, shape, and habits. For example, some of these unusual creatures may range from a minimum of merely two to three inches, while some huge varieties may ultimately grow to a maximum length of twelve feet.

Some of these reptiles have startling habits such as the ability to snap off their tails if they are seized. Some species may rear up on their hind legs and scamper away if they become frightened.

Most lizards benefit mankind by eating unwanted insects that, in most cases, are harmful to mankind. Although numerous superstitions abound concerning these strange creatures, only two types are definitely known to be poisonous.

Some lizards lay eggs that have a tough, leathery shell, while others bear living young. The eggs are typically laid where they may be incubated by the warmth emitted from the sun.

Since lizards are cold-blooded animals, they cannot stand extreme variations in temperature. If the sun becomes extremely hot, the lizard must pursue the solace of an overhead shelter such as a rock or bush.

The boomerang is perhaps the most remarkable weapon invented by any of the primitive tribes of the world. This unusual piece of equipment is fashioned from hardwood and is designed in various shapes and sizes. Most models are smooth and curved and range from two to four feet in length. They are normally flat on one side and convex on the opposite side. It is believed that the first prototype of this strange weapon was designed by the native tribes of aborigines in Australia.

There are two main types of boomerangs commonly used by men and women in sports and hunting today. These are classified into two categories, which are the return and nonreturn types. The return type is principally used for sport and amusement and is seldom used by professionals for hunting purposes. The nonreturn type is used for hunting and is capable of doing great damage to an animal for distances up to 400 feet.

With very little formal practice even a novice can become adept at using a return-type boomerang.

2/Form B

(Scoring Sheet on pp. 224–225)

Test 2: Reading Passages
Forms C and D

Oral Reading Passages

Silent Reading Passages

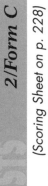

PP

C

ORAL

Sam is a boy.

He has a dog.

The dog's name is Tim.

Tim is a black dog.

He has a pink nose.

Sam goes to school.

The dog stays at home.

2/Form C

(Scoring Sheet on p. 228)

TESTS

PP

D
SILENT

Mary lives in a house.

She has a kitten.

The kitten's name is Tab.

Tab sleeps with Mary.

He likes to play ball.

The ball is yellow.

Mary and Tab have fun.

(Scoring Sheet on p. 229)

2/Form D

C
ORAL

2/Form C

(Scoring Sheet on p. 230)

Dave and Tom live in a large city.
They live with their father and mother.
Their house is near a park. Many kids
play football in the park.

Dave and Tom like to play football
there too. Dave can run faster than Tom.

Dave and Tom's mother goes to
school. She is going to be a teacher. Her
school is far from their home. She goes
to school in a car.

Ann's class went to visit a fire station. One of the firemen was at the door. He said he was happy to see the class.

He showed the class a big fire truck. Then he showed them a car. The car and truck were both red. The big truck had a long ladder on it.

Then the class went back to school. They were very happy. They told their teacher they wanted to go again.

(Scoring Sheet on p. 231)

2/Form D

TESTS

Dale lives on a large animal farm with his father and mother. His father has many cows, horses, sheep, and pigs on the farm. One of the animals belongs to Dale. It is a pet pig. The pig is black with a white ring around its back. It has a very short curly tail.

When Dale goes for a walk the pig likes to walk with him. Sometimes when Dale goes to school his pig will follow him. The children at school all laugh when they see the pig with Dale. Many of the boys and girls say they would like to have a pet pig too.

Emily has a little black dog with curly hair. The little dog's name is Chester. He has long ears and a short tail. He lives in a little house behind Emily's big house. Sometimes when he is extra good he gets to come in the big house.

The dog does not like cats. Sometimes when he sees a cat he will run after it. The cat can run faster than the dog, so he does not catch it.

When the dog is hungry he begins to bark. When Emily hears him barking she brings him some food.

(Scoring Sheet on p. 233)

2/Form D

TESTS

Judy's class was going on a trip to visit an airport. Before they left they read some books about airplanes and airplane pilots. Everyone in the class was excited when it came time to go.

The class rode to the airport in a big yellow bus. After the bus stopped, the first person to get off was Judy's teacher. She told the class that they must all stay together so that none of the students would get lost.

First, they visited the ticket counter and learned how passengers buy their tickets. Then a pilot came and told them he would take them on a large airplane. After they were inside the airplane, everyone was surprised because it was so large. When Judy's class got back to school they all said they wanted to visit the airport again.

Many people would like to live on a farm so they could be around animals. If you had ever lived on a farm you would know that life is often not easy. Most farmers have to get up very early. In the morning a farmer has to feed and milk his cows. After doing this, the farmer has to go to his fields and work long hours plowing his land or planting his crops. After working hard all day, the farmer has to come home and milk his cows again.

In the winter when it is cold the farmer does not have to work in his fields. But when it is cold he has to work hard at keeping his animals warm.

Today's farmer has to learn how to do many things. He has to know how to care for animals, repair machines, and make the best use of his time.

A desert is a place where the weather is dry and often hot. Some people think it is a place where there is nothing but sand. This is true sometimes, but some deserts have many kinds of plants and animals living in them. The kinds of plants and animals living there usually do not require much water. For example, some desert plants can store water in their leaves and exist for long periods of time without rain.

Some animals that live in the desert get all of the water they need by eating the leaves of plants that have water in them. People who have been lost in the desert have died because they had no water to drink. Some of these people would not have died if they had known how to survive. People who know how to survive in such a dry place often know how to obtain water from cactus plants.

A person may enjoy living in the desert because he thinks it is a beautiful place, but another person may think the same place is not pretty at all.

One of the biggest jobs ever started was the building of the Panama Canal. The Panama Canal was known as "The Big Ditch." It was called "The Big Ditch" because it was a ditch with water in it and carried ships from one side of Panama to the other side, or from one ocean to another. By going through the Panama Canal, ships did not have to sail all the way around the continent of South America to get from one ocean to another.

When people first started building the Panama Canal there were many dangers from disease. People were getting Yellow Fever, which is a disease carried by a certain kind of mosquito. One man was a hero while the Panama Canal was being built. He discovered a way to get rid of the mosquitos that were carrying Yellow Fever. After these insects were killed, Yellow Fever was no longer spread from one person to another. By the time the Panama Canal was finished, very few people were dying from Yellow Fever.

(Scoring Sheet on pp. 240–241)

2/Form D

TESTS

**C
ORAL**

2/Form C

TESTS

(Scoring Sheet on pp. 242–243)

There are about a hundred different kinds of monkeys. Some may be as large as a big dog, while others are so small that you could hold them in your hand. Some monkeys have bright colored faces and when they become excited these colors become brighter. Certain types of monkeys live in pairs or sometimes in clans of up to a hundred or more. Many monkeys can be tamed when they are young, but they have bad tempers when they grow old. The night or owl monkey is so named because it sleeps in the daytime and roams about at night.

Some monkeys are like humans because they make sounds to indicate they are angry. The howler monkey produces a sound that can be heard for a distance of two miles. This type has a "boss" that is usually the strongest and largest male of the group. When the boss loses his job he may be forced to leave the group and wander alone.

Potatoes, along with wheat and rice, are one of the most important food crops in the world. Nearly every year the world grows about 10 billion bushels of potatoes. In some countries potatoes are used as food for animals as well as for people. In America they are usually consumed only by humans. The potatoes that people eat are almost always baked, boiled, or fried.

Potatoes are often grown in places where it is not quite warm enough for corn. In the Far Eastern countries, few are grown because the climate is too warm and because rice has more food value.

When the Spanish first came to South America they found the Indians growing potatoes. It was not until many years later that this new food became popular with the Spanish.

A king in France made this food popular by wearing the flowers of the plant in his buttonhole.

(Scoring Sheet on pp. 244–245)

2/Form D

A mole is a small animal about six inches long. Moles have a long snout like a pig, a short thick neck, and a pink tail. Their ears are not visible but are concealed in their fur.

If a mole is placed on the ground it will begin to scramble about looking for a soft spot to dig. When it begins to dig, it will disappear in less than a minute. Moles often ruin lawns and gardens by making ridges in them caused from their burrowing through the ground.

Most of a mole's life is spent in darkness because it lives underground. A mole's home is usually a nest made from grasses and leaves. Its home is nearly always located beneath something like a rock, tree stump, or stone wall, which gives it more protection.

Moles are most commonly found in the northern half of the world.

Cottontails and jackrabbits are two of the most commonly known wild animals in the world. Most people do not realize that certain animals such as the jackrabbit and snowshoe rabbit are naturally not rabbits but hares. A hare is an animal with longer ears and it is heavier and larger than a rabbit.

A mother rabbit spends considerably more time in building her nest than a mother hare. The female hare, which is called a doe, has two or three litters of young during the year.

There are usually four to six babies born in each litter. Young hares are born with their eyes open and can care for themselves in a few days. The infant rabbit is born with its eyes closed and does not see for about a week.

Both the rabbit and the hare are well equipped to detect their enemies. They have long sensitive ears for excellent hearing and eyes that enable them to see in every direction.

(Scoring Sheet on pp. 248–249)

2/Form D

TEST 2

Among the animals of the world, one of the most talented is the spider. With its silken webs it can construct suspension bridges, beautiful designs, and insect traps. The spider might be thought of as one of nature's greatest engineers.

Spiders can be found in all parts of the world except where it is extremely cold. They cannot survive in cold or polar regions covered with snow because of a lack of food.

People sometimes mistakenly refer to spiders as insects. Unlike insects, which have six legs and three body segments, spiders have eight legs and two body segments.

Although there are many different kinds of spiders in the United States, only two of these are considered dangerous. These are the Black Widow and the Brown House Spider. Spiders are useful to humans because they destroy many kinds of harmful insects.

Millions of cats have homes, but there are many who are strays. They are still the second most popular type of pet in America. People who raise cats and enter them in shows are called members of the "American Cat Fancy." A cat must have earned four winner's ribbons to become a champion.

Cats are meat eaters and are equipped with special teeth to tear meat into chunks. Once the meat has been torn into small chunks, it is swallowed without chewing. Cats are excellent hunters and can jump as high as seven feet in the air. One purpose of a cat's tail is to enable it to balance itself when it jumps. If a cat is turned upside down and dropped, it will always turn over and land on its feet.

Some cats have been known to live to be 19 or 20 years old; however, the average life of a cat is about 14 years.

(Scoring Sheet on pp. 252–253)

2/Form D

The ostrich, which roams wild in Africa, is the biggest living bird. A fully developed male is extremely large, often standing as tall as seven or eight feet. The eggs from which the young are hatched are also quite large, with a weight of about three pounds.

Most humans consider this giant bird to be awkward and ugly. Although it is not a beautiful bird, it was once highly prized for its fluffy feathers or plumes. Knights of long ago used them as decorations on their helmets and their ladies used them to adorn their dresses.

The ostrich is a flightless bird; however, in running it may attain speeds of up to fifty miles per hour. This large bird often roams over the plains with other animals such as zebras and antelopes. If it fears danger it is likely to dash off, warning other animals. If it is forced to defend itself, it will often kick using its strong legs and sharp claws.

D
SILENT

There is no other natural substance that has the ability of rubber to stretch or bend and then snap back into shape. This ability makes this important product very useful in modern transportation.

Most of the natural rubber is obtained from the rubber tree. The inner bark of the rubber tree secretes a milky fluid called latex. There are a number of other tropical vines and shrubs that secrete a substance similar to latex, but it is of little economic value.

Most of the trees that produce rubber are grown in an area close to the equator. Rubber trees are normally found in countries with a low altitude. Some of these trees may grow as fast as nine feet per year. When a rubber tree has obtained a growth of about six inches in diameter, it is ready to be tapped for latex.

Although some materials have replaced rubber, it is still one of the most widely used products in the world.

(Scoring Sheet on pp. 256–257)

2/Form D

TESTS

A rather unusual fish that can fly through the air for relatively extensive distances is called the flying fish. It may fly distances of merely a few feet, but may also soar through the air for distances ranging up to 200 yards. This particular type of fish usually only flies when it is pursued by a predator. The peculiar flying fish may stay aloft only momentarily but it may remain airborne for a duration of up to ten or fifteen seconds. Among the creatures of the ocean who prey on the flying fish are tuna, sharks, dolphins, and porpoises.

If the flying fish is endangered, it is able to use its tail to strike a sharp blow on the water's surface to give it added momentum in making its ascent. When the fish makes its exodus from the water, it may attain speeds of up to 35 miles per hour. Once the fish is airborne, it spreads its pectoral fins and proceeds to use them as wings. These fins are not actually wings but elastic membranes that enable them to be flexible.

There are approximately 65 species of this unique fish, which commonly inhabits only the warm waters of the Atlantic Ocean.

One of our most important and familiar forms of energy is light. Some researchers believe that millions of years ago the sun was responsible for the various chemical reactions that led to the beginning of life. Light is instrumental in photosynthesis, which is a process by which plants utilize light to form chemical compounds necessary for their survival. A large percentage of the living organisms on earth are dependent on photosynthesis for their food supply.

Light is also important in providing the earth's surface and atmosphere with warmth, which is important in maintaining a proper temperature range for habitation. Without a source of light, the temperature of the earth would be so low that survival for man would be impossible.

If an object is to be visible, light must travel from that object to the eye, which then senses that light. An object that provides a source of light in itself is said to be luminous. The moon is typical of an object that is not luminous in itself but is only seen because it reflects light from the sun. In contrast, the sun and other stars emit their own light energy and would be classified as luminous.

(Scoring Sheet on pp. 260–261)

2/Form D

TEST 3b: CONCEPTS ABOUT PRINT

This is a sentence.

B

word

(Scoring Sheet on p. 267)

3b

These sentences are used to demonstrate that when we read, we begin at the upper left and move to the right, then we do a return sweep to begin the next sentence, as we read down the page.

TEST 3c: LETTER KNOWLEDGE

3c1

f   l   t   k   s

i   o   j   z

y   x   v   w

3c2

b   p   d   q   g

n   u   r   m

a   h   c   e

(Scoring Sheet on p. 268)

3c1, 3c2

TEST 4a: QUICK CHECK FOR BASIC SIGHT WORDS

1. I	10. want	19. thing	28. leave
2. the	11. those	20. run	29. should
3. was	12. went	21. thank	30. there
4. down	13. both	22. once	31. sure
5. these	14. then	23. wish	32. always
6. saw	15. shall	24. think	33. carry
7. than	16. upon	25. every	34. present
8. start	17. while	26. ran	35. such
9. this	18. draw	27. another	36. hurt

4a

(Scoring Sheet on p. 269)

TEST 5: PHONICS

5a APPLICATION OF PHONICS SKILLS IN CONTEXT

Ron has a job. He will make the fur of the cat shine. He will use a brush. Ron can fix a cage. He can pat a wet nose. He may hug a cute cub.

Ron may perk up a sad white bird with a nice word. Then Ron will clean dirt from the ground in the owl barn. He can see a fawn rest by a tree. He may bring a toy on a chain to a girl cub. The cub will make a strange noise. Ron will smile. He likes all the things he can do to work and play at the zoo.

(Scoring Sheet on p. 276–277)

5a

5b INITIAL CONSONANTS

1.	l	w	h	t	b	6.	h	b	f	k	t
2.	c	b	k	q	d	7.	t	f	a	j	k
3.	m	l	t	n	b	8.	d	b	p	r	t
4.	c	k	g	b	d	9.	k	c	f	s	r
5.	b	d	p	k	g	10.	t	h	g	i	k

5c INITIAL BLENDS AND DIGRAPHS

1.	cr	gl	gr	tr	dr	6.	sh	cr	bl	ch	sl
2.	bl	tr	br	gl	fr	7.	dr	th	tl	fl	ch
3.	sp	sn	sm	st	sc	8.	dr	bl	cr	pr	br
4.	sh	st	ch	sl	cn	9.	sm	sp	ch	sh	cr
5.	bl	pr	gl	pl	sl	10.	tr	dr	th	ch	tw

5d ENDING SOUNDS

1.	q	r	t	k	d	6.	nt	nk	st	ng	rk
2.	k	b	q	d	t	7.	st	ch	ss	ck	sh
3.	b	p	t	k	d	8.	sk	st	sh	ss	ck
4.	r	u	o	l	k	9.	st	nk	ng	nt	rd
5.	d	b	k	t	p	10.	nd	rd	pt	ld	rt

5e VOWELS

1.	a	e	i	o	u	6.	a	e	i	o	u
2.	e	i	o	u	a	7.	e	i	o	u	a
3.	i	o	u	a	e	8.	i	o	u	a	e
4.	o	u	a	e	i	9.	o	u	a	e	i
5.	u	a	e	i	o	10.	u	o	a	e	i

5f PHONOGRAMS

1.	ang	and	ime	ing	ame
2.	in	ime	ame	ind	ain
3.	ite	ipe	ike	ice	eek
4.	ick	og	uck	ock	eep
5.	up	eek	ipe	eep	ime
6.	it	ate	ight	ipe	ice
7.	ung	ine	ang	ing	ind
8.	ad	ade	age	and	ape
9.	ean	ime	ad	ang	ame
10.	elp	in	ill	all	ell

5g BLENDING

at   in

t   +   in

h + at   m + at

ch + in   sh + in

tr + in   str + at

bl + at   f + in

th + at   d + in

(Scoring Sheet on pp. 277–278)

5b–5i

TESTS

5h SUBSTITUTION

fan	track	hat	rade	bib
ran	shack	hit	rode	bif
tan	spack	hot	ride	bid
ban	frack	het	rude	big
jan	chack	hut		bim
lan	plack			
van	stack			
can	whack			

5i VOWEL PRONUNCIATION

boat	crown	serve
paint	trout	stir
own	hawk	born
soil	haul	word
coy	card	burn

TEST 6: STRUCTURAL ANALYSIS

6a APPLICATION OF STRUCTURAL ANALYSIS SKILLS IN CONTEXT

6a1

It was a cold winter day. The trees were bare and birds could be seen in the countryside. A grasshopper hopped across the road to hide from the cold and the foxes curled up to keep warm. A brown field mouse and her babies came running out of a hole in the ground. The babies were fighting with each other. Mother mouse looked unhappy as she sat on a big overgrown stump. It was dangerous for the mice to stay above ground but the active children wanted their lunches. Mother mouse was also nervous about her children eating the poisonous plants that were in the field. The children were curious and the plants looked so attractive.

Just that morning, Mother mouse had a disagreement with Father mouse. The question was whether or not the children should run in the field in the daytime.

(Scoring Sheet on p. 279)

6a1

TESTS

6a2

What should have been a great day turned out to be a disappointing one for David King. He found out that he would be the new quarterback for Friday night's game. Unfortunately, he was going to be taking his best friend Ron's place. Ron had gotten a disqualification notice because his grades dropped at the end of the first report. Ron felt that his concentration was poor because of his older brother's recent motorcycle crash. David was sorry about Ron's dismissal from the team, but was shocked by the resentment he saw on Ron's face when he found out who his replacement would be. This was the unfriendliest that Ron had ever treated David.

David thought about the rest of his rather uneventful day as he walked home. He turned on the flashlight he carried with him, for it had grown quite dark. David stopped short when he heard a loud and frightening scream coming from the vacant mansion just up the road.

The place had been empty for three years and was in bad shape. Fixing it up had been estimated to be costlier than most families could afford. David had always felt that the mansion had a mysterious look about it. The man who had built and lived in the mansion was believed to be knowledgeable in the ways of witchcraft. His disappearance three years ago had shocked the people of the town. What made it even scarier was that it happened on a Halloween night when so many children were out on the streets. The imaginative minds of several of the neighbors had come up with many strange stories about what had happened to old Flint.

6c INFLECTIONAL ENDINGS

bake	pale	slow
baker	paler	slower
baked	paling	slowest
bakes	palest	slowly
		slows

6d PREFIXES

play	mote	form
replay	remote	conform
display	promote	inform
misplay	demote	deform
take	tend	pack
retake	intend	unpack
intake	contend	prepack
mistake	extend	repack
	distend	
	pretend	

(Scoring Sheet on pp. 281–282)

6c–6h

TESTS

6e SUFFIXES

<u>joy</u>	<u>invent</u>	<u>base</u>	<u>elect</u>
joyous	inventive	basement	election
joyful	inventable	baseness	elective
joyless		baseless	

6f COMPOUND WORDS

overdone	motorplane
laterthought	clockrunner
baskethouse	

6g AFFIXES

uncall	treeness
proclaim	sunning
indeem	bookful
demark	raytion
prestrain	darkous

6h SYLLABICATION

automotive	premeditate
displacement	imperfection
conformation	unreasonable
remarkable	misplaying
impeachable	complicated

TEST 7: KNOWLEDGE OF CONTRACTIONS

1. let's	25. wouldn't
2. didn't	26. she'll
3. it's	27. here's
4. won't	28. couldn't
5. that's	29. they're
6. can't	30. they'd
7. wasn't	31. you'll
8. isn't	32. she'd
9. hadn't	33. weren't
10. don't	34. I'd
11. I'll	35. you've
12. we'll	36. you'd
13. I've	37. we'd
14. he'll	38. anybody'd
15. hasn't	39. there'll
16. haven't	40. we've
17. aren't	41. who'll
18. I'm	42. he'd
19. he's	43. who'd
20. we're	44. doesn't
21. you're	45. where's
22. what's	46. they've
23. there's	47. they'll
24. she's	

(Scoring Sheet on p. 283)

7

TEST 8: EL PASO PHONICS SURVEY

GENERAL DIRECTIONS

1. Before beginning the test, make sure the student has instant recognition of the test words that appear in the box at the top of the first page of the Test Sheet. These words should be known immediately by the student. If they are not, reschedule the test at a later date, after the words have been taught and the student has learned them.

2. Give the student the El Paso Phonics Survey Test Sheet pages.

3. Point to the letter in the first column and have the student say the name of that letter (not the sound it represents). Then point to the word in the middle column and have the student pronounce it. Then point to the nonsense word in the third column and have the student pronounce it.

4. If the student can give the name of the letter, the word in the middle column, and the nonsense word in the third column, mark the answer sheet with a plus (+). If he or she cannot pronounce the nonsense word after giving the name of the letter and the word in the middle column, mark the answer sheet with a minus (–), or you may wish to write the word phonetically as the student pronounced it.

5. If the student can tell you the name of the letter and the small word in the middle column but cannot pronounce the nonsense word, you may want to have him or her give the letter sound in isolation. If he or she can give the sound in isolation, either the student is unable to "blend" or does not know the letter well enough to give its sound and blend it at the same time.

6. Whenever a superior letter appears on the Scoring Sheet—for example, [a]3 in item number 3—you may want to refer to the Special Directions sheet.

7. To the right of each answer blank on the Scoring Sheet, you will note a grade-level designation under the heading "PEK." This number represents the point at which most basal reading series would have already taught that sound. Therefore, at that point you should expect it to be known. The designation 1.9 means the ninth month of the first year, and so forth.

8. When the student comes to two- or three-letter consonant digraphs or blends, as with *qu* in number 22, he or she is to say "*q-u*" as with the single letters. *Remember:* The student never gives letter sounds in isolation when engaged in actual reading.

9. When the student comes to the vowels (number 59), he or she is to say "short *a*," and so forth, and then the nonsense word in column two. If the student does not know that the breve (˘) over the vowels means short *a, e,* and so forth, then explain this. Do the same with the long vowels, where the macron (¯) appears.

10. All vowels and vowel combinations are put with only one or two of the first eight consonants tested. If any of these first eight consonants are not known, they should be taught before you attempt to test for vowel knowledge.

11. You will note that words appear to the right of some of the blanks on the Scoring Sheet. These words illustrate the correct consonant or vowel sound that should be heard when the student responds.

12. Only phonic elements that have a high enough utility to make them worthwhile learning have been included. For example, the vowel pair *ui* appears very seldom,

▶ and when it does it may stand for the short *i* sound as in *build* or the long *oo* sound as in *fruit*. Therefore, there is no reason to teach it as a sound. However, some letters, such as *oe*, may stand for several sounds but most often stand for one particular sound. In the case of *oe*, the long *o* sound should be used. In cases such as this, the most common sound is illustrated by a word to the right of the blank on the Scoring Sheet. If the student gives another correct sound for the letter(s), then say, "Yes, but what is another way that we could say this nonsense word?" The student must then say it as illustrated in the small word to the right of the blank on the Scoring Sheet. Otherwise, count the answer as wrong.

13. Stop the test after five consecutive misses or if the student appears frustrated at missing a number of items even though he or she has not missed five consecutive items.

SPECIAL DIRECTIONS

[a]3. If the student uses another *s* sound as in *sugar* (*sh*) in saying the nonsense word *sup*, ask, "What is another *s* sound?" The student must use the *s* as in *sack*.

[b]15. If the student uses the soft *c* sound as in *cigar* in saying the nonsense word *cam*, ask, "What is another *c* sound?" The student must use the hard *c* sound as in *coat*.

[c]16. If the student uses the soft *g* sound as in *gentle* in saying the nonsense word *gup*, ask, "What is another *g* sound?" The student must use the hard *g* sound as in *gate*.

[d]17. Ask, "What is the *y* sound when it comes at the beginning of a word?"

[e]23. The student must use the *ks* sound of *x*, and the nonsense word *mox* must rhyme with *box*.

[f]33. If the student uses the *th* sound heard in *that*, ask, "What is another *th* sound?" The student must use the *th* sound heard in *thing*.

[g]34. If the student uses the *hoo* sound of *wh* in saying the nonsense word *whup*, ask, "What is another *wh* sound?" The student must use the *wh* sound as in *when*.

[h]69. The student may give either the *oo* sound heard in *moon* or the *oo* sound heard in *book*. Be sure to note which one is used.

[i]70. If the same *oo* sound is given this time as was given for item 69, say, "Yes, that's right, but what is another way we could pronounce this nonsense word?" Whichever sound was *not* used in item 69 must be used here; otherwise, it is incorrect.

[j]71. The student may give either the *ea* sound heard in *head* or the *ea* sound heard in *meat*. Be sure to note which one is used.

[k]72. If the same *ea* sound is given this time as was given for item 71, say, "Yes, that's right, but what is another way we could pronounce this nonsense word?" Whichever sound was *not* used in item 71 must be used here; otherwise, it is incorrect.

[l]78. The student may give either the *ow* sound heard in *cow* or the *ow* sound heard in *crow*. Be sure to note which one is used.

[m]79. If the same *ow* sound is given this time as was given for item 78, say, "Yes, that's right, but what is another way we could pronounce this nonsense word?" Whichever sound was not used in item 78 must be used here; otherwise, it is incorrect.

(Scoring Sheet on pp. 284–285)

8

TEST

TEST 8: EL PASO PHONICS SURVEY

Test Words | in up am

1.	p	am	pam	22.	qu	am	quam
2.	n	up	nup	23.	m	ox	mox
3.	s	up	sup	24.	pl	up	plup
4.	t	up	tup	25.	fr	in	frin
5.	r	in	rin	26.	fl	am	flam
6.	m	in	min	27.	st	up	stup
7.	b	up	bup	28.	bl	in	blin
8.	d	up	dup	29.	tr	in	trin
9.	w	am	wam	30.	gr	up	grup
10.	h	up	hup	31.	br	in	brin
11.	f	in	fin	32.	sh	up	shup
12.	j	in	jin	33.	th	up	thup
13.	k	am	kam	34.	wh	up	whup
14.	l	in	lin	35.	ch	am	cham
15.	c	am	cam	36.	dr	up	drup
16.	g	up	gup	37.	pr	am	pram
17.	y	in	yin	38.	sl	up	slup
18.	v	am	vam	39.	cl	in	clin
19.	z	in	zin	40.	gl	am	glam
20.	c	in	cin	41.	sm	in	smin
21.	g	in	gin	42.	sk	am	skam

▶

43.	cr	in	crin		67.	ū	pune
44.	tw	am	twam		68.	ō	sote
45.	sn	up	snup		69.	oo	oot
46.	sch	am	scham		70.	oo	oot
47.	sp	am	spam		71.	ea	eap
48.	sc	up	scup		72.	ea	eam
49.	str	am	stram		73.	ai	ait
50.	thr	up	thrup		74.	ay	tay
51.	shr	up	shrup		75.	oe	poe
52.	squ	am	squam		76.	oa	oan
53.	sw	up	swup		77.	ee	eem
54.	spr	am	spram		78.	ow	owd
55.	spl	in	splin		79.	ow	fow
56.	wr	in	wrin		80.	or	orm
57.	dw	in	dwin		81.	ir	irt
58.	scr	up	scrup		82.	ur	urd
59.	ă	tam			83.	aw	awp
60.	ĭ	rit			84.	oi	doi
61.	ĕ	nep			85.	ou	tou
62.	ŏ	sot			86.	ar	arb
63.	ŭ	tum			87.	oy	moy
64.	ī	tipe			88.	er	ert
65.	ē	rete			89.	ew	bew
66.	ā	sape			90.	au	dau

(Scoring Sheet on pp. 284–285)

8

TEST 9: QUICK WORD LIST SURVEY

wratbeling

dawsnite

pramminciling

whetsplitter

gincule

cringale

slatrungle

twayfrall

spreanplit

goanbate

streegran

glammertickly

grantellean

aipcid

Scoring Sheets

TEST 1: SAN DIEGO QUICK ASSESSMENT
OR GRADED WORD LIST (GWL)

GRADED WORD LIST (GWL) SCORING SHEET

Name _____   Date _____

School _____   Tester _____

PP

see _____
play _____
me _____
at _____
run _____
go _____
and _____
look _____
can _____
here _____

P

you _____
come _____
not _____
with _____
jump _____
help _____
is _____
work _____
are _____
this _____

1

road _____
live _____
thank _____
when _____
bigger _____
how _____
always _____
night _____
spring _____
today _____

2

our _____
please _____
myself _____
town _____
early _____
send _____
wide _____
believe _____
quietly _____
carefully _____

3

city _____
middle _____
moment _____
frightened _____
exclaimed _____
several _____
lonely _____
drew _____
since _____
straight _____

4

decided _____
served _____
amazed _____
silent _____
wrecked _____
improved _____
certainly _____
entered _____
realized _____
interrupted _____

(Test Sheet on p. 128)

▶

5 📖

scanty	_____
business	_____
develop	_____
considered	_____
discussed	_____
behaved	_____
splendid	_____
acquainted	_____
escaped	_____
grim	_____

6 📖

bridge	_____
commercial	_____
abolish	_____
trucker	_____
apparatus	_____
elementary	_____
comment	_____
necessity	_____
gallery	_____
relativity	_____

7 📖

amber	_____
dominion	_____
sundry	_____
capillary	_____
impetuous	_____
blight	_____
wrest	_____
enumerate	_____
daunted	_____
condescend	_____

8 📖

capacious	_____
limitation	_____
pretext	_____
intrigue	_____
delusion	_____
immaculate	_____
ascent	_____
acrid	_____
binocular	_____
embankment	_____

9 📖

conscientious	_____
isolation	_____
molecule	_____
ritual	_____
momentous	_____
vulnerable	_____
kinship	_____
conservatism	_____
jaunty	_____
inventive	_____

RESULTS OF GRADED WORD LIST

Independent Reading Level	Grade _____	Highest level at which one or no words were missed
Instructional Reading Level	Grade _____	Level at which two words were missed
Frustration Reading Level	Grade _____	Lowest level at which three or more words were missed

*From Margaret LaPray and Ramon Ross, "The Graded Word List: Quick Gauge of Reading Ability," *Journal of Reading* (January 1969), pp. 305–307. Reprinted with permission of the International Reading Association and the authors.

(Test Sheet on p. 128)

SCORING   **1**

Test 2: Reading Passages
Forms A and B

Oral Reading Passages

Silent Reading Passages

PP

A
ORAL

Jan *has* a dog.

The dog's name *is* Pat.

He can run fast.

One day Pat *ran away.*

Jan looked *for him.*

The dog wanted *to eat.*

Soon he came home.

(31 Words) (Number of word recognition errors _____) *(19 Dolch Words)*

Questions:

F   1. _____ What does Jan have? (A dog)
F   2. _____ What is the dog's name? (Pat)
F   3. _____ What can the dog do? (Run or run fast)
F   4. _____ What did Jan do when the dog ran away? (She looked for him)
F   5. _____ What did the dog want? (To eat)

Number of Questions Missed	Number of Word Recognition Errors				Reading Level		
	0	1	2–3	4			
0	+	*	*	×		+	Independent
1	*	*	×	×		*	Instructional
2	*	×	×	×		×	Frustration
3	×	×	×	×			
4	×	×	×	×			
5+	×	×	×	×			

_____ Check here if this passage was used for the Listening Comprehension Test.

Listening Comprehension result: *(70 percent or higher to pass)*

_____ Percent   _____ **Passed**   _____ **Failed**

PP

B

SILENT

Bob likes to play ball.

He plays with Sam.

They play at school.

It is far away.

The boys ride a bus.

It takes them to school.

It also takes them home.

(32 Words)

Time: _____
    (in seconds)

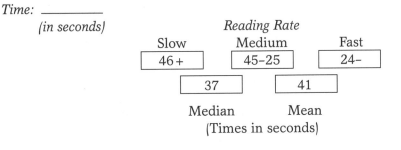

Reading Rate

Slow	Medium	Fast
46 +	45–25	24–

37	41

Median   Mean

(Times in seconds)

Questions:

F   1. _____ What does Bob like to do? (Play, play ball, play with Sam, or play ball with Sam)

F   2. _____ Who does Bob play with? (Sam)

F   3. _____ Where do the boys play? (At school)

F   4. _____ Where is the school? (Far away)

F   5. _____ What do the boys ride in? (A bus)

Number of Questions Missed		*Reading Level*	
0	Independent	Independent	
1–2	Instructional	Instructional	
3+	Frustration	Frustration	

_____ Check here if this passage was used for the Listening Comprehension Test.

Listening Comprehension result: *(70 percent or higher to pass)*

_____ Percent   _____ **Passed**   _____ **Failed**

(Test Sheet on p. 131)

2/Form B

SCORING

1A
ORAL

Tuff *was a big brown* bear. *He* lived *in a big* park. *He* liked *to eat* honey *best of all. He* also liked *to eat* bread.

Some people *were in the* park having *a* picnic. *They were* sitting *by a big* table. Tuff *went to the* picnic *too. When the* people *saw him they were* afraid. *They all* jumped *up and ran away. Then the* bear *ate all of their* food.

(71 Words) (Number of word recognition errors _____) *(49 Dolch Words)*

Questions:

F   1. _____ Who was Tuff? (A big brown bear, a bear, or a brown bear)
F   2. _____ Where did he live? (In a big park, or in a park)
F   3. _____ What did he like to eat best of all? (Honey—If student says "bread" say, "But what did he like best of all?" Student must say "honey.")
F   4. _____ What did he also like to eat? (Bread)
F   5. _____ What were the people doing in the park? (Having a picnic)
F   6. _____ Where were the people sitting? (By a table, or by a big table)
F   7. _____ Where did Tuff go? (To the picnic too)
F   8. _____ What did the people think when they saw Tuff? (They were afraid)
F   9. _____ What did they do when they saw Tuff? (They jumped up and ran away, or they ran away)
F 10. _____ What did the bear do then? (He ate all of their food, or he ate the food)

Number of Questions Missed	Number of Word Recognition Errors						Reading Level	
	0–1	2	3–4	5	6	7		
0	+	*	*	*	*	×		
1	+	*	*	*	×	×	+ Independent	
2	*	*	*	×	×	×	* Instructional	
3	*	*	×	×	×	×	× Frustration	
4	*	×	×	×	×	×		
5+	×	×	×	×	×	×		

_____ Check here if this passage was used for the Listening Comprehension Test.

Listening Comprehension result: (*70 percent or higher to pass*)

_____ Percent   _____ **Passed**   _____ **Failed**

1B
SILENT

Steve was going to have a birthday party. He asked all of his good friends to come. His mother made a big cake for him. She put eight candles on it.

Steve's dog was in the house that day. Soon Steve's friends were at the door. The dog began to bark. He was afraid of all of Steve's friends. Steve told his dog to go to his room. Then the children began playing some games.

(75 Words)

Time: _____
        (in seconds)

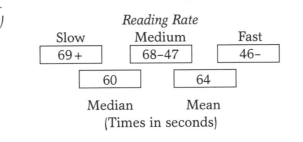

Reading Rate

Slow	Medium	Fast
69+	68–47	46–

60   64

Median   Mean
(Times in seconds)

Questions:

F   1. _____ What was Steve going to have? (A party, or a birthday party)
F   2. _____ Who did he ask to come? (His friends, or his good friends, or all of his good friends)
F   3. _____ What did his mother make for him? (A cake, or a big cake, or a birthday cake)
F   4. _____ What did his mother put on the cake? (Eight candles, or some candles)
F   5. _____ Where was Steve's dog that day? (In the house)
F   6. _____ Who came to the door? (Steve's friends, or his friends)
F   7. _____ What did the dog do? (He began to bark, or started barking)
F   8. _____ Who was the dog afraid of? (Steve's friends, or the children)
F   9. _____ What did Steve tell his dog to do? (To go to his room)
F 10. _____ What did the children begin to do? (To play, or to play some games)

Number of Questions Missed		*Reading Level*	
0–1	Independent	Independent	
2–4	Instructional	Instructional	
5+	Frustration	Frustration	

_____ Check here if this passage was used for the Listening Comprehension Test.

Listening Comprehension result: *(70 percent or higher to pass)*

_____ Percent   _____ **Passed**   _____ **Failed**

(Test Sheet on p. 133)

SCORING **2/Form B**

2A ORAL

Bob *and his* father *like to work on old* cars. *His* father *has five old* cars *that* belong *to him. One of them is black with a white* top.

Bob *is very* young, *so* none *of the* cars belong *to him. He would like to have his* own car *when he* gets *big.*

Sometimes Bob *and his* father *go to a* car *show. At the* car *show there are many* old cars.

One time Bob's father took *his black and white* car *to the car show. One of the* men looked *at the* cars *to see which one was best. He gave* Bob's father *a* prize *because his* car *was so pretty.*

(112 Words) (Number of word recognition errors _____) *(79 Dolch Words)*

Questions:

F 1. _____ What do Bob and his father like to do? (Work on old cars)
F 2. _____ How many old cars does Bob's father have? (Five)
F 3. _____ What color is one of his cars? (Black and white, or black with a white top)
F 4. _____ Why do none of the cars belong to Bob? (Because he is young, or because he is too young)
F 5. _____ What would Bob like to have when he gets big? (His own car)
F 6. _____ Where do Bob and his father go sometimes? (To a car show)
F 7. _____ What is at the car show? (Many old cars, old cars, or many cars)
F 8. _____ What did Bob's father take to the car show? (His car, or his black and white car)
F 9. _____ Why did the man look at the cars? (To see which one was best, or prettiest)
F 10. _____ Why did the man give Bob's father a prize? (Because his car was so pretty)

Number of Questions Missed	Number of Word Recognition Errors						Reading Level		
	0–1	2–3	4–6	7–8	9–10	11			
0	+	*	*	*	*	×	+	Independent	
1	+	*	*	*	×	×	*	Instructional	
2	*	*	*	×	×	×	×	Frustration	
3	*	*	×	×	×	×			
4	×	×	×	×	×	×			
5+	×	×	×	×	×	×			

_____ Check here if this passage was used for the Listening Comprehension Test.

Listening Comprehension result: *(70 percent or higher to pass)*

_____ Percent _____ **Passed** _____ **Failed**

**2B
SILENT**

Kay was waiting by the door for the mail to come. Her father had promised to write her a letter. He told Kay the letter would have a blue stamp on it.

Kay saw the woman walking toward the house. She was carrying a big bag on her side. She reached in her bag and gave Kay some letters. One of the letters had Kay's name on it. When Kay read the letter she was very happy. She was so happy when she read it that she began to jump up and down. In the letter Father told Kay he was going to buy her a pony.

(107 Words)

Time: _____
        (in seconds)

                            Reading Rate
         Slow   Medium   Fast
        | 73 + | | 72–53 | | 52– |

              | 63 | | 63 |
             Median   Mean
          (Times in seconds)

Questions:

F 1. _____ Why was Kay waiting by the door? (For the mail to come or for a letter)
F 2. _____ Who had promised to write her a letter? (Her father, or Father)
F 3. _____ What had her father told her the letter would have on it? (A blue stamp)
F 4. _____ Who did Kay see walking toward her house? (A woman or mail carrier or similar title)
F 5. _____ What was the woman carrying on her side? (A big bag)
F 6. _____ What did the woman do? (She reached in her bag and gave Kay some letters, or she gave Kay some letters)
F 7. _____ How did Kay know that one of the letters was for her? (Because it had her name on it, or because it had a blue stamp on it)
F 8. _____ How did Kay feel when she opened the letter? (Happy)
F 9. _____ What did she do because she was so happy? (She began to jump up and down)
F 10. _____ What did Father tell Kay in the letter? (That he was going to buy her a pony)

Number of Questions Missed		Reading Level	
0–1	Independent	Independent	
2–4	Instructional	Instructional	
5+	Frustration	Frustration	

_____ Check here if this passage was used for the Listening Comprehension Test.

Listening Comprehension result: (*70 percent or higher to pass*)

_____ Percent   _____ **Passed**   _____ **Failed**

(Test Sheet on p. 135)   **2/Form B**

**3A
ORAL**

Kathy *had always* wanted *to go for a ride on an* airplane. *One* day *her* father told *her that she could ride on an* airplane *to* visit *her* grandmother *and* grandfather. *She was very* happy *and could* hardly wait *to get* started.

When the time *came to go, her* father *went to the* ticket counter *and* paid *for the* airplane ticket. *Her* mother helped *her get on the* airplane. *Then a* lady told *her to* buckle *her* seat belt *and she* even helped *her with it.*

Soon the airplane *was going very fast down the* runway. Kathy *was* afraid *at first but soon the* airplane *was in the* air. Kathy peered *out of the* window *at the* ground below, *where the* houses *and* cars looked *very small. The* lady *gave* Kathy something *to drink and a* sandwich *to eat.*

(139 Words) (Number of word recognition errors _____) *(90 Dolch Words)*

Questions:

F 1. _____ What had Kathy always wanted to do? (Go for a ride on an airplane)
F 2. _____ Who told Kathy that she could ride on an airplane? (Her father)
F 3. _____ Who was Kathy going to visit? (Her grandmother and grandfather)
F 4. _____ How did Kathy feel about going? (She was very happy, happy, and/or she could hardly wait to get started)
F 5. _____ Who helped Kathy get on the airplane? (Her mother)
F 6. _____ What did the lady tell Kathy when she got on the airplane? (To buckle her seat belt)
F 7. _____ How did Kathy feel when the airplane started going very fast? (She was afraid)
V 8. _____ What did the word *peered* mean when it said, "Kathy peered out of the window"? (She looked, or she looked out of the window)
I 9. _____ Why did the houses and cars look small below? (Because they were up in the air, far away, or high up in the air)
F 10. _____ What did the lady give Kathy? (A drink and a sandwich) (Student must get both)

Number of Questions Missed	Number of Word Recognition Errors						Reading Level	
	0–2	3–4	5–7	8–10	11–13	14		
0	+	*	*	*	*	×	+	Independent
1	+	*	*	*	×	×	*	Instructional
2	*	*	*	×	×	×	×	Frustration
3	*	*	×	×	×	×		
4	*	×	×	×	×	×		
5+	×	×	×	×	×	×		

_____ Check here if this passage was used for the Listening Comprehension Test.
Listening Comprehension result: *(70 percent or higher to pass)*

_____ Percent _____ **Passed** _____ **Failed**

(Test Sheet on p. 136)

SCORING 2/Form A

3B
SILENT

Dick and his father liked to go camping. Dick asked his father if they could go camping in the woods. His father told him they would go the next Saturday.

When Saturday came they got up early and rode in the car until they found an excellent place to camp. Father decided that they would put up their tent by a small river. They put up their tent and then gathered some wood to start a fire. After the fire was burning, Father got some food ready and Dick helped him cook it over the fire.

After they finished eating they watched the fire until it was time to go to sleep. When Dick and Father had gone to sleep, something made a terribly loud noise and woke them up. Dick was afraid but Father laughed because it was only an airplane flying over them.

(145 Words)

Time: _____
       (in seconds)

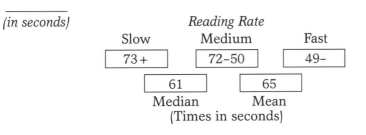

Reading Rate

Slow	Medium	Fast
73 +	72–50	49–

61	65
Median	Mean

(Times in seconds)

Questions:

F   1. _____ What did Dick and his father like to do? (Go camping)
F   2. _____ What did Dick ask his father? (If they could go camping)
F   3. _____ What did his father tell him? (That they would go the next Saturday)
F   4. _____ How did they get to the place where they camped? (They rode in the car, or in a car)
V   5. _____ What did it mean when it said they found an "excellent" place to camp? (A good place to camp)
F   6. _____ Where did they put up their tent? (By a small river, or by a river)
F   7. _____ What did they do with the wood they gathered? (Started a fire)
F   8. _____ Why did they start a fire? (To cook some food, or to cook)
F   9. _____ What woke them up? (An airplane, or a loud noise)
I   10. _____ What did Father do that would make you think he was not afraid? (He laughed)

Number of Questions Missed		*Reading Level*	
0–1	Independent	Independent	
2–4	Instructional	Instructional	
5+	Frustration	Frustration	

_____ Check here if this passage was used for the Listening Comprehension Test.

Listening Comprehension result: (*70 percent or higher to pass*)

_____ Percent   _____ **Passed**   _____ **Failed**

(Test Sheet on p. 137)   **2/Form B**

**4A
ORAL**

Some people enjoy exploring *the many* caves *in this* country. *This can be a* lot *of* fun *but it can* also *be* dangerous *because you* might *get* lost. *Many* people *have been* lost *in* caves *because they did not know what to do to find their* way *out.*

One thing *that* people *who* explore caves often *take with them is a* ball *of* string. *The* string serves *an* important purpose *in* keeping *them from* getting lost. *They* tie *one* end *of the* string *to a* stake outside *the* cave *and* unroll *the* string *as they walk* along. *This* way, *when they want to* leave *the* cave, *all they have to do to find their* way *out is to* follow *the* string.

Some caves *may* appear *small at the* opening, *but when you get* inside *there may be many* giant rooms *or* caverns *in them. One of the* largest known caves *in the* world *is* Mammoth Cave *in* Kentucky. *It* contains enormous caverns *and* underground rivers, *and may take up as much* space *as* 78 square miles.

(176 Words) (Number of word recognition errors _____) *(109 Dolch Words)*

Questions:

F 1. _____ What do some people enjoy doing? (Exploring caves)
F 2. _____ Why can exploring caves be dangerous? (Because you might get lost)
F 3. _____ Why have many people been lost in caves? (Because they did not know how to find their way out, or because they did not use string to follow)
F 4. _____ What do people who explore caves often take with them? (A ball of string) (Tell student if he or she does not know)
F 5. _____ What is the string tied to outside the cave? (To a stake)
F 6. _____ How do they use the string to find their way out? (They follow it, or follow the string that has been unrolled)
V 7. _____ What is a cavern? (A large room in a cave, or a cave)
F 8. _____ Where is one of the largest known caves? (In Kentucky)
F 9. _____ What else does Mammoth Cave contain besides enormous caverns? (Underground rivers, or rivers)
I 10. _____ Why would someone who explored caves need to be brave? (Because it is dangerous, or because one might get lost)

▶

Number of Questions Missed	Number of Word Recognition Errors						Reading Level
	0–2	3–6	7–9	10–13	14–16	17	
0	+	✳	✳	✳	✳	✕	
1	+	✳	✳	✳	✕	✕	
2	✳	✳	✳	✕	✕	✕	
3	✳	✳	✕	✕	✕	✕	
4	✳	✕	✕	✕	✕	✕	
5+	✕	✕	✕	✕	✕	✕	

	Reading Level	
+	Independent	
✳	Instructional	
✕	Frustration	

_____ Check here if this passage was used for the Listening Comprehension Test.

Listening Comprehension result: (*70 percent or higher to pass*)

_____ Percent   _____ **Passed**   _____ **Failed**

4B SILENT

One of people's best friends in North America is the bird. Birds are valuable to the farmer and gardener because they eat insects and weed seeds. Birds are also important to the hunter because they provide meat for his table.

When people first came to this country, there were many game birds. However, when the settlers started hunting birds for sport some kinds of birds were nearly all killed off. We now have much smaller numbers of wild turkey than we had in the past. In fact, some birds such as the passenger pigeon had all been killed or died by 1914.

In England a man might have been put in prison for taking wild birds' eggs from land owned by another man. A man might have even been hanged for killing a deer on someone else's land. The Indians in North America only killed wild game to eat.

(149 Words)

Time: _____
        (in seconds)

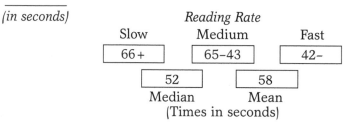

Reading Rate

Slow	Medium	Fast
66+	65–43	42–

52	58
Median	Mean

(Times in seconds)

Questions:

F 1. _____ What is one of people's best friends in North America? (Birds, or the bird)

V 2. _____ What does the word *valuable* mean in this reading passage? (Worth a lot, or similar synonym)

F 3. _____ Why are birds valuable to the farmer and gardener? (Because they eat insects and weed seeds)

F 4. _____ Why are birds valuable to the hunter? (Because they provide meat, or because they provide meat for the table)

F 5. _____ What happened to many birds when settlers started to hunt them for sport? (They were nearly all killed)

F 6. _____ What kind of bird do we still have but in much smaller numbers than we did in the past? (Wild turkeys)

F 7. _____ What birds had all been killed or died by 1914? (The passenger pigeon)

F 8. _____ What might have happened in England to a man who took wild birds' eggs from a man who owned the land they were on? (He might have been put in prison)

F 9. _____ What might they have done to a man who killed a deer on someone else's land? (Hanged him, or killed him)

I 10. _____ Why do you think the Indians would not have killed off most of the wild game in North America? (Because they only killed game to eat)

▶ *Number of Questions Missed*   *Reading Level*

0–1	Independent	Independent
2–4	Instructional	Instructional
5+	Frustration	Frustration

_____ Check here if this passage was used for the Listening Comprehension Test.

Listening Comprehension result: (*70 percent or higher to pass*)

_____ Percent   _____ **Passed**   _____ **Failed**

**5A
ORAL**

The elephant is the largest animal in the world that lives on land. A full-grown elephant may have a weight of about four tons and may be nine feet tall. Because elephants are so large, they have no natural enemies other than man. Since elephants have so few enemies, they are usually easy to get along with and almost always act friendly.

Elephants usually live in herds with around thirty members of all ages. A female, or lady elephant, is called a cow. The herd usually has a cow as its leader, who is in charge of all the other elephants. During the hottest part of the day, the herd will huddle together and attempt to find shade. Near sundown the entire herd usually goes to a nearby river or lake for a drink. Elephants normally continue to stay together in a herd for most of their lives.

(148 Words) (Number of word recognition errors _____)

Questions:

F   1. _____ What is the largest animal in the world that lives on land? (The elephant)
F   2. _____ How heavy might a full-grown elephant be? (About four tons)
F   3. _____ Why do elephants have no natural enemies other than man? (Because they are so large)
F   4. _____ Why are elephants almost always easy to get along with or why do they act friendly? (Because they have no or few enemies or because they are so large)
V   5. _____ What is a herd? (A group of something, a group of elephants, or a good synonym)
F   6. _____ How many elephants usually live in a herd? (About thirty)
F   7. _____ Who is usually the leader of an elephant herd? (A cow, a female, or a lady elephant)
F   8. _____ What do elephants do during the hottest part of the day? (They huddle together and/or attempt to find shade)
F   9. _____ What do elephants usually do near sundown? (Go to get a drink or go to a nearby river or lake)
I   10. _____ What did it say that would make you think elephants usually like each other? (They stay together for most of their lives, they stay together, or they stay in a herd)

SCORING 2/Form A
(Test Sheet on p. 140)

▶

Number of Questions Missed	Number of Word Recognition Errors					
	0–2	3–5	6–8	9–11	12–14	15
0	+	*	*	*	*	×
1	+	*	*	*	×	×
2	*	*	*	×	×	×
3	*	*	×	×	×	×
4	*	×	×	×	×	×
5+	×	×	×	×	×	×

Reading Level

+	Independent	
*	Instructional	
×	Frustration	

_____ Check here if this passage was used for the Listening Comprehension Test.

Listening Comprehension result: (*70 percent or higher to pass*)

_____ Percent   _____ **Passed**   _____ **Failed**

5B
SILENT

The first aircraft that man invented was the balloon. The first balloon was sent into the air by experimenters in France in 1783. It was a large bag made of paper and went about 6,000 feet into the air. It had been filled with hot air and smoke from a fire made by burning straw. A balloon rises into the air because it is filled with a gas that is lighter than the air outside.

Some balloons carry engines that turn a propeller, which drives them through the air. This type of balloon can be driven by a pilot and is called a dirigible or an airship.

For quite a long period of time airships were used to carry passengers. Because airships are rather slow and often dangerous, they are now used very little for transportation. Many people still enjoy riding in balloons as a sport because it is so thrilling.

(151 Words)

Time: _____
       (in seconds)

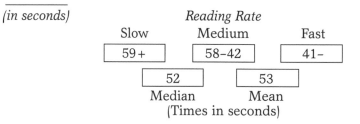

Reading Rate

Slow	Medium	Fast
59+	58–42	41–

52	53
Median	Mean

(Times in seconds)

Questions:

F   1. _____ What was the first aircraft invented by man? (The balloon)
F   2. _____ When did experimenters send the first balloon into the air? (In 1783)
F   3. _____ What was the first balloon made of? (Paper)
F   4. _____ What was the first balloon filled with? (Hot air, or hot air and smoke)
F   5. _____ Why are engines sometimes put on balloons? (To turn a propeller, or to drive them through the air)
F   6. _____ What is a balloon that can be driven by a pilot called? (A dirigible, or an airship)
F   7. _____ What were airships used for, for quite a long period of time? (To carry passengers, or for transportation)
V   8. _____ What does the word *transportation* mean? (A means of carrying people, or a means of carrying things from place to place)
F   9. _____ Why are airships no longer used for transportation? (Because they are slow and/or dangerous)
I   10. _____ Why do you think balloons may still be used for a long time? (Because they are thrilling, or because people still enjoy riding in them)

SCORING **2/Form B** *(Test Sheet on p. 141)*

▶

▶

Number of Questions Missed		Reading Level	
0–1	Independent	Independent	
2–4	Instructional	Instructional	
5+	Frustration	Frustration	

_____ Check here if this passage was used for the Listening Comprehension Test.

Listening Comprehension result: (*70 percent or higher to pass*)

_____ Percent   _____ **Passed**   _____ **Failed**

6A ORAL

The beaver is the largest rodent in North America. The weight of an adult may range from 35 to 70 pounds. The hair or coat of the beaver is dense and waterproof, which allows it to swim in cold water without getting cold.

A beaver has sharp teeth that wear away as it uses them to cut down trees. These teeth keep growing as long as the animal lives. The back feet of a beaver are webbed, which help make it a good swimmer. Because of its large lungs that carry oxygen, it can stay submerged in water for as long as 15 minutes. The tail of a beaver is wide and flat and is covered with a scaly skin. When danger approaches, a beaver will warn the others by slapping the surface of the water with its tail.

The dams and canals made by beavers are useful in conserving both water and soil.

(154 Words) (Number of word recognition errors _____)

Questions:

F 1. _____ What is the largest rodent in North America? (The beaver)
F 2. _____ How much might an adult beaver weigh? (From 35 to 70 pounds)
F 3. _____ What is it about the coat or hair of a beaver that allows it to swim in cold water without discomfort? (It is dense and/or waterproof)
F 4. _____ What happens to a beaver's teeth as it cuts down trees? (They wear away)
I 5. _____ How do you know that a beaver's teeth never completely wear away? (Because it said they keep growing as long as the animal lives)
F 6. _____ What is it about a beaver's back feet that enables it to be an excellent swimmer? (They are webbed)
V 7. _____ What does the word *submerged* mean in this passage? (Staying under, or going underwater)
F 8. _____ What does the tail of a beaver look like? (It is broad and flat and covered with a scaly skin) (Student must give at least two facts)
F 9. _____ How does a beaver warn other beavers that danger is near? (It slaps the surface of the water with its tail)
F 10. _____ Why are the dams and canals built by beavers useful to man? (Because they help to conserve water and soil)

Number of Questions Missed	Number of Word Recognition Errors					
	0–2	3–5	6–8	9–11	12–14	15
0	+	*	*	*	*	×
1	+	*	*	*	×	×
2	*	*	*	×	×	×
3	*	*	×	×	×	×
4	*	×	×	×	×	×
5+	×	×	×	×	×	×

Reading Level

+	Independent	
*	Instructional	
×	Frustration	

_____ Check here if this passage was used for the Listening Comprehension Test.

Listening Comprehension result: (*70 percent or higher to pass*)

_____ Percent   _____ **Passed**   _____ **Failed**

[Test Sheet on p. 142]

2/Form A

SCORING

**6B
SILENT**

One of the most useful insects that can be made to work for man is the bee. Two of the most important ways in which the bee benefits us are in the making of honey and the growing of fruit and flowers.

The three types of bees in each hive are the workers, the queen, and the drones. Probably the most interesting members of the bee colony are the workers. The workers do several interesting jobs such as cleaning the hive, acting as nurses, and protecting the hive from enemies. When the worker bees are about ten days old, they begin to make short excursions away from the hive. When they first leave they learn to find their way back by becoming familiar with landmarks such as trees and houses. During these trips from the hive the bees learn to gather nectar from flowers. The nectar from the flowers is then made into honey.

One man discovered that bees do a certain kind of dance to inform other bees where flowers with nectar are located.

(175 Words)

Time: _____
          (in seconds)

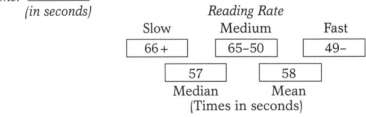

Reading Rate

Slow	Medium	Fast
66 +	65–50	49–

Median	Mean
57	58

(Times in seconds)

Questions:

F   1. _____   What is one of the most useful insects that can be made to work for man? (The bee)

F   2. _____   What are two of the most important ways in which the bee benefits us? (In making honey and in the growing of fruit and/or flowers)

F   3. _____   What are the three types of bees in each hive? (The workers, the queen, and the drones) (Students must get at least two)

F   4. _____   What type of bee is probably the most interesting? (The worker)

F   5. _____   What are some jobs of the worker? (Cleaning the hive, acting as nurse, protecting the hive, and making honey) (Students must get at least two)

V   6. _____   What does the word *excursions* mean in this reading passage? (Trips, or any other appropriate synonym)

F   7. _____   When bees first leave the hive, how do they find their way back? (By becoming familiar with landmarks, or by watching for trees and houses)

F   8. _____   What do bees do on their trips from the hive? (Look for nectar, or gather nectar)

F   9. _____   How old are the worker bees when they first begin to make short excursions away from the hive? (Ten days old)

I 10. _____   How do we know that bees can communicate with each other? (Because it said they do a dance to tell the other bees where flowers, or flowers with nectar, are located)

(Test Sheet on p. 143)

SCORING 2/Form B

▶

Number of Questions Missed		Reading Level	
0–1	Independent	Independent	
2–4	Instructional	Instructional	
5+	Frustration	Frustration	

_____ Check here if this passage was used for the Listening Comprehension Test.

Listening Comprehension result: (*70 percent or higher to pass*)

_____ Percent   _____ **Passed**   _____ **Failed**

7A ORAL

There are four types of poisonous snakes in North America. One of these is the rattlesnake, which belongs to a family that is often called pit viper. This family of snakes has a deep pit between the eye and nostril on each side of its face. Inside the pit there is a membrane that is sensitive to heat. This membrane enables the snake to locate and strike at any animal with warm blood.

A rattlesnake coils itself into a loop and then strikes with lightning speed. It kills by sinking its poison fangs into its prey.

A rattlesnake gets its name from a series of loosely fitted rings at the end of its tail. A new ring or rattle is formed each time a snake sheds its skin. After the snake sheds its skin the first time, a rattle is formed, which is called a button.

(146 Words) (Number of word recognition errors _____)

Questions:

F 1. _____ How many types of poisonous snakes are there in North America? (Four)

F 2. _____ To what family of snakes does the rattlesnake belong? (The pit viper) (Tell the student if he or she does not know)

F 3. _____ Why is it called pit viper? (Because it has a pit between the eye and nostril on each side of its face, or because it has a pit on its face)

F 4. _____ What is inside the pit? (A membrane that is sensitive to heat, something that senses heat, or a membrane)

F 5. _____ What is the purpose of the heat-sensitive membrane? (It helps the snake locate warm-blooded animals, or warm things)

I 6. _____ Why do you think you might not be able to get away from a snake when it strikes? (Because it said it strikes with lightning speed, or because it strikes so fast)

V 7. _____ What does the word *prey* mean? (What the rattlesnake kills, or something the rattlesnake eats)

F 8. _____ Where does the rattlesnake get its name? (From the series of loosely fitted rings at the end of its tail, or from the rattles on its tail)

F 9. _____ When is a new rattle formed? (Each time the snake sheds its skin)

F 10. _____ What is the first rattle that is formed called? (A button)

Number of Questions Missed	Number of Word Recognition Errors					
	0–2	3–5	6–8	9–11	12–14	15
0	+	*	*	*	*	×
1	+	*	*	*	×	×
2	*	*	*	×	×	×
3	*	*	×	×	×	×
4	*	×	×	×	×	×
5+	×	×	×	×	×	×

Reading Level

+	Independent	
*	Instructional	
×	Frustration	

_____ Check here if this passage was used for the Listening Comprehension Test.

Listening Comprehension result: (*70 percent or higher to pass*)

_____ Percent   _____ **Passed**   _____ **Failed**

(Test Sheet on p. 144)

2/Form A

SCORING

One of the most useful animals in the world is the camel. The camel has helped men living in deserts for thousands of years. One advantage of using camels is that they can travel for great distances without needing water. Because the camel can carry heavy loads of freight, it is sometimes referred to as the "ship of the desert."

The camel is ugly and stupid and has a bad temper. When a camel is loaded for work, it will often show its disapproval by bellowing loudly and by kicking and biting.

There are two kinds of camels; these are the single-humped and the two-humped. The hump contains a great deal of fat and does not have any bone in it. When a camel is required to go without food, the fat in its hump can furnish it with energy for several days.

The main reason camels can go without water for so long is that they do not sweat.

(162 Words)

Time: _____
    (in seconds)

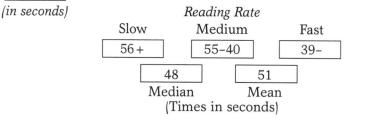

▶ *Questions:*

F 1. _____ What is one of the most useful animals in the world? (The camel)

F 2. _____ How long has the camel been helping man? (For thousands of years)

F 3. _____ What is one of the advantages of using camels? (They can travel great distances without water, can go for a long time without water, or can carry heavy loads)

F 4. _____ Why is the camel sometimes called the "ship of the desert"? (Because it can carry heavy loads, or heavy loads of freight)

I 5. _____ Why do you think you might not like working with camels? (Because they are ugly, stupid, bad-tempered, and they bite and kick) (The student should name at least two reasons)

V 6. _____ What does the word *bellowing* mean in this reading passage? (Making a loud noise)

F 7. _____ What are the two kinds of camels mentioned in this passage? (The single- or one-humped and the two-humped)

F 8. _____ What does the hump contain a great deal of? (Fat)

F 9. _____ Where does a camel get its energy when it is required to go without food for several days? (From the fat in its hump, or from its hump)

F 10. _____ What is the main reason camels can go without water for so long? (They do not sweat)

Number of Questions Missed		*Reading Level*	
0–1	Independent	Independent	
2–4	Instructional	Instructional	
5+	Frustration	Frustration	

_____ Check here if this passage was used for the Listening Comprehension Test.

Listening Comprehension result: (*70 percent or higher to pass*)

_____ Percent   _____ **Passed**   _____ **Failed**

(Test Sheet on p. 145)

2/Form B

8A
ORAL

The most prominent feature in the sky at night is the moon, which is the earth's natural satellite. Astronomers, however, might think our moon is small and insignificant. They would be likely to feel our moon is small because the moons of other planets are so much larger.

People began to study lunar geography when the telescope was invented. One of the earliest of these astronomers was Galileo, who began looking at the moon in 1609. Later researchers found large craters, mountains, plains, and long valleys on the surface of the moon.

Manned vehicle landings were made on the moon in 1969. These were attempted because people were not satisfied with the information they had obtained by looking through telescopes. Rock samples taken from these explorations of the moon's surface have provided us with a great deal of knowledge about the age of the moon.

Because of our natural curiosity, few people would be willing to predict what we may accomplish in space.

(163 Words) (Number of word recognition errors _____)

Questions:

F   1. _____ What is the most prominent feature in the sky at night? (The moon)
F   2. _____ Why might an astronomer think our moon is small and insignificant? (Because the moons of other planets are so much larger)
V   3. _____ What does *lunar* mean in this passage? (It refers to the moon)
F   4. _____ Who was one of the earliest astronomers? (Galileo)
F   5. _____ When did Galileo begin to study the moon? (In 1609)
F   6. _____ What did later researchers find on the surface of the moon? (Craters, mountains, plains, and valleys) (Students must name at least two)
F   7. _____ When were the first manned vehicle landings made on the moon? (In 1969)
F   8. _____ Why did people make the first manned landings on the moon? (Because they were not satisfied with the information they had obtained by looking through telescopes)
F   9. _____ What did the rock samples taken from the moon's surface provide us with? (Information about the age of the moon)
I 10. _____ Why do you think many more space explorations may be made in the future? (Because of man's curiosity)

Number of Questions Missed	Number of Word Recognition Errors					
	0–2	3–5	6–8	9–12	13–15	16
0	+	*	*	*	*	×
1	+	*	*	*	×	×
2	*	*	*	×	×	×
3	*	*	×	×	×	×
4	*	×	×	×	×	×
5+	×	×	×	×	×	×

Reading Level

+	Independent	
*	Instructional	
×	Frustration	

_____ Check here if this passage was used for the Listening Comprehension Test.

Listening Comprehension result: (*70 percent or higher to pass*)

_____ Percent   _____ **Passed**   _____ **Failed**

**8B
SILENT**

No substance has been more eagerly sought after than gold. Because it is rare and durable, gold has been widely accepted as money. In past years gold coins were circulated, but this practice ceased in 1934. Gold is still kept by many nations because they know it will retain its value.

Another important use of gold is in the making of jewelry and metalwork. When gold is made into jewelry it is usually mixed with another metal to form an alloy. Alloys of gold are used because in its pure form gold is too soft to withstand the wear caused from regular usage.

Tiny quantities of gold occur in most soils and rocks throughout the world. However, in most cases the amount of gold is so small that it is not worth extracting. Gold is often found in association with metals such as copper.

(144 Words)

Time: _____
       (in seconds)

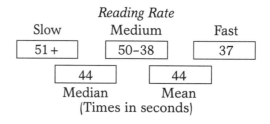

Reading Rate

Slow	Medium	Fast
51 +	50–38	37

	44	44	
	Median	Mean	

(Times in seconds)

Questions:

V   1. _____   What does the word *sought* in this passage mean? (Looked for, or an appropriate synonym)

F   2. _____   Why has gold been widely accepted as money? (Because it is rare and/or durable)

F   3. _____   In what year did they stop circulating gold coins? (In 1934)

F   4. _____   Why do many nations still keep gold? (Because they know it will retain or keep its value)

F   5. _____   Other than for money, what is another use of gold? (In the making of jewelry and/or metalwork)

F   6. _____   What is done with gold to form an alloy? (It is mixed with another metal)

F   7. _____   Why is gold made into an alloy sometimes? (Because it is too soft in its natural form)

I   8. _____   Why do you think it might not be a good idea to make a ring out of pure gold? (Because it would wear out easily, or it would not last a long time)

F   9. _____   Why has some gold not been taken from soils and rocks? (Because the amount is so small, or it would not be worth extracting)

F 10. _____   What metal is gold often found in association with? (Copper)

▶

Number of Questions Missed		Reading Level	
0–1	Independent	Independent	
2–4	Instructional	Instructional	
5+	Frustration	Frustration	

_____ Check here if this passage was used for the Listening Comprehension Test.

Listening Comprehension result: (*70 percent or higher to pass*)

_____ Percent   _____ **Passed**   _____ **Failed**

(Test Sheet on p. 147)

2/Form B

SCORING

There are approximately 3,000 types of lizards, which vary considerably in such characteristics as size, color, shape, and habits. For example, some of these unusual creatures may range from a minimum of merely two to three inches, while some huge varieties may ultimately grow to a maximum length of twelve feet.

Some of these reptiles have startling habits such as the ability to snap off their tails if they are seized. Some species may rear up on their hind legs and scamper away if they become frightened.

Most lizards benefit mankind by eating unwanted insects that, in most cases, are harmful to mankind. Although numerous superstitions abound concerning these strange creatures, only two types are definitely known to be poisonous.

Some lizards lay eggs that have a tough, leathery shell, while others bear living young. The eggs are typically laid where they may be incubated by the warmth emitted from the sun.

Since lizards are cold-blooded animals, they cannot stand extreme variations in temperature. If the sun becomes extremely hot, the lizard must pursue the solace of an overhead shelter such as a rock or bush.

(186 Words) (Number of word recognition errors_____)

SCORING 2/Form A
(Test Sheet on p. 148)

Questions:

F 1. _____ In what ways do lizards vary? (In size, shape, color, and habits) (Student must get at least three)

F 2. _____ What is the maximum length you might expect a lizard to be? (Twelve feet)

F 3. _____ What happens to some lizards if they are seized by the tail? (It snaps off)

F 4. _____ Why might some lizards rear up on their hind legs and scamper away? (Because they are frightened, or scared)

F 5. _____ How do some lizards help us? (By eating harmful insects, or by eating insects)

I 6. _____ Why do you think that most lizards would not harm us? (Because there are only two kinds that are poisonous)

F 7. _____ What is the shell of a lizard's egg like? (Tough and/or leathery)

V 8. _____ What does the word *incubated* mean? (Hatched, or an appropriate synonym or explanation)

F 9. _____ What characteristic of lizards keeps them from being able to stand extreme variations in temperature? (They are cold-blooded)

F 10. _____ What would a lizard likely to do if it became extremely hot? (Pursue the solace of a rock or bush, go where it was not hot, or go where it was cool)

Number of Questions Missed	Number of Word Recognition Errors						Reading Level		
	0–2	3–6	7–10	11–13	14–17	18			
0	+	*	*	*	*	×	+	Independent	
1	+	*	*	*	×	×	*	Instructional	
2	*	*	*	×	×	×	×	Frustration	
3	*	*	×	×	×	×			
4	*	×	×	×	×	×			
5+	×	×	×	×	×	×			

_____ Check here if this passage was used for the Listening Comprehension Test.

Listening Comprehension result: (*70 percent or higher to pass*)

_____ Percent   _____ **Passed**   _____ **Failed**

(Test Sheet on p. 148)

2/Form A

SCORING

**9B
SILENT**

The boomerang is perhaps the most remarkable weapon invented by any of the primitive tribes of the world. This unusual piece of equipment is fashioned from hardwood and is designed in various shapes and sizes. Most models are smooth and curved and range from two to four feet in length. They are normally flat on one side and convex on the opposite side. It is believed that the first prototype of this strange weapon was designed by the native tribes of aborigines in Australia.

There are two main types of boomerangs commonly used by men and women in sports and hunting today. These are classified into two categories, which are the return and nonreturn types. The return type is principally used for sport and amusement and is seldom used by professionals for hunting purposes. The nonreturn type is used for hunting and is capable of doing great damage to an animal for distances up to 400 feet.

With very little formal practice even a novice can become adept at using a return-type boomerang.

(174 Words)

Time: _____
   (in seconds)

Reading Rate

Slow	Medium	Fast
53 +	52–36	35–

45	48
Median	Mean

(Times in seconds)

(Test Sheet on p. 149)

SCORING *2/Form B*

Questions:

F 1. _____ What was probably the most remarkable weapon invented by any of the primitive tribes of the world? (The boomerang)

F 2. _____ What is the boomerang usually made of? (Hardwood, or wood)

F 3. _____ How long would you expect a boomerang to be? (From two to four feet in length)

V 4. _____ What does the term *convex* mean in this reading passage? (Curved, or rounded)

F 5. _____ Where do we believe the first boomerangs came from, or where were they first used? (In Australia)

F 6. _____ How many types of boomerangs are commonly in use today? (Two) (Tell student if he or she does not know)

F 7. _____ What are these two types of boomerangs called? (The return type and the nonreturn type) (Students must get both)

F 8. _____ What is the return type of boomerang used for? (For sport, or amusement) (Student must get one)

F 9. _____ What is the nonreturn type of boomerang used for? (Hunting)

I 10. _____ Why do you think that more people in the United States learn to throw a return type rather than a nonreturn type of boomerang? (Because they are easier to learn to throw, because they are used for sport, or because they are not used for hunting)

Number of Questions Missed		*Reading Level*	
0–1	Independent	Independent	
2–4	Instructional	Instructional	
5+	Frustration	Frustration	

_____ Check here if this passage was used for the Listening Comprehension Test.

Listening Comprehension result: (*70 percent or higher to pass*)

_____ Percent   _____ **Passed**   _____ **Failed**

(Test Sheet on p. 149)   **2/Form B**

SCORING

Test 2: Reading Passages Forms C and D

Oral Reading Passages

Silent Reading Passages

PP

C
ORAL

Sam *is a* boy.

He has a dog.

The dog's name *is* Tim.

Tim *is a black* dog.

He has a pink nose.

Sam *goes to* school.

The dog stays *at home.*

(32 Words) (Number of word recognition errors _____) *(17 Dolch Words)*

Questions:

F   1. _____ Who is Sam? (A boy)
F   2. _____ What does Sam have? (A dog)
F   3. _____ What is the dog's name? (Tim)
F   4. _____ What color is the dog? (Black, or black with a pink nose)
F   5. _____ Where does Sam go? (To school)

Number of Questions Missed	Number of Word Recognition Errors				Reading Level	
	0	1	2–3	4		
0	+	*	*	×	+	Independent
1	*	*	×	×	*	Instructional
2	*	×	×	×	×	Frustration
3	×	×	×	×		
4	×	×	×	×		
5+	×	×	×	×		

(Test Sheet on p. 152)

SCORING 2/Form C

_____ Check here if this passage was used for the Listening Comprehension Test.

Listening Comprehension result: (*70 percent or higher to pass*)

_____ Percent   _____ **Passed**   _____ **Failed**

PP

D

SILENT

Mary lives in a house.

She has a kitten.

The kitten's name is Tab.

Tab sleeps with Mary.

He likes to play ball.

The ball is yellow.

Mary and Tab have fun.

(32 Words)

Time: _____
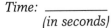
        (in seconds)

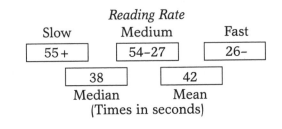

Questions:

F   1. _____ Where does Mary live? (In a house)
F   2. _____ What does Mary have? (A kitten)
F   3. _____ What is the kitten's name? (Tab)
F   4. _____ Who does Tab sleep with? (Mary)
F   5. _____ What color is the ball? (Yellow)

Number of Questions Missed		*Reading Level*	
0	Independent	Independent	
1–2	Instructional	Instructional	
3+	Frustration	Frustration	

_____ Check here if this passage was used for the Listening Comprehension Test.

Listening Comprehension result: *(70 percent or higher to pass)*

_____ Percent   _____ **Passed**   _____ **Failed**

(Test Sheet on p. 153)

SCORING   **2/Form D**

1C
ORAL

Dave *and* Tom *live in a* large city. *They live with their* father *and* mother. *Their* house *is* near *a* park. *Many* kids *play* football *in the* park.

Dave *and* Tom *like to play* football *there too.* Dave *can run* faster than Tom. Dave *and* Tom's mother *goes to* school. *She is going to be a* teacher. *Her* school *is far from their* home. *She goes to* school *in a* car.

(71 Words) (Number of word recognition errors _____) *(39 Dolch Words)*

Questions:

F 1. _____ In what kind of city do Dave and Tom live? (A large city)
F 2. _____ Who do they live with? (Their father and mother)
F 3. _____ Where is their house or what is it near? (Near a park)
F 4. _____ What do many kids do in the park? (Play football)
F 5. _____ What do Dave and Tom like to do? (Play too, play in the park, or play football too)
F 6. _____ Which of the boys can run faster? (Dave)
F 7. _____ What does Dave and Tom's mother do? (Goes to school)
F 8. _____ What is she going to be? (A teacher)
F 9. _____ Where is her school? (Far from their home)
F 10. _____ How does she get to school? (In a car)

Number of Questions Missed	Number of Word Recognition Errors					
	0–2	3–6	7–10	11–13	14–17	18
0	+	*	*	*	*	×
1	+	*	*	*	×	×
2	*	*	*	×	×	×
3	*	*	×	×	×	×
4	*	×	×	×	×	×
5+	×	×	×	×	×	×

Reading Level

+	Independent	
*	Instructional	
×	Frustration	

_____ Check here if this passage was used for the Listening Comprehension Test.

Listening Comprehension result: *(70 percent or higher to pass)*

_____ Percent _____ **Passed** _____ **Failed**

1D
SILENT

Ann's class went to visit a fire station. One of the firemen was at the door. He said he was happy to see the class.

He showed the class a big fire truck. Then he showed them a car. The car and truck were both red. The big truck had a long ladder on it.

Then the class went back to school. They were very happy. They told their teacher they wanted to go again.

(75 Words)

Time: _____
        (in seconds)

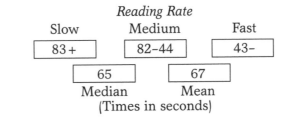

	Reading Rate	
Slow	Medium	Fast
83+	82–44	43–

65	67
Median	Mean

(Times in seconds)

Questions:

F   1. _____ What did Ann's class go to visit? (A fire station)
F   2. _____ Who was at the door to meet them? (One of the firemen, or a fireman)
F   3. _____ What did he say to the class? (He was happy to see them)
F   4. _____ What did the fireman show the class first? (A big fire truck, a truck, or a big truck)
F   5. _____ Then what did he show them? (A car)
F   6. _____ What color were the car and truck? (Red)
F   7. _____ What did the big truck have on it? (A ladder, a long ladder, or a big ladder)
F   8. _____ Where did the class go after they left the fire station? (Back to school)
F   9. _____ How did the class feel? (Happy, or very happy)
F 10. _____ What did they tell their teacher? (That they wanted to go back again)

Number of Questions Missed		Reading Level	
0–1	Independent	Independent	
2–4	Instructional	Instructional	
5+	Frustration	Frustration	

_____ Check here if this passage was used for the Listening Comprehension Test.

Listening Comprehension result: (*70 percent or higher to pass*)

_____ Percent   _____ **Passed**   _____ **Failed**

(Test Sheet on p. 155)

SCORING 2/Form D

2C
ORAL

Dale lives *on a* large animal farm *with his* father *and* mother. *His* father *has many* cows, horses, sheep, *and* pigs *on the* farm. *One of the* animals belongs *to* Dale. *It is a* pet pig. *The* pig *is black with a white* ring *around its* back. *It has a very* short curly tail.

When Dale *goes for a walk the* pig likes *to walk with him.* Sometimes *when* Dale *goes to* school *his* pig *will* follow *him. The* children *at* school *all laugh when they see the* pig *with* Dale. *Many of the* boys *and* girls *say they would like to have a* pet pig *too.*

(107 Words) (Number of word recognition errors _____) *(67 Dolch Words)*

Questions:

F   1. _____ Where does Dale live? (On a large animal farm, on an animal farm, or on a farm)

F   2. _____ Who does Dale live with? (His father and mother)

F   3. _____ What kinds of animals does his father have? (Cows, horses, sheep, and pigs) (Students must name at least two)

F   4. _____ Who does one of the animals belong to? (Dale)

F   5. _____ What kind of animal does Dale have for a pet? (A pig)

F   6. _____ What does his pet pig look like? (It is black with a white ring around its back, or it is black and white)

F   7. _____ What does the pig's tail look like? (It is very short and curly, or short and/or curly)

F   8. _____ When Dale goes for a walk what does the pig do? (Follows him, or walks with him)

F   9. _____ What do the children at school do when they see the pig with Dale? (They laugh)

I 10. _____ What did it say that would make you think the boys and girls like the pet pig? (It told how the boys and girls said they would like to have a pet pig too)

Number of Questions Missed	Number of Word Recognition Errors						Reading Level	
	0–1	2–3	4–5	6–8	9	10		
0	+	*	*	*	*	×	+	Independent
1	+	*	*	*	×	×	*	Instructional
2	*	*	*	×	×	×	×	Frustration
3	*	*	×	×	×	×		
4	*	×	×	×	×	×		
5+	×	×	×	×	×	×		

_____ Check here if this passage was used for the Listening Comprehension Test.

Listening Comprehension result: (*70 percent or higher to pass*)

_____ Percent   _____ **Passed**   _____ **Failed**

SCORING 2/Form C
(Test Sheet on p. 156)

2D
SILENT

Emily has a little black dog with curly hair. The little dog's name is Chester. He has long ears and a short tail. He lives in a little house behind Emily's big house. Sometimes when he is extra good he gets to come in the big house.

The dog does not like cats. Sometimes when he sees a cat he will run after it. The cat can run faster than the dog, so he does not catch it.

When the dog is hungry he begins to bark. When Emily hears him barking she brings him some food.

(97 Words)

Time: _____
      (in seconds)

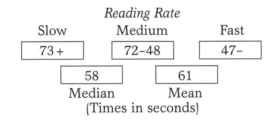

Reading Rate

Slow	Medium	Fast
73+	72–48	47–

58	61
Median	Mean

(Times in seconds)

Questions:

F   1. _____ What does Emily have? (A dog, a little dog, or a little black dog)

F   2. _____ What does he look like? (He is black, has curly hair, long ears, and a short tail) (Student must get at least two answers)

F   3. _____ Where does the dog live? (In a little house, or behind Emily's house)

F   4. _____ When does the dog get to come in the big house? (When he is good, or when he is extra good)

F   5. _____ What does the dog not like? (Cats)

F   6. _____ What does he sometimes do when he sees a cat? (He runs after it)

F   7. _____ Why can't the dog catch the cat? (It runs faster than the dog)

F   8. _____ What does the dog do when he is hungry? (He barks)

F   9. _____ What does Emily do when she hears the dog barking? (She brings him food)

I 10. _____ Why do you think cats do not like the dog? (Because he chases them, or runs after them)

Number of Questions Missed		*Reading Level*	
0–1	Independent	Independent	
2–4	Instructional	Instructional	
5+	Frustration	Frustration	

_____ Check here if this passage was used for the Listening Comprehension Test.

Listening Comprehension result: (*70 percent or higher to pass*)

_____ Percent   _____ **Passed**   _____ **Failed**

(Test Sheet on p. 157)   **2/Form D**   SCORING

3C ORAL

Judy's class *was going on a* trip *to* visit *an* airport. *Before they* left *they read some* books *about* airplanes *and* airplane pilots. Everyone *in the* class *was* excited *when it came* time *to go.*

The class rode *to the* airport *in a big yellow* bus. *After the* bus stopped, *the first* person *to get off was* Judy's teacher. *She* told *the* class *that they must all* stay *together so that* none *of the* students *would get* lost.

First, they visited *the* ticket counter *and* learned *how* passengers *buy their* tickets. *Then a* pilot *came and* told *them he would take them* on a large airplane. *After they were* inside *the* airplane, everyone *was* surprised *because it was so* large. *When* Judy's class *got* back *to* school *they all said they* wanted *to* visit *the* airport *again.*

(137 Words) (Number of word recognition errors _____) *(85 Dolch Words)*

Questions:

F   1. _____ Where was Judy's class going? (To visit an airport)
F   2. _____ What did they do before they left? (They read some books, or they read some books about airplanes and airplane pilots)
F   3. _____ How did the class feel when it was time to go? (They were excited)
F   4. _____ How did the class get to the airport? (They rode in a bus, or in a big yellow bus)
F   5. _____ Who was the first person to get off the bus? (Judy's teacher, or the teacher)
F   6. _____ What did the teacher tell the class when they first got off the bus? (That they must stay together, or that they must stay together so they would not get lost)
F   7. _____ What did they visit first? (The ticket counter)
V   8. _____ In this story it said the students learned how the passengers buy their tickets. What is a passenger? (Someone who rides on an airplane)
F   9. _____ When the pilot came to meet the class, what did he tell them? (He told them he would take them on an airplane, or on a large airplane)
I   10. _____ What did the class say that would make you think they liked their visit to the airport? (They said they wanted to visit the airport again)

Number of Questions Missed	Number of Word Recognition Errors					
	0–2	3–4	5–7	8–10	11–13	14
0	+	*	*	*	*	×
1	+	*	*	*	×	×
2	*	*	*	×	×	×
3	*	*	×	×	×	×
4	*	×	×	×	×	×
5+	×	×	×	×	×	×

Reading Level

+	Independent	
*	Instructional	
×	Frustration	

_____ Check here if this passage was used for the Listening Comprehension Test.

Listening Comprehension result: (*70 percent or higher to pass*)

_____ Percent   _____ **Passed**   _____ **Failed**

Many people would like to live on a farm so they could be around animals. If you had ever lived on a farm you would know that life is often not easy. Most farmers have to get up very early. In the morning a farmer has to feed and milk his cows. After doing this, the farmer has to go to his fields and work long hours plowing his land or planting his crops. After working hard all day, the farmer has to come home and milk his cows again.

In the winter when it is cold the farmer does not have to work in his fields. But when it is cold he has to work hard at keeping his animals warm.

Today's farmer has to learn how to do many things. He has to know how to care for animals, repair machines, and make the best use of his time.

(151 Words)

Time: _____
        (in seconds)

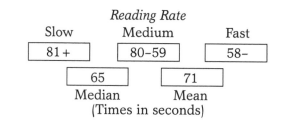

Reading Rate

Slow	Medium	Fast
81+	80–59	58–

65	71
Median	Mean

(Times in seconds)

Questions:

F   1. _____ Why do many people think they would like to live on a farm? (So they could be around animals)

F   2. _____ When do most farmers get up? (Early, or very early)

F   3. _____ What kind of work do many farmers have to do in the morning? (Feed and/or milk their cows)

F   4. _____ What do farmers often work long hours doing during the day? (Either or both—plowing their fields, or planting their crops)

F   5. _____ What do many farmers have to do after working all day in their fields? (Milk the cows again)

F   6. _____ When does the farmer not have to work in his fields? (In the wintertime)

F   7. _____ What does the farmer have to do with his animals when it is cold? (Try to keep them warm)

F   8. _____ What are some of the things a farmer has to know today? (How to care for animals, repair machines, and make the best use of his time) (Student must name at least two)

I   9. _____ Why do you think today's farmer does not have much free time? (Because he has to spend so much time working)

V 10. _____ This reading passage said that the farmer has to know how to repair machines. What does *repair* mean? (To fix, or a proper synonym)

▶

Number of Questions Missed		*Reading Level*	
0–1	Independent	Independent	☐
2–4	Instructional	Instructional	☐
5+	Frustration	Frustration	☐

_____ Check here if this passage was used for the Listening Comprehension Test.

Listening Comprehension result: (*70 percent or higher to pass*)

_____ Percent   _____ **Passed**   _____ **Failed**

4C
ORAL

A desert *is a* place *where the* weather *is* dry *and* often *hot. Some* people *think it is a* place *where there is* nothing *but* sand. *This is* true sometimes, *but some* deserts *have many* kinds *of* plants *and* animals living *in them. The* kinds *of* plants *and* animals living *there* usually *do not* require *much* water. *For* example, *some* desert plants *can* store water *in their* leaves *and* exist *for long* periods *of* time without rain.

Some animals *that live in the* desert *get all of the* water *they* need *by* eating *the* leaves *of* plants *that have* water *in them.* People *who have been* lost *in the* desert *have* died *because they had no* water *to drink. Some of these* people *would not have* died *if they had* known *how to* survive. People *who know how to* survive *in* such *a* dry place often *know how to* obtain water *from* cactus plants.

A person *may* enjoy living *in the* desert *because he* thinks *it is* beautiful, *but* another person *may think the* same place *is not pretty at all.*

(183 Words) (Number of word recognition errors _____) *(110 Dolch Words)*

Questions:

F 1. _____ What do we call a place that is dry and often hot? (A desert)
F 2. _____ What do some people think a desert is? (A place where there is nothing but sand, or a place that is beautiful)
F 3. _____ What do some deserts have living in them? (Plants and animals)
F 4. _____ What is it about some plants and animals that enables them to live in the desert? (They do not need much water)
F 5. _____ Where do some desert plants store water? (In their leaves)
F 6. _____ Where do some animals that live in the desert get their water? (From the leaves of plants)
F 7. _____ What has sometimes happened to people who have been lost in the desert? (They have died, they had no water to drink, or they have died because they had no water to drink)
V 8. _____ What does the word *survive* mean? (To live, or stay alive)
F 9. _____ Why did it say someone might enjoy living in the desert? (Because it is beautiful, or because the person thought it was beautiful)
I 10. _____ Why do you think it would be a good idea to learn how to survive in the desert? (So that you would not die if you were lost, or a similar answer)

▶

▶

Number of Questions Missed	Number of Word Recognition Errors					
	0–2	3–6	7–10	11–13	14–17	18
0	+	*	*	*	*	×
1	+	*	*	*	×	×
2	*	*	*	×	×	×
3	*	*	×	×	×	×
4	*	×	×	×	×	×
5+	×	×	×	×	×	×

Reading Level

+	Independent	
*	Instructional	
×	Frustration	

_____ Check here if this passage was used for the Listening Comprehension Test.

Listening Comprehension result: (*70 percent or higher to pass*)

_____ Percent   _____ **Passed**   _____ **Failed**

**4D
SILENT**

One of the biggest jobs ever started was the building of the Panama Canal. The Panama Canal was known as "The Big Ditch." It was called "The Big Ditch" because it was a ditch with water in it and carried ships from one side of Panama to the other side, or from one ocean to another. By going through the Panama Canal, ships did not have to sail all the way around the continent of South America to get from one ocean to another.

When people first started building the Panama Canal there were many dangers from disease. People were getting Yellow Fever, which is a disease carried by a certain kind of mosquito. One man was a hero while the Panama Canal was being built. He discovered a way to get rid of the mosquitos that were carrying Yellow Fever. After these insects were killed, Yellow Fever was no longer spread from one person to another. By the time the Panama Canal was finished, very few people were dying from Yellow Fever.

(173 Words)

Time: _____
       (in seconds)

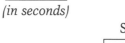

                            Reading Rate
         Slow   Medium   Fast
       | 71 + | | 70–50 | | 49– |
                | 60 | | 63 |
              Median   Mean
              (Times in seconds)

Questions:

F 1. _____ What was one of the biggest jobs ever started? (Building the Panama Canal)

F 2. _____ What was another name for the Panama Canal? ("The Big Ditch")

V 3. _____ What is a ditch? (A canal, or something with water in it)

F 4. _____ Why did they dig the Panama Canal? (To carry ships from one side of Panama to the other, from ocean to ocean, or to keep from going all the way around the continent to South America)

V 5. _____ What does the word *disease* mean in this reading passage? (A sickness) (Tell the student if he or she does not know)

F 6. _____ What disease were men getting when they started digging the Panama Canal? (Yellow Fever)

F 7. _____ How is the disease called Yellow Fever carried? (By a mosquito)

F 8. _____ Why was one man a hero while the Panama Canal was being built? (He discovered a way to get rid of the mosquito that caused Yellow Fever, or he found a cure for it)

F 9. _____ When did most people stop dying from Yellow Fever? (By the time the Panama Canal was finished, or when the mosquitos were dead)

I 10. _____ Why do you think people were happy to get rid of the mosquito that caused Yellow Fever? (Because fewer or no people would get sick or die)

SCORING *2/Form D* (Test Sheet on p. 161)

Number of Questions Missed		Reading Level	
0–1	Independent	Independent	
2–4	Instructional	Instructional	
5+	Frustration	Frustration	

_____ Check here if this passage was used for the Listening Comprehension Test.

Listening Comprehension result: (*70 percent or higher to pass*)

_____ Percent _____ **Passed** _____ **Failed**

5C ORAL

There are about a hundred different kinds of monkeys. Some may be as large as a big dog, while others are so small that you could hold them in your hand. Some monkeys have bright colored faces and when they become excited these colors become brighter. Certain types of monkeys live in pairs or sometimes in clans of up to a hundred or more. Many monkeys can be tamed when they are young, but they have bad tempers when they grow old. The night or owl monkey is so named because it sleeps in the daytime and roams about at night.

Some monkeys are like humans because they make sounds to indicate they are angry. The howler monkey produces a sound that can be heard for a distance of two miles. This type has a "boss" that is usually the strongest and largest male of the group. When the boss loses his job he may be forced to leave the group and wander alone.

(164 Words) (Number of word recognition errors _____)

Questions:

F 1. _____ How many different kinds of monkeys are there? (About a hundred, or a hundred)

F 2. _____ How big are some of the biggest monkeys? (As large as a big dog)

F 3. _____ What happens to some monkeys' faces when they become excited? (They become brighter)

V 4. _____ What does the word *clan* mean in this passage? (A group, or appropriate synonym)

F 5. _____ What happens to monkeys if they are not tamed before they grow old? (They get bad tempers, or become mean)

F 6. _____ Why is one kind of monkey called the night or owl monkey? (Because it sleeps in the daytime and/or roams about at night)

F 7. _____ How did this reading passage say some monkeys are like humans? (They make sounds to indicate they are angry)

I 8. _____ How do you know that some monkeys can make loud sounds? (Because they can be heard for two miles)

F 9. _____ What is the largest and strongest male of the group called? (The boss)

F 10. _____ What happens to the boss if he loses his job? (He may be forced to wander alone, to go off alone, or to be by himself)

Number of Questions Missed	Number of Word Recognition Errors					
	0–1	3–5	6–8	9–12	13–15	16
0	+	*	*	*	*	×
1	+	*	*	*	×	×
2	*	*	*	×	×	×
3	*	*	×	×	×	×
4	*	×	×	×	×	×
5+	×	×	×	×	×	×

Reading Level

+	Independent	
*	Instructional	
×	Frustration	

_____ Check here if this passage was used for the Listening Comprehension Test.

Listening Comprehension result: (*70 percent or higher to pass*)

_____ Percent   _____ **Passed**   _____ **Failed**

(Test Sheet on p. 162)

2/Form C

SCORING

**5D
SILENT**

Potatoes, along with wheat and rice, are one of the most important food crops in the world. Nearly every year the world grows about 10 billion bushels of potatoes. In some countries potatoes are used as food for animals as well as for people. In America they are usually consumed only by humans. The potatoes that people eat are almost always baked, boiled, or fried.

Potatoes are often grown in places where it is not quite warm enough for corn. In the Far Eastern countries, few are grown because the climate is too warm and because rice has more food value.

When the Spanish first came to South America they found the Indians growing potatoes. It was not until many years later that this new food became popular with the Spanish.

A king in France made this food popular by wearing the flowers of the plant in his buttonhole.

(149 Words)

Time: _____
   (in seconds)

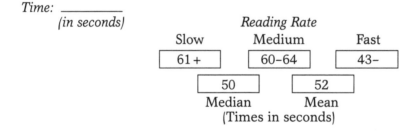

Reading Rate

Slow	Medium	Fast
61 +	60–64	43–

50	52
Median	Mean

(Times in seconds)

SCORING 2/Form D

(Test Sheet on p. 163)

▶

▶ *Questions:*

F 1. _____ What three crops are among the most important in the world? (Potatoes, wheat, and rice) (Student must get at least two)

F 2. _____ How many bushels of potatoes does the world grow each year? (10 billion)

F 3. _____ In some countries potatoes are used for food for people and what else? (Animals)

V 4. _____ What does the word *consumed* mean in this reading passage? (Eaten, or used)

F 5. _____ What are some ways that potatoes are prepared when they are eaten by humans? (They are baked, boiled, or fried) (Student must get at least two)

F 6. _____ This reading passage said potatoes are often grown where it is not warm enough for what crop? (Corn)

F 7. _____ Why are few potatoes grown in Far Eastern countries? (Because the climate is too warm, or because it is too warm and because rice has more food value) (Student must get one of the two)

F 8. _____ Whom did the Spanish find growing potatoes when they came to South America? (The Indians)

I 9. _____ How do we know that potatoes were not already a popular food with the Spanish when they found the Indians growing them? (Because the reading passage said they did not become popular for many years later)

F 10. _____ How did a king in France make potatoes popular? (By wearing the flowers of the plant in his buttonhole)

Number of Questions Missed		*Reading Level*	
0–1	Independent	Independent	
2–4	Instructional	Instructional	
5+	Frustration	Frustration	

_____ Check here if this passage was used for the Listening Comprehension Test.

Listening Comprehension result: (*70 percent or higher to pass*)

_____ Percent   _____ **Passed**   _____ **Failed**

(Test Sheet on p. 163)   **2/Form D**

A mole is a small animal about six inches long. Moles have a long snout like a pig, a short thick neck, and a pink tail. Their ears are not visible but are concealed in their fur.

If a mole is placed on the ground it will begin to scramble about looking for a soft spot to dig. When it begins to dig, it will disappear in less than a minute. Moles often ruin lawns and gardens by making ridges in them caused from their burrowing through the ground.

Most of a mole's life is spent in darkness because it lives underground. A mole's home is usually a nest made from grasses and leaves. Its home is nearly always located beneath something like a rock, tree stump, or stone wall, which gives it more protection.

Moles are most commonly found in the northern half of the world.

(147 Words) (Number of word recognition errors _____)

Questions:

F 1. _____ About how long is a mole? (Six inches)
F 2. _____ What does a mole look like? (It has a long snout, a short thick neck, and a pink tail) (Student must name at least two)
V 3. _____ What does *concealed* mean in this reading passage? (Hidden)
F 4. _____ What will a mole do if it is placed on the ground? (It will begin to scramble and/or look for a place to dig, or look for a soft spot)
F 5. _____ How long will it take a mole to disappear when it is placed on the ground? (Less than a minute)
I 6. _____ Why do you think people might not like moles? (Because they ruin lawns and/or gardens)
F 7. _____ Where does a mole spend most of its life? (In darkness and/or underground)
F 8. _____ What does a mole usually use to make its nest? (Grasses and leaves)
F 9. _____ Why do moles usually build their homes beneath rocks, tree stumps, or stone walls? (To give them more protection, or to make them more safe)
F 10. _____ Where are moles most commonly found? (In the northern half of the world)

Number of Questions Missed	Number of Word Recognition Errors					
	0–2	3–5	6–8	9–11	12–14	15
0	+	*	*	*	*	×
1	+	*	*	*	×	×
2	*	*	*	×	×	×
3	*	*	×	×	×	×
4	*	×	×	×	×	×
5+	×	×	×	×	×	×

Reading Level

+	Independent	
*	Instructional	
×	Frustration	

_____ Check here if this passage was used for the Listening Comprehension Test.

Listening Comprehension result: (*70 percent or higher to pass*)

_____ Percent   _____ **Passed**   _____ **Failed**

6D
SILENT

Cottontails and jackrabbits are two of the most commonly known wild animals in the world. Most people do not realize that certain animals such as the jackrabbit and snowshoe rabbit are actually not rabbits but hares. A hare is an animal with longer ears and it is heavier and larger than a rabbit.

A mother rabbit spends considerably more time in building her nest than a mother hare. The female hare, which is called a doe, has two or three litters of young during the year.

There are usually four to six babies born in each litter. Young hares are born with their eyes open and can care for themselves in a few days. The infant rabbit is born with its eyes closed and does not see for about a week.

Both the rabbit and the hare are well equipped to detect their enemies. They have long sensitive ears for excellent hearing and eyes that enable them to see in every direction.

(162 Words)

Time: _____
       (in seconds)

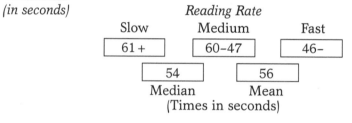

Reading Rate

Slow	Medium	Fast
61 +	60–47	46–

Median	Mean
54	56

(Times in seconds)

SCORING **2/Form D**

(Test Sheet on p. 165)

▶

▶ *Questions:*

F   1. _____ Name two of the most commonly known wild animals in the world. (Cottontails and jackrabbits, or hares and rabbits)

F   2. _____ In this passage it said that jackrabbits and snowshoe rabbits are not actually rabbits. What are they? (Hares)

F   3. _____ In their looks, what is the difference between a hare and a rabbit? (A hare has longer ears and/or is larger and heavier than a rabbit)

I   4. _____ Why do you think a mother rabbit takes better care of her young than a mother hare? (Because she spends more time in building her nest, or because young hares are born with their eyes open and can care for themselves in a few days, or because the infant rabbit is born with its eyes closed and does not see for about a week)

F   5. _____ What is a female hare called? (A doe)

F   6. _____ How many babies does a female hare usually have in each litter? (Four to six, or four, five, or six)

F   7. _____ How long is it before a young hare can care for itself? (A few days)

V   8. _____ What does the word *infant* mean? (A baby, or a very young rabbit)

F   9. _____ How long does it take for a baby or infant rabbit to open its eyes? (About a week)

F 10. _____ Why are hares and rabbits able to detect their enemies? (They have long sensitive ears for hearing and/or can see in every direction, or they can hear and/or see well)

Number of Questions Missed		*Reading Level*	
0–1	Independent	Independent	
2–4	Instructional	Instructional	
5+	Frustration	Frustration	

_____ Check here if this passage was used for the Listening Comprehension Test.

Listening Comprehension result: (*70 percent or higher to pass*)

_____ Percent   _____ **Passed**   _____ **Failed**

**7C
ORAL**

Among the animals of the world, one of the most talented is the spider. With its silken webs it can construct suspension bridges, beautiful designs, and insect traps. The spider might be thought of as one of nature's greatest engineers.

Spiders can be found in all parts of the world except where it is extremely cold. They cannot survive in cold or polar regions covered with snow because of a lack of food.

People sometimes mistakenly refer to spiders as insects. Unlike insects, which have six legs and three body segments, spiders have eight legs and two body segments.

Although there are many different kinds of spiders in the United States, only two of these are considered dangerous. These are the Black Widow and the Brown House Spider. Spiders are useful to humans because they destroy many kinds of harmful insects.

(141 Words) (Number of word recognition errors _____)

Questions:

F 1. _____ What might be considered one of the most talented animals in the world? (The spider)

F 2. _____ What are some things that spiders are able to construct with their webs? (Suspension bridges, beautiful designs, and insect traps, or bridges, designs, and traps) (Student must name at least two)

I 3. _____ Why might the spider be thought of as one of the world's greatest engineers? (Because it is able to build so many things, or because of its ability to build)

F 4. _____ Where would you not expect to find spiders? (Where it is extremely cold)

V 5. _____ What does the word *talented* mean in this reading passage? (Skillful, able to do many things, gifted, or an appropriate synonym)

F 6. _____ What do people often mistakenly call spiders? (Insects)

F 7. _____ How are spiders different from insects? (Spiders have eight legs while insects have six, and spiders have two body segments while insects have three) (Student must explain at least one difference)

F 8. _____ How many kinds of poisonous spiders are there in the United States? (Two)

F 9. _____ What are the two kinds of dangerous spiders in the United States? (The Black Widow and the Brown House Spider)

F 10. _____ Why are spiders useful to humans? (Because they destroy many harmful insects, or because they kill insects)

Number of Questions Missed	Number of Word Recognition Errors					
	0–2	3–5	6–7	8–10	11–13	14
0	+	*	*	*	*	×
1	+	*	*	*	×	×
2	*	*	*	×	×	×
3	*	*	×	×	×	×
4	*	×	×	×	×	×
5+	×	×	×	×	×	×

Reading Level

+	Independent	
*	Instructional	
×	Frustration	

_____ Check here if this passage was used for the Listening Comprehension Test.

Listening Comprehension result: (*70 percent or higher to pass*)

_____ Percent   _____ **Passed**   _____ **Failed**

7D
SILENT

Millions of cats have homes, but there are many who are strays. They are still the second most popular type of pet in America. People who raise cats and enter them in shows are called members of the "American Cat Fancy." A cat must have earned four winner's ribbons to become a champion.

Cats are meat eaters and are equipped with special teeth to tear meat into chunks. Once the meat has been torn into small chunks, it is swallowed without chewing. Cats are excellent hunters and can jump as high as seven feet in the air. One purpose of a cat's tail is to enable it to balance itself when it jumps. If a cat is turned upside down and dropped, it will always turn over and land on its feet.

Some cats have been known to live to be 19 or 20 years old; however, the average life of a cat is about 14 years.

(157 Words)

Time: _____
(in seconds)

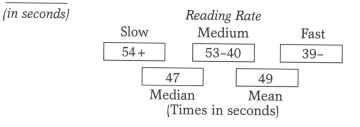

Reading Rate

Slow	Medium	Fast
54 +	53–40	39–

47	49
Median	Mean

(Times in seconds)

Questions:

V 1. _____ What is meant by a *stray*? (Something without a home, or a cat without a home)

I 2. _____ How do you know from reading this passage that cats are not the most popular type of pet in America? (Because it said that cats are the second most popular type of pet in America)

F 3. _____ What must a cat have to become a champion? (Four winner's ribbons)

F 4. _____ For what purpose do cats have special teeth? (For tearing meat into chunks)

F 5. _____ What do cats do with meat once it has been torn into chunks? (Swallow it, or swallow it without chewing it)

F 6. _____ How high can cats jump? (Seven feet)

F 7. _____ What is one purpose of the cat's tail? (To enable it to balance while it jumps, or to enable it to balance)

F 8. _____ What will happen to a cat if it is turned upside down and dropped? (It will turn over and land on its feet, or it will land on its feet)

F 9. _____ How long have some of the oldest cats been known to live? (For 19 or 20 years)

F 10. _____ How long is the average life of a cat? (About 14 years)

SCORING **2/Form D**
(Test Sheet on p. 167)

▶

Number of Questions Missed		Reading Level	
0–1	Independent	Independent	
2–4	Instructional	Instructional	
5+	Frustration	Frustration	

_____ Check here if this passage was used for the Listening Comprehension Test.

Listening Comprehension result: (*70 percent or higher to pass*)

_____ Percent   _____ **Passed**   _____ **Failed**

The ostrich, which roams wild in Africa, is the biggest living bird. A fully developed male is extremely large, often standing as tall as seven or eight feet. The eggs from which the young are hatched are also quite large, with a weight of about three pounds.

Most humans consider this giant bird to be awkward and ugly. Although it is not a beautiful bird, it was once highly prized for its fluffy feathers or plumes. Knights of long ago used them as decorations on their helmets and their ladies used them to adorn their dresses.

The ostrich is a flightless bird; however, in running it may attain speeds of up to fifty miles per hour. This large bird often roams over the plains with other animals such as zebras and antelopes. If it fears danger it is likely to dash off, warning other animals. If it is forced to defend itself, it will often kick using its strong legs and sharp claws.

(163 Words) (Number of word recognition errors _____)

Questions:

F 1. _____ What is the largest living bird? (The ostrich)
F 2. _____ How tall might we expect a fully developed male ostrich to be? (Seven or eight feet)
F 3. _____ How much might we expect an ostrich egg to weigh? (About three pounds)
F 4. _____ What do most humans think of the ostrich? (They think it is awkward and/or ugly)
F 5. _____ Why was the ostrich once highly prized? (For its fluffy feathers or plumes, or for its feathers and/or plumes)
F 6. _____ For what purpose were ostrich feathers once used? (For decorations for clothing and/or for knights to use in their helmets)
V 7. _____ What does *flightless* mean? (Unable to fly)
F 8. _____ What other animals might one expect to find ostriches with? (Zebras and antelopes)
I 9. _____ Why might other animals like to have ostriches around them? (To warn them of danger)
F 10. _____ How do ostriches defend themselves? (By kicking, or by using their sharp claws)

▶

Number of Questions Missed	Number of Word Recognition Errors					
	0–2	3–5	6–8	9–12	13–15	16
0	+	*	*	*	*	×
1	+	*	*	*	×	×
2	*	*	*	×	×	×
3	*	*	×	×	×	×
4	*	×	×	×	×	×
5+	×	×	×	×	×	×

Reading Level

+	Independent	
*	Instructional	
×	Frustration	

_____ Check here if this passage was used for the Listening Comprehension Test.

Listening Comprehension result: (*70 percent or higher to pass*)

_____ Percent   _____ **Passed**   _____ **Failed**

**8D
SILENT**

There is no other natural substance that has the ability of rubber to stretch or bend and then snap back into shape. This ability makes this important product very useful in modern transportation.

Most of the natural rubber is obtained from the rubber tree. The inner bark of the rubber tree secretes a milky fluid called latex. There are a number of other tropical vines and shrubs that secrete a substance similar to latex, but it is of little economic value.

Most of the trees that produce rubber are grown in an area close to the equator. Rubber trees are normally found in countries with a low altitude. Some of these trees may grow as fast as nine feet per year. When a rubber tree has obtained a growth of about six inches in diameter, it is ready to be tapped for latex.

Although some materials have replaced rubber, it is still one of the most widely used products in the world.

(162 Words)

Time: _____
      (in seconds)

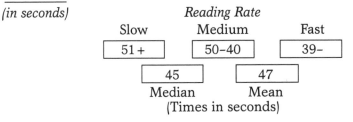

Reading Rate

Slow	Medium	Fast
51 +	50–40	39–

45	47
Median	Mean

(Times in seconds)

Questions:

F   1. _____ What are some of the abilities of rubber that no other natural substance has? (Stretch, bend, and snap back into shape) (Student must name at least two)

F   2. _____ In what part of industry do these abilities make rubber very useful? (In modern transportation, or in transportation)

F   3. _____ From what do we get most of our natural rubber? (From the rubber tree)

F   4. _____ What is the milky fluid collected from rubber? (Latex)

V   5. _____ What does the word *secrete* mean? (To give off, or a similar synonym)

F   6. _____ Where are most of the trees that produce rubber grown? (In an area close to the equator, or close to the equator)

F   7. _____ Rubber trees are usually found in countries with what types of altitude? (Low)

F   8. _____ How fast might we expect some rubber trees to grow? (Nine feet per year)

F   9. _____ How large in diameter must a tree be before it is tapped for latex? (Six inches)

I   10. _____ From what you read in this passage, why do you think it would be hard to do without rubber? (Because it is one of the most widely used products in the world, or because it is so important in transportation)

SCORING 2/Form D
(Test Sheet on p. 169)

▶ | *Number of Questions Missed* | *Reading Level* |
|---|---|
| 0–1 | Independent | Independent | ☐ |
| 2–4 | Instructional | Instructional | ☐ |
| 5+ | Frustration | Frustration | ☐ |

_____ Check here if this passage was used for the Listening Comprehension Test.

Listening Comprehension result: (*70 percent or higher to pass*)

_____ Percent   _____ **Passed**   _____ **Failed**

(Test Sheet on p. 169)

SCORING 2/Form D

**9C
ORAL**

A rather unusual fish that can fly through the air for relatively extensive distances is called the flying fish. It may fly distances of merely a few feet, but may also soar through the air for distances ranging up to 200 yards. This particular type of fish usually only flies when it is pursued by a predator. The peculiar flying fish may stay aloft only momentarily but it may remain airborne for a duration of up to ten or fifteen seconds. Among the creatures of the ocean who prey on the flying fish are tuna, sharks, dolphins, and porpoises.

If the flying fish is endangered, it is able to use its tail to strike a sharp blow on the water's surface to give it added momentum in making its ascent. When the fish makes its exodus from the water, it may attain speeds of up to 35 miles per hour. Once the fish is airborne, it spreads its pectoral fins and proceeds to use them as wings. These fins are not actually wings but elastic membranes that enable them to be flexible.

There are approximately 65 species of this unique fish, which commonly inhabits only the warm waters of the Atlantic Ocean.

(202 Words) (Number of word recognition errors _____)

Questions:

F 1. _____ What is the name of the unusual fish in this reading passage? (Flying fish)
F 2. _____ What is the longest distance this fish may be able to soar through the air? (Up to 200 yards, or 200 yards)
F 3. _____ When does this particular fish usually fly? (When it is chased, or when it is pursued by a predator)
F 4. _____ How long can this fish stay in the air if it wants to? (From ten to fifteen seconds, or either ten or fifteen seconds)
F 5. _____ What kinds of ocean creatures prey on the flying fish? (Tuna, sharks, dolphins, and porpoises) (Student must get at least three)
F 6. _____ What does the flying fish do to give it added momentum in its ascent? (It strikes its tail on the water)
V 7. _____ What does the word *exodus* mean in this reading passage? (Leaving, or taking off from the water)
F 8. _____ What does the flying fish use its pectoral fins for? (To fly, or as wings)
F 9. _____ What are the fins made of that allow them to be flexible? (An elastic membrane)
I 10. _____ Why could we not expect to find this fish in the cold waters around the polar regions? (Because it lives only in the warm waters of the Atlantic Ocean, or because it lives in warm water)

Number of Questions Missed	Number of Word Recognition Errors						Reading Level	
	0–3	4–7	8–11	12–15	16–19	20		
0	+	*	*	*	*	×	+	Independent
1	+	*	*	*	×	×	*	Instructional
2	*	*	*	×	×	×	×	Frustration
3	*	*	×	×	×	×		
4	*	×	×	×	×	×		
5+	×	×	×	×	×	×		

_____ Check here if this passage was used for the Listening Comprehension Test.

Listening Comprehension result: (*70 percent or higher to pass*)

_____ Percent   _____ **Passed**   _____ **Failed**

(Test Sheet on p. 170)

SCORING *2/Form C*

**9D
SILENT**

One of our most important and familiar forms of energy is light. Some researchers believe that millions of years ago the sun was responsible for the various chemical reactions that led to the beginning of life. Light is instrumental in photosynthesis, which is a process by which plants utilize light to form chemical compounds necessary for their survival. A large percentage of the living organisms on earth are dependent on photosynthesis for their food supply.

Light is also important in providing the earth's surface and atmosphere with warmth, which is important in maintaining a proper temperature range for habitation. Without a source of light, the temperature of the earth would be so low that survival for man would be impossible.

If an object is to be visible, light must travel from that object to the eye, which then senses that light. An object that provides a source of light in itself is said to be luminous. The moon is typical of an object that is not luminous in itself but is only seen because it reflects light from the sun. In contrast, the sun and other stars emit their own light energy and would be classified as luminous.

(198 Words)

Time: _____
   (in seconds)

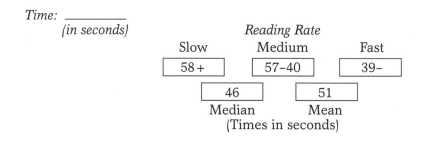

Reading Rate

Slow	Medium	Fast
58 +	57–40	39–

46	51
Median	Mean

(Times in seconds)

Questions:

F   1. _____ What is one of the most important and familiar forms of energy? (Light, or the sun)

F   2. _____ What do some researchers believe was responsible for the chemical reactions that led to the beginning of life? (The sun)

F   3. _____ What is the process called in which plants utilize light to form chemical compounds necessary for life? (Photosynthesis)

F   4. _____ Other than causing chemical reactions, what does light do that is important for maintaining habitation on the earth? (It helps maintain a proper temperature)

F   5. _____ What would happen to man if it were not for the light source that we have? (He could not inhabit the earth, or it would get too cold to live)

F   6. _____ In order for an object to be visible what must happen? (Light must travel from that source to the eye)

F   7. _____ What is the word that refers to an object that provides its own source of light? (Luminous)

F   8. _____ What object was mentioned that is not luminous? (The moon)

V   9. _____ What does the word *emit* mean? (To send out, give off, or a similar synonym)

I   10. _____ Why do you think the moon does not provide us with a great deal of energy? (Because it does not emit or give off light, or because it is not luminous)

Number of Questions Missed		Reading Level	
0–1	Independent	Independent	
2–4	Instructional	Instructional	
5+	Frustration	Frustration	

_____ Check here if this passage was used for the Listening Comprehension Test.

Listening Comprehension result: (*70 percent or higher to pass*)

_____ Percent   _____ **Passed**   _____ **Failed**

(Test Sheet on p. 171)

SCORING 2/Form D

TEST 3: EMERGENT LITERACY TESTS

Student _____   School _____

Teacher _____   Grade _____ Age _____

Examiner _____   Test Dates _____   _____

                                                    1st Test   2nd Test

DIRECTIONS/SCORING	NUMBER CORRECT	

	1st Test	2nd Test
3a. Phonemic Awareness		

3a1. Rhyme Production

Model Item. Say: **"Words that rhyme sound the same at the end. Here are some words that rhyme. Some are not real words. Listen:** *fit, dit, rit, sit, kit.***"**

Practice Item #1. Say: **"Now I will say two words and you say one that rhymes. It doesn't have to be a real word. It can be a silly one. Listen:** *rake, take . . .***"** (Student says rhyming word. If student gives incorrect response, prompt or assist as needed.)

Practice Item #2. Say: **"Good. Let's try it again. I will say two words and you say one that rhymes. Listen:** *fat, rat . . .***"** (If student is successful, go on. If not, go to alternate test.)

Test Items. Say: **"Good. Let's do some more."** (Indicate + or – in each space next to the test words. If the student misses 3 consecutive items, stop testing.)

see – bee _____	much – touch _____		
buy – shy _____	blue – grew _____		
big – pig _____	hope – soap _____		
head – bed _____	top – mop _____	/8	/8

DIRECTIONS/SCORING	NUMBER CORRECT	

3a. Phonemic Awareness

	1st Test	2nd Test

3a2.   Rhyme Recognition [ALTERNATE TEST]

Give this test *only* when the student fails the previous test.

Model Item. Say: **"Words that rhyme sound the same at the end. Here are some words that rhyme. Some are not real words. Listen:** *cat*, *sat*, *mat*, *fat*, *rat*. **Now I will say two words and if they rhyme, I'll put my thumb up. If they don't rhyme, I'll put my thumb down. Listen:** *big – pig*." (Put your thumb up after you say the words.) **"Now watch while I do another one:** "*dog – tree*." (Thumb down.)

Practice Item #1. Say: **"Now you try it. Listen:** *my – fly*." (If the student gives the correct response, give the second practice item. If not, demonstrate again as described in the model item.)

Practice Item #2. Say: **"Good. Now I will say two more words and if they rhyme, you put your thumb up. If they don't rhyme, put your thumb down. Listen:** *take – house*." (If the student gives the correct response, go on to the test items below. If not, cease testing.)

Test Items. Say: **"Good. Let's do some more. Remember, put your thumb up if the words rhyme and put your thumb down if the words don't rhyme."** (Indicate + or – in each space next to the test words. If the student misses 3 consecutive items, stop testing.)

top – mop	_____	**sat – rat**	_____		
try – man	_____	**blue – true**	_____		
hill – take	_____	**fan – fog**	_____		
red – my	_____	**see – be**	_____	/8	/8

3a2

SCORING

DIRECTIONS/SCORING	NUMBER CORRECT	

	1st Test	2nd Test

3a. Phonemic Awareness

3a3. Initial Sound Recognition

Model Item. Say: **"Now we're going to listen for sounds at the beginning of words. The first sound in** *sit* **is s-s-s-s. The word** *sit* **starts with s-s-s-s. You tell me the beginning sound of** *sit***."** (If the student gets it right, say: **"Very good."** If not, repeat the instructions. Be prepared for the possibility that the student may give you a rhyming word instead of the beginning sound. If this occurs, reemphasize the beginning sound.)

Practice Item. Say: **"Now I will say two words and you tell me the beginning sound of these words. f-ish . . . f-un."** (Emphasize the beginning sound, but do not distort it too much.) If necessary, ask: **"What sound do you hear at the beginning?"** (If the student gets the item right, go on to the test items. If not, try one more example: sock – sun. If the student fails on this item, cease testing.)

Test Items. Say: **"Good. Let's do some more."** (Indicate + or – in each space next to the test words. If the student misses 3 consecutive items, stop testing.)

jump – just _____	**land – lake** _____		
duck – door _____	**talk – tell** _____		
sun – see _____	**bat – ball** _____		
car – can _____	**pink – pig** _____	/8	/8

3a3

SCORING

DIRECTIONS/SCORING	**NUMBER CORRECT**	
	1st Test	2nd Test

3a. Phonemic Awareness

3a4. Phoneme Blending

Model Item. Say: **"I have a robot friend. He can say words in a funny way. When he says** *bad,* **he says /b/ – /a/ – /d/. When he says** *fan,* **he says /f/ – /a/ – /n/."** Emphasize and distinctly separate each of the letter sounds, but do not distort the sounds. For example, for **bad,** do not say: **/buh/ – /aaa/ – /duh/.**)

Practice Item. Say: **"Now I'm going to say words like a robot and you tell me what the words really are. Okay?** /c/ – /a/ – /t/, [pause for student's response] /b/ – /i/ – /g/, [pause for student's response] /s/ – /ee/ – /m/."** (Student should say *cat, big,* and *seem.*)

Test Items. Say: **"Good. Let's do some more."** (Indicate + or – in each space next to the test words. If the student misses 3 consecutive items, stop testing.)

/c/ – /a/ – /t/	_____	/s/ – /u/ – /n/	_____
/b/ – /oa/ – /t/	_____	/m/ – /o/ – /m/	_____
/st/ – /o/ – /p/	_____	/f/ – /ee/ – /l/	_____
/g/ – /i/ – /v/	_____	/r/ – /ae/ – /z/	_____
(give)		(raze)	

/8   /8

3a4

DIRECTIONS/SCORING	NUMBER CORRECT	

3a. Phonemic Awareness

3a5. Phoneme Segmentation

	1st Test	2nd Test

Model Item. Say: "**Now** *you* **get to be the robot. I'm going got say a word and I want you to say all the sounds of the word like my robot friend does. So if I say** *pat*, **you would say /p/ – /a/ – /t/.**" (Pronounce the whole word slowly and clearly, separating the sounds as you say the word.)

Practice Item. Say: "**Okay, you try it. The word is** *cat*. **Say it like my robot friend does.**" (Student should say /c/ – /a/ – /t/. If necessary, try one or two more practice items.)

Test Items. Say: "**Good. Let's do some more.**" (Indicate + or – in each space next to the test words. If the student misses 3 consecutive items, stop testing.)

sit _____   dog _____

ham _____   wide _____

big _____   rope _____

take _____   just _____   /8   /8

DIRECTIONS/SCORING	NUMBER CORRECT	

3b. Concepts about Print

	1st Test	2nd Test

Test Items. Place the Concepts about Print Test Sheet in front of the student and say: **"Look at this page. I'm going to ask you some questions about it."** (In the spaces to the *left* of the test questions, indicate + or –. Cease testing if the student clearly does not understand these concepts.)

_____ 1. **"Use your finger to point and show me the TOP of the page."**

_____ 2. **"Show me the BOTTOM of the page."**

_____ 3. **"Look here** (use your finger to circle the area *above* the line) **and show me where there is a LETTER all by itself."**

_____ 4. **"Show me where there is a WORD by itself."**

_____ 5. **"Show me where there is a SENTENCE."**

_____ 6. **"Now look here** (use your finger to circle the area *below* the line) **and show me where I would START reading here."**

_____ 7. **"Show me with your finger where I would go if I were reading this."**

_____ 8. (Point to the end of the first line, at the word *that*.) **"Where would I go next if I am reading from here?"** (Answer: *when*)

_____ 9. **"Point to the place I will be when I finish reading this."** (Answer: *page*)

_____ 10. **"Can you read any of the words on this page?"** (Mark "+" if the student reads one or more words correctly.)

Anecdotal Comments: _____

_____

_____

/10	/10

(Test Sheet on p. 172)

3b

SCORING

▶

DIRECTIONS	RESPONSES—CIRCLE INCORRECT RESPONSES			NUMBER CORRECT	

3c. Letter Knowledge

3cl. Letters (Auditory Stimulus)

				1st Test	2nd Test
Test Items. Place the 3c Test Sheet in front of the student and say: **"Point to the letter** *t* **. . . , the letter** *o.* **. . ."** Continue for each letter listed in order.	t	o	i		
	f	x	y		
	l	k	v		
	s	j	w		
	z			/13	/13

13 = Mastery

3c2. Letters (Visual Stimulus)

				1st Test	2nd Test
Test Items. Place the 3c Test Sheet in front of the student and say: **"Now you say the letters as I point to them."** Point to each letter on Test 3c2. Continue for each letter listed.	b	p	d		
	q	g	n		
	u	r	m		
	a	h	c		
	e			/13	/13

13 = Mastery

TEST 4a: QUICK CHECK FOR BASIC SIGHT WORDS

SCORING SHEET

Student _____   School _____

Teacher _____   Grade _____ Age _____

Examiner _____   Test Dates _____ _____
                                                   Pretest   Posttest

Directions: Place the Test Sheet in front of the student and say: **"I want you to read the words on this list out loud. Start here** (point to the word *I* in the upper left-hand corner) **and read each word as you go DOWN the columns."** Provide assistance if the student loses place. As the student reads, mark those words read correctly with a plus (+) and those read incorrectly with a minus (–). If the student pauses more than approximately **one** second before saying a word, count it as wrong. If the student says he or she does not know an answer, mark it with the letters *DK* (for "Don't Know"). If the student skips a word completely, mark it with the letters *NR* (for "No Response"). If the student misses **any** words on this test, he or she should be given Test 4b. If the student pronounces approximately half or more of the words on Test 4b correctly, then also administer Test 4c.

1. I _____		19. thing _____	
2. the _____		20. run _____	
3. was _____		21. thank _____	
4. down _____		22. once _____	
5. these _____		23. wish _____	
6. saw _____		24. think _____	
7. than _____		25. every _____	
8. start _____		26. ran _____	
9. this _____		27. another _____	
10. want _____		28. leave _____	
11. those _____		29. should _____	
12. went _____		30. there _____	
13. both _____		31. sure _____	
14. then _____		32. always _____	
15. shall _____		33. carry _____	
16. upon _____		34. present _____	
17. while _____		35. such _____	
18. draw _____		36. hurt _____	

(Test Sheet on p. 174)

4a

SCORING

TEST 4b: BASIC SIGHT WORDS

SCORING SHEETS

Name _____   Date _____

School _____   Tester _____

Scores: (Pretest) _____/220 (Posttest) _____/220

Directions: Turn on the tape recorder and place the microphone on the table. Tell the student what you are going to do. Flash the cards to the student at a rate of one to two words per second in the order in which they appear on the list. After you have completed the flashing of the cards, play back the tape and mark the Scoring Sheet with (+) for correct and (−) for incorrect responses.

List I	Pre	Post
1. the		
2. to		
3. and		
4. he		
5. a		
6. I		
7. you		
8. it		
9. of		
10. in		
11. was		
12. said		
13. his		
14. that		
15. she		
16. for		
17. on		
18. they		
19. but		
20. had		
*	/20	/20

List II	Pre	Post
1. at		
2. him		
3. with		
4. up		
5. all		
6. look		
7. is		
8. her		
9. there		
10. some		
11. out		
12. as		
13. be		
14. have		
15. go		
16. we		
17. am		
18. then		
19. little		
20. down		
*	/20	/20

List III	Pre	Post
1. do		
2. can		
3. could		
4. when		
5. did		
6. what		
7. so		
8. see		
9. not		
10. were		
11. get		
12. them		
13. like		
14. one		
15. this		
16. my		
17. would		
18. me		
19. will		
20. yes		
*	/20	/20

* Number of words read correctly

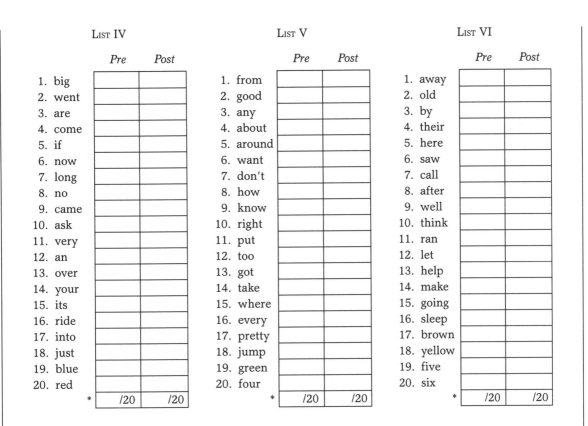

LIST IV

	Pre	Post
1. big		
2. went		
3. are		
4. come		
5. if		
6. now		
7. long		
8. no		
9. came		
10. ask		
11. very		
12. an		
13. over		
14. your		
15. its		
16. ride		
17. into		
18. just		
19. blue		
20. red		
*	/20	/20

LIST V

	Pre	Post
1. from		
2. good		
3. any		
4. about		
5. around		
6. want		
7. don't		
8. how		
9. know		
10. right		
11. put		
12. too		
13. got		
14. take		
15. where		
16. every		
17. pretty		
18. jump		
19. green		
20. four		
*	/20	/20

LIST VI

	Pre	Post
1. away		
2. old		
3. by		
4. their		
5. here		
6. saw		
7. call		
8. after		
9. well		
10. think		
11. ran		
12. let		
13. help		
14. make		
15. going		
16. sleep		
17. brown		
18. yellow		
19. five		
20. six		
*	/20	/20

LIST VII

	Pre	Post
1. walk		
2. two		
3. or		
4. before		
5. eat		
6. again		
7. play		
8. who		
9. been		
10. may		
11. stop		
12. off		
13. never		
14. seven		
15. eight		
16. cold		
17. today		
18. fly		
19. myself		
20. round		
*	/20	/20

LIST VIII

	Pre	Post
1. tell		
2. much		
3. keep		
4. give		
5. work		
6. first		
7. try		
8. new		
9. must		
10. start		
11. black		
12. white		
13. ten		
14. does		
15. bring		
16. goes		
17. write		
18. always		
19. drink		
20. once		
*	/20	/20

LIST IX

	Pre	Post
1. soon		
2. made		
3. run		
4. gave		
5. open		
6. has		
7. find		
8. only		
9. us		
10. three		
11. our		
12. better		
13. hold		
14. buy		
15. funny		
16. warm		
17. ate		
18. full		
19. those		
20. done		
*	/20	/20

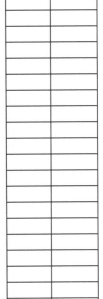

* Number of words read correctly

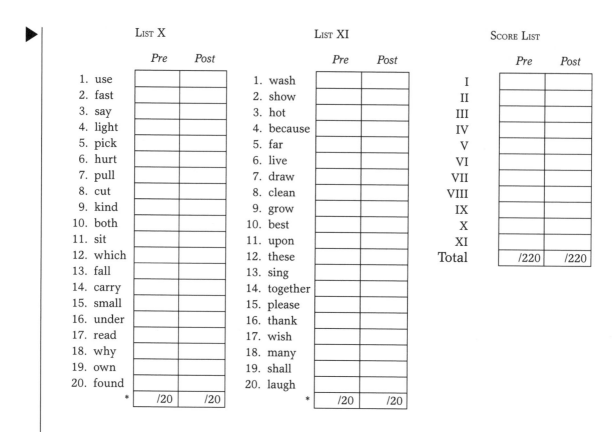

LIST X	Pre	Post
1. use		
2. fast		
3. say		
4. light		
5. pick		
6. hurt		
7. pull		
8. cut		
9. kind		
10. both		
11. sit		
12. which		
13. fall		
14. carry		
15. small		
16. under		
17. read		
18. why		
19. own		
20. found		
*	/20	/20

LIST XI	Pre	Post
1. wash		
2. show		
3. hot		
4. because		
5. far		
6. live		
7. draw		
8. clean		
9. grow		
10. best		
11. upon		
12. these		
13. sing		
14. together		
15. please		
16. thank		
17. wish		
18. many		
19. shall		
20. laugh		
*	/20	/20

SCORE LIST	Pre	Post
I		
II		
III		
IV		
V		
VI		
VII		
VIII		
IX		
X		
XI		
Total	/220	/220

* Number of words read correctly

TEST 4c: BASIC SIGHT WORD PHRASES

SCORING SHEETS

Name _____   Date _____

School _____   Tester _____

Scores: (Pretest) _____/143 (Posttest) _____/143

Directions: Turn on the tape recorder and place the microphone on the table. Tell the student what you are going to do. Flash the cards to the student at a rate of two seconds per phrase in the order in which they appear on the list. After you have completed the flashing of the cards, play back the tape and mark the Scoring Sheet with (+) for correct and (–) for incorrect responses.

List I

	Pre	Post
1. he had to		
2. she said that		
3. to the		
4. you and I		
5. but they said		
6. on a		
7. for his		
8. of that		
9. that was in		
10. it was		
*	/10	/10

List II

	Pre	Post
1. look at him		
2. as little		
3. at all		
4. I have a		
5. have some		
6. there is		
7. down there		
8. then we have		
9. to go		
10. to be there		
11. look up		
12. look at her		
13. we go out		
14. I am		
*	/14	/14

List III

	Pre	Post
1. look at me		
2. can you		
3. a little one		
4. you will see		
5. what is that		
6. my *cat*		
7. I will get		
8. when did he		
9. like this		
10. get them		
11. so you will see		
12. I could		
13. we were		
14. would not		
15. yes, I do		
*	/15	/15

List IV

	Pre	Post
1. a big ride		
2. went into		
3. if I ask		
4. come over with		
5. they went		
6. I am very		
7. there are blue		
8. a long *book*		
9. an *apple*		
10. your red *book*		
11. its *name*		
12. they came		
13. just now		
*	/13	/13

* Number of phrases read correctly

4c

SCORING

LIST V

	Pre	Post
1. I take every		
2. the four green		
3. they don't want		
4. right around		
5. a good jump		
6. a pretty *rabbit*		
7. I know how		
8. where can I		
9. the *duck* got		
10. it is about		
11. don't put any		
12. take from		
13. too little		
*	/13	/13

LIST VI

	Pre	Post
1. ran away		
2. let me help		
3. going to sleep		
4. five yellow *ducks*		
5. the old *turtle*		
6. by their *mother*		
7. call after six		
8. the brown *rabbit*		
9. I am well		
10. will think		
11. will make		
12. you saw		
13. here it is		
*	/13	/13

LIST VII

	Pre	Post
1. we eat		
2. two may walk		
3. on or off		
4. before seven		
5. today is cold		
6. play by myself		
7. don't stop		
8. it is round		
9. who is eight		
10. have never been		
11. can fly again		
*	/11	/11

LIST VIII

	Pre	Post
1. black and white		
2. start a new		
3. must try once		
4. don't keep much		
5. it does go		
6. always drink *milk*		
7. will bring ten		
8. *Lad* goes		
9. write and tell		
10. work is first		
11. can give it		
*	/11	/11

* Number of phrases read correctly

LIST IX

	Pre	*Post*
1. open and find		
2. *Jill* ate the		
3. those are done		
4. is funny		
5. buy us three		
6. this is only		
7. gave a warm		
8. soon we ate		
9. had a full		
10. run and hold		
11. made a big		
12. it is better		
13. our *duck*		
*	/13	/13

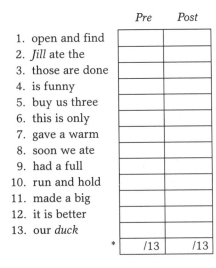

LIST X

	Pre	*Post*
1. sit with both		
2. you use it		
3. carry a small		
4. the cut hurt		
5. the fast *car*		
6. then the light		
7. which will fall		
8. pull it in		
9. had found		
10. under here		
11. be kind		
12. pick it up		
13. *Bill* can read		
14. my own *bed*		
15. why is it		
16. I can say		
*	/16	/16

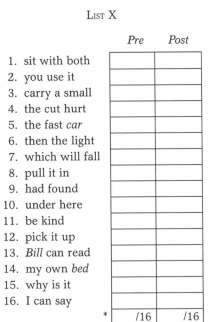

LIST XI

	Pre	*Post*
1. wash in hot		
2. because it is		
3. grow best		
4. once upon		
5. sing and laugh		
6. please thank		
7. we draw these		
8. shall we know		
9. the wish is		
10. we clean		
11. they live		
12. too far		
13. all together		
14. many *turtles*		
	/14	/14

SCORE LIST

	Pre	*Post*
I		
II		
III		
IV		
V		
VI		
VII		
VIII		
IX		
X		
XI		
Total	/143	/143

* Number of phrases read correctly

4c

SCORING

TEST 5: PHONICS

Student _____   School _____

Teacher _____   Grade _____ Age _____

Examiner _____   Test Dates _____ _____
                                                  Pretest   Posttest

5a Application of Phonics Skills in Context

Place Test 5a in front of the student. Say: "Read this story aloud until I say stop." (Do not assist the student by pronouncing unknown words.) Write the mispronunciations on the story below and note the weak skill areas.

Ron has a <u>job</u>. He will <u>make</u> the <u>fur</u> of the <u>cat shine</u>. He will <u>use</u> a <u>brush</u>. Ron can <u>fix</u> a <u>cage</u>. He can <u>pat</u> a <u>wet nose</u>. He <u>may hug</u> a <u>cute cub</u>.

Ron may <u>perk up</u> a <u>sad white bird</u> with a <u>nice word</u>. Then Ron will <u>clean dirt</u> from the <u>ground</u> in the <u>owl barn</u>. He can see a <u>fawn rest</u> by a <u>tree</u>. He may <u>bring</u> a <u>toy</u> on a <u>chain</u> to a <u>girl</u> cub. The cub will make a <u>strange noise</u>. Ron will <u>smile</u>. He <u>likes</u> all the <u>things</u> he can do to <u>work</u> and <u>play</u> at the <u>zoo</u>.

RESPONSES—CIRCLE THE LETTER(S) REPRESENTING THE SOUNDS STUDENTS READ INCORRECTLY

Beginning Single Consonants	**Ending Single Consonants**	**Beginning Consonant Blends**	**Ending Consonant Blends**
b (barn, bird)	b (cub, job)	cl (clean)	nd (ground)
hard c (cage, cat, cub, cute)	soft c (nice)	pl (play)	ng (bring)
d (dirt)	d (sad)	br (bring, brush)	rd (bird, word)
f (fawn, fix, fur)	soft g (cage, strange)	gr (ground)	rk (park, work)
hard g (girl)	hard g (hug)	tr (tree)	rl (girl)
h (hug)	k (make, perk)	sm (smile)	rn (barn)
j (job)	l (owl, smile)	str (strange)	rt (dirt)
l (likes)	n (chain, clean, fawn, Ron, shine)	_____/7	st (rest)
m (make, may)	p (up)		_____/8
n (nice, noise, nose)	r (fur)	**Beginning Consonant Digraphs**	**Ending Consonant Digraph**
p (pat, perk)	s (likes, noise, nose, things, use)	ch (chain)	sh (brush)
r (rest, Ron)	t (cat, cute, pat, wet, white)	sh (shine)	_____/1
s (sad)	x (fix)	th (things)	
t (toy)		wh (white)	
w (wet, word, work)			
z (zoo)			
_____/16	_____/13	_____/4	

5a–5i

(Test Sheet on p. 175)

SCORING

Short Vowels	Long Vowels	Vowel Combinations	
a (cat, pat, sad)	a (cage, make, strange)	ar (barn)	aw (fawn)
e (rest, wet)	e (tree)	er (perk)	ea (clean)
i (fix)	i (likes, nice, shine, smile, white)	ir (bird, dirt, girl)	oi (noise)
o (job, Ron)	o (nose)	or (word, work)	oo (zoo)
u (brush, cub, hug, up)	u (cute, use)	ur (fur)	ou (ground)
		ai (chain)	ow (owl)
_____/5	_____/5	ay (may, play)	oy (toy)
		_____/14	

NUMBER CORRECT

Total		Pretest	Posttest
____/16 Beginning Single Consonants			
____/13 Ending Single Consonants			
____/7 Beginning Consonant Blends			
____/8 Ending Consonannt Blends			
____/8 Beginning Consonant Diagraphs			
____/1 Ending Consonant Diagraph			
____/5 Short Vowels			
____/5 Long Vowels			
____/14 Vowel Combinations		/73	/73
		65 = Mastery	

	RESPONSES—CIRCLE INCORRECT RESPONSES	NUMBER CORRECT	
DIRECTIONS			
		Pretest	Posttest
5b Initial Consonants (Sound–Symbol) Place Test 5b in front of the student. Say: "Look at number 1 and point to the letter you hear at the beginning of *water* . . . , *dog.* . . ." Continue for each word listed.	1. water 5. book 9. sit 2. dog 6. kite 10. hide 3. nice 7. fat 4. goat 8. put	/10 9 = Mastery	/10
5c Initial Blends & Digraphs (Sound–Symbol) Place Test 5c in front of the student. Say: "Look at number 1 and point to the letters you hear at the beginning of *great* . . . , *blue.* . . ." Continue for each word listed.	1. great 5. plum 9. spell 2. blue 6. church 10. those 3. small 7. thumb 4. short 8. bring	/10 9 = Mastery	/10
5d Ending Sounds (Sound–Symbol) Place Test 5d in front of the student. Say: "Look at number 1 and point to the letter or letters you hear at the end of *bat* . . . , *bed.* . . ." Continue for each word listed.	1. bat 5. tab 9. pant 2. bed 6. sing 10. card 3. drop 7. bush 4. cool 8. mask	/10 8 = Mastery	/10

(Test Sheet on pp. 175–178)

5a–5i

SCORING

DIRECTIONS	RESPONSES—CIRCLE INCORRECT RESPONSES			NUMBER CORRECT	
				Pretest	Posttest
5e Vowels (Sound–Symbol) Place Test 5e in front of the student. Say: "Look at number 1 and point to the vowel you hear in *tip . . . , mule. . . ."* Continue for each word listed.	1. tip 5. mope 9. cup 2. mule 6. tape 10. keep 3. snap 7. pet 4. dot 8. fine			/10	/10
	9 = Mastery				
5f Phonograms (Sound–Symbol) Place Test 5f in front of the student. Say: "Look at number 1 and point to the ending part you hear: *ame . . . , ime. . . ."* Continue for each part listed.	1. ame 5. eep 9. ang 2. ime 6. ight 10. ill 3. ike 7. ing 4. ock 8. ade			/10	/10
	9 = Mastery				
5g Blending (Symbol–Sound) Place Test 5g in front of the student. Make sure the student can pronounce the two phonograms *at* and *in.* Say: "You are going to blend letters with *at* and *in.* The first one is *t* plus *in* or *tin.* Now you blend the rest. Some of these are real words; some are not."	1. h + at 5. th + at 9. f + in 2. ch + in 6. m + at 10. d + in 3. tr + in 7. sh + in 4. bl + at 8. str + at			/10	/10
	9 = Mastery				
5h Substitution (Symbol–Sound) Place Test 5h in front of the student. Say: "Read these words. I will tell you the first one in each column in case you don't know it. Some are real words, some are not."	fan track hat rade bib r sh i o f t sp o i d b fr e u g j ch u m l pl v st c wh			/25	/25
	22 = Mastery				
5i Vowel Pronunciation (Symbol–Sound) Place Test 5i in front of the student. Say: "Read as many of these words as you can."	boat crown serve paint trout stir own hawk born soil haul word coy card burn			/15	/15
	13 = Mastery				

TEST 6: STRUCTURAL ANALYSIS

Student _____   School _____

Teacher _____   Grade _____ Age _____

Examiner _____   Test Dates _____ _____
                                              Pretest   Posttest

6a Application of Structural Analysis Skills in Context

Place Test 6a1 or 6a2 in front of the student. Say: "Read this story aloud until I say 'stop.'" (Do not assist the student by pronouncing unknown words.)

The first story is easier than the second. Stop if the story becomes too difficult. In both stories, the words requiring the structural analysis are underlined. Write the mispronunciations on the story below and note the weak skill areas.

6a1

It was a cold winter day. The <u>trees</u> were bare and <u>birds</u> could be seen in the <u>countryside</u>. A <u>grasshopper hopped</u> across the road to hide from the cold and the <u>foxes curled</u> up to keep warm. A brown field mouse and her babies came <u>running</u> out of a hole in the ground. The babies were <u>fighting</u> with each other. Mother mouse looked <u>unhappy</u> as she sat on a big <u>overgrown</u> stump. It was <u>dangerous</u> for the mice to stay above ground but the <u>active</u> children <u>wanted</u> their <u>lunches</u>. Mother mouse was also <u>nervous</u> about her children <u>eating</u> the <u>poisonous plants</u> that were in the fields. The children were <u>curious</u> and the plants <u>looked</u> so <u>attractive</u>.

Just that <u>morning</u> Mother mouse had a <u>disagreement</u> with Father mouse. The <u>question</u> was whether or not the children should run in the field in the <u>daytime</u>.

RESPONSES—CIRCLE INCORRECT RESPONSES				NUMBER CORRECT	
Inflectional Endings	**Compounds**	**Suffixes**	**Syllabication**	**6a1**	
trees	fighting	countryside	active	dangerous		
birds	wanted	grasshopper	nervous	poisonous		
hopped	lunches	overgrown	question	curious		
foxes	eating	daytime		attractive		
curled	plants	**Prefix**		disagreement		
babies	looked	unhappy			
running	morning			/27	/27
				24 = Mastery	

(Test Sheet on pp. 179)

SCORING **6a–6h** ▶

6a2

What should have been a great day <u>turned</u> out to be a <u>disappointing</u> one for David King. He found out that he would be the new <u>quarterback</u> for Friday <u>night's</u> game. <u>Unfortunately</u>, he was <u>going</u> to be <u>taking</u> his best friend Ron's place. Ron had <u>gotten</u> a <u>disqualification notice</u> because his <u>grades dropped</u> at the end of the first <u>report</u>. Ron felt that his <u>concentration</u> was poor because of his <u>older brother's recent motorcycle crash</u>. David was sorry about Ron's <u>dismissal</u> from the team, but was <u>shocked</u> by the <u>resentment</u> he saw on Ron's face when he found out who his <u>replacement</u> would be. This was the <u>unfriendliest</u> that Ron had ever <u>treated</u> David.

David thought about the rest of his rather <u>uneventful</u> day as he <u>walked</u> home. He turned on the <u>flashlight</u> he <u>carried</u> with him, for it had grown quite dark. David <u>stopped</u> short when he heard a loud and <u>frightening</u> scream <u>coming</u> from the vacant <u>mansion</u> just up the road.

The place had been empty for <u>years</u> and was in bad shape. <u>Fixing</u> it up had been <u>estimated</u> to be <u>costlier</u> than most <u>families</u> could afford. David had always felt that the mansion had a <u>mysterious</u> look about it. The man who had built and <u>lived</u> in the mansion was <u>believed</u> to be <u>knowledgeable</u> in the ways of <u>witchcraft</u>. His <u>disappearance</u> three years ago had shocked the people of the town. What made it even <u>scarier</u> was that it <u>happened</u> on a <u>Halloween</u> night when so many children were out on the <u>streets</u>. The <u>imaginative minds</u> of <u>several</u> of the <u>neighbors</u> had come up with many strange <u>stories</u> about what had happened to old Flint.

RESPONSES—CIRCLE INCORRECT RESPONSES

Inflectional Endings	Compounds	Syllabication		NUMBER CORRECT 6a2
turned carried	quarterback	disappointing	estimated	
night's stopped	motorcycle	Unfortunately	costlier	
going coming	flashlight	disqualification	mysterious	
taking years	witchcraft	concentration	believed	
Ron's Fixing	**Prefixes**	dismissal	knowledgeable	
gotten families	report	resentment	disappearance	/53 /53
grades lived	recent	replacement	Halloween	48 = Mastery
dropped scarier	**Suffixes**	unfriendliest	imaginative	
older happened	notice	uneventful	several	
brother's streets	mansion	frightening	neighbors	**Total Score**
shocked minds				
treated stories				/80 /80
walked				72 = Mastery

DIRECTIONS	RESPONSES—CIRCLE INCORRECT RESPONSES						NUMBER CORRECT	

6b Hearing Word Parts
Say: "How many syllables do you hear in the word *cowboy . . . , intention . . . , steam . . . , disagreement . . . , randomly?"*

		Pretest	Posttest
1. cowboy (2)	4. disagreement (4)		
2. intention (3)	5. randomly (3)		
3. steam (1)		/5	/5

4 = Mastery

6c Inflectional Endings
Place Test 6c in front of the student. Say: "Read these words. I will read the first one in each column."

bake	pale	slow		
er	er	er		
ed	ing	est		
s	est	ly		
		s	/10	/10

9 = Mastery

6d Prefixes
Place Test 6d in front of the student. Say: "Read these words. I will read the first one in each column."

play	mote	form	take	tend	pack		
re	re	con	re	in	un		
dis	pro	in	in	con	pre		
mis	de	de	mis	ex	re		
				dis			
				pre		/20	/20

18 = Mastery

6e Suffixes
Place Test 6e in front of the student. Say: "Read these words. I will read the first one in each column."

joy	invent	base	elect		
ous	ive	ment	ion		
ful	able	ness	ive		
less		less		/10	/10

9 = Mastery

6f Compound Words
Place Test 6f in front of the student. Say: "Read as many of these words as you can. Some are not real words." (It is more important for the student to recognize the separate units of the words than to pronounce them perfectly.)

overdone	motorplane		
laterthought	clockrunner		
baskethouse		/5	/15

14 = Mastery

(Test Sheet on pp. 181–182)

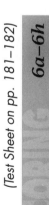

6a–6h

SCORING

DIRECTIONS	RESPONSES—CIRCLE INCORRECT RESPONSES		NUMBER CORRECT	
			Pretest	Posttest
6g Affixes Place Test 6g in front of the student. Say: "Read as many of these words as you can. Some are not real words." (It is more important for the student to recognize the separate units of the words than to pronounce them perfectly.)	uncall proclaim indeem demark prestrain	treeness sunning bookful raytion darkous	 /10 9 =	 /10 Mastery
6h Syllabication Place Test 6h in front of the student. Say: "Read as many of these words as you can."	automotive displacement conformation remarkable impeachable	premeditate imperfection unreasonable misplaying complicated	 /10 9 =	 /10 Mastery

TEST 7: KNOWLEDGE OF CONTRACTIONS

SCORING SHEET

Student _____   School _____

Teacher _____   Grade _____ Age _____

Examiner _____   Test Dates _____ _____
                                                Pretest   Posttest

Directions: Say, "Here is a list of contractions. I want you to begin with number one and say the contraction, and then tell me what two words it stands for." Following each contraction are two lines. If the student is able to pronounce the contraction correctly, put a plus (+) in the first blank. If he can then tell you what two words it stands for, put a plus (+) in the second blank. Mark wrong answers with a minus (–).

1. let's	____	____		25. wouldn't	____	____
2. didn't	____	____		26. she'll	____	____
3. it's	____	____		27. here's	____	____
4. won't	____	____		28. couldn't	____	____
5. that's	____	____		29. they're	____	____
6. can't	____	____		30. they'd	____	____
7. wasn't	____	____		31. you'll	____	____
8. isn't	____	____		32. she'd	____	____
9. hadn't	____	____		33. weren't	____	____
10. don't	____	____		34. I'd	____	____
11. I'll	____	____		35. you've	____	____
12. we'll	____	____		36. you'd	____	____
13. I've	____	____		37. we'd	____	____
14. he'll	____	____		38. anybody'd	____	____
15. hasn't	____	____		39. there'll	____	____
16. haven't	____	____		40. we've	____	____
17. aren't	____	____		41. who'll	____	____
18. I'm	____	____		42. he'd	____	____
19. he's	____	____		43. who'd	____	____
20. we're	____	____		44. doesn't	____	____
21. you're	____	____		45. where's	____	____
22. what's	____	____		46. they've	____	____
23. there's	____	____		47. they'll	____	____
24. she's	____	____				

Number of Words Pronounced (from left columns)   ____ /47

Number of Words Known (from right columns)   ____ /47

Total Score   ____ /94

(Test Sheet on p. 183)

TEST 8: EL PASO PHONICS SURVEY

SCORING SHEET

Student _____   School _____

Teacher _____   Grade _____ Age _____

Examiner _____   Test Dates _____ _____
                                                    Pretest   Posttest

Mark Answers as Follows   *PEK   Point at which phonic element*
Pass +   *is expected to be known*
Fail – (or write word as pronounced)

		Answers	PEK			Answers	PEK
Initial Consonant Sounds							
1. p	pam	_____	1.9	12. j	jin	_____	1.9
2. n	nup	_____	1.9	13. k	kam	_____	1.9
[a]3. s	sup	_____	1.9	14. l	lin	_____	1.9
4. t	tup	_____	1.9	[b]15. c	cam	_____	1.9
5. r	rin	_____	1.9	[c]16. g	gup	_____	1.9
6. m	min	_____	1.9	[d]17. y	yin	_____	1.9
7. b	bup	_____	1.9	18. v	vam	_____	1.9
8. d	dup	_____	1.9	19. z	zin	_____	1.9
9. w	wam	_____	1.9	20. c	cin	_____	2.5 (sin)
10. h	hup	_____	1.9	21. g	gin	_____	2.9 (jim)
11. f	fin	_____	1.9	22. qu	quam	_____	1.9
Ending Consonant X							
[e]23. x	mox	_____	1.9				
Initial Consonant Clusters							
24. pl	plup	_____	1.9				
25. fr	frin	_____	1.9	42. sk	skam	_____	2.5
26. fl	flam	_____	1.9	43. cr	crin	_____	2.5
27. st	stup	_____	1.9	44. tw	twam	_____	2.5
28. bl	blin	_____	1.9	45. sn	snup	_____	2.5
29. tr	trin	_____	1.9	46. sch	scham	_____	2.5
30. gr	grup	_____	1.9	47. sp	spam	_____	2.9
31. br	brin	_____	1.9	48. sc	scup	_____	2.9
32. sh	shup	_____	1.9	49. str	stram	_____	2.9
[f]33. th	thup	_____	1.9 (thing)	50. thr	thrup	_____	2.9
[g]34. wh	whup	_____	1.9 (when)	51. shr	shrup	_____	2.9
35. ch	cham	_____	1.9 (church)	52. squ	squam	_____	2.9
36. dr	drup	_____	2.5	53. sw	swup	_____	3.5
37. pr	pram	_____	2.5	54. spr	spram	_____	3.5
38. sl	slup	_____	2.5	55. spl	splin	_____	3.5
39. cl	clin	_____	2.5	56. wr	wrin	_____	4.5
40. gl	glam	_____	2.5	57. dw	dwin	_____	4.5
41. sm	smin	_____	2.5	58. scr	scrup	_____	4.5

Superior letters preceding list numbers indicate notes in the El Paso Phonics Survey: Special Directions.

▶   **Answers   PEK**   **Answers   PEK**

Vowels, Vowel Teams, and Special Letter Combinations

59.	ă	tam	_____	1.9	75.	oe	poe	_____ 2.5 (hoe)
60.	ĭ	rit	_____	1.9	76.	oa	oan	_____ 2.5 (soap)
61.	ĕ	nep	_____	1.9	77.	ee	eem	_____ 2.5 (heed)
62.	ŏ	sot	_____	1.9	[l]78.	ow	owd	_____ 2.5 (cow or crow)
63.	ŭ	tum	_____	1.9	[m]79.	ow	fow	_____ 2.5 (cow or crow)
64.	ī	tipe	_____	2.5	80.	or	orm	_____ 2.5 (corn)
65.	ē	rete	_____	2.5	81.	ir	irt	_____ 2.5 (hurt)
66.	ā	sape	_____	2.5	82.	ur	urd	_____ 2.5 (hurt)
67.	ū	pune	_____	2.5	83.	aw	awp	_____ 2.9 (paw)
68.	ō	sote	_____	2.5	84.	oi	doi	_____ 2.9 (boy)
[h]69.	oo	oot	_____	2.5 (moon or book)	85.	ou	tou	_____ 2.9 (cow)
[i]70.	oo	oot	_____	2.5 (moon or book)	86.	ar	arb	_____ 2.9 (harp)
[j]71.	ea	eap	_____	2.5 (head or meat)	87.	oy	moy	_____ 2.9 (boy)
[k]72.	ea	eam	_____	2.5 (head or meat)	88.	er	ert	_____ 2.9 (her)
73.	ai	ait	_____	2.5 (ape)	89.	ew	bew	_____ 2.9 (few)
74.	ay	tay	_____	2.5 (hay)	90.	au	dau	_____ 2.9 (paw)

TEST 9: QUICK WORD LIST SURVEY

SCORING SHEET

Student _____   School _____

Teacher _____   Grade _____ Age _____

Examiner _____   Test Dates _____ _____
                                                    Pretest   Posttest

Pronunciation of Quick Survey Words

1. răt´-bĕl-ĭng
2. däs´-nīt
3. prăm´-mĭn-sĭl-ĭng
4. hwĕt´-splĭt-ter
5. jĭn´-kyo͞ol
6. crĭn´-gāl
7. slăt´-rŭn-gəl
8. twā´-fräl
9. sprēn´-plĭt
10. gōn´-bāt
11. strē´-grăn
12. glăm´-mer-tĭck-ly
13. grăn´-tĕl-lēn
14. āp´-sĭd

Pronunciation Key

l – litt<u>le</u>   er – h<u>er</u>

ə – <u>a</u>bout   hw – <u>wh</u>at

ä – f<u>a</u>ther   kyo͞o – <u>cu</u>te

Directions: Write the student's pronunciation for each word in the first space below. Indicate with a + or a – if the pronunciation is correct in the second space.

	Pronunciation	**+ or –**		**Pronunciation**	**+ or –**
1.	_____	_____	8.	_____	_____
2.	_____	_____	9.	_____	_____
3.	_____	_____	10.	_____	_____
4.	_____	_____	11.	_____	_____
5.	_____	_____	12.	_____	_____
6.	_____	_____	13.	_____	_____
7.	_____	_____	14.	_____	_____

TEST 10: READING INTERESTS SURVEY

SCORING SHEET

Student _____   School _____

Teacher _____   Grade _____ Age _____

Examiner _____   Test Dates _____   _____
                                                  Pretest   Posttest

TEST 10a READING INTERESTS SURVEY—ELEMENTARY

I. Open-Ended Questions

I like school if _____ .

I wish _____ .

When I grow up _____ .

Reading makes me _____ .

Books are _____ .

I like to read when _____ .

Teachers should _____ .

II. Reading Interests

I like to read about:

_____ Science   _____ Dogs

_____ Biography   _____ Mysteries

_____ Sports   _____ Science Fiction

_____ People   _____ Riddles

_____ History   _____ Plays

_____ Horses   _____ Monsters

_____ Fantasy   _____ Poetry

I do *not* like to read about _____ .

If I had my choice, I would really like to read about _____

_____ .

III. Reading Experiences

The last book I read was _____ .

My three favorite books are _____

_____ .

People in my family read: _____

_____ Books   _____ Magazines   _____ Newspapers

I watch television or play video games about _____ hours per day.

The hours I watch television or play video games are from _____ to _____ .

I visit the public library:

_____ Often   _____ Seldom   _____ Never

10a

SCORING

▶ **TEST 10b READING INTERESTS SURVEY—ADULT   SCORING SHEET**

I. Open-Ended Questions

What are your favorite activities? _____

_____

What are your career or educational goals? _____

_____

How do you feel about school? _____

_____

How do you feel about your classes and your instructors? _____

_____

_____

II. Reading Interests

What do you enjoy reading about? _____

_____

What do you *not* enjoy reading about? _____

_____

What do you tend to read—books? magazines? newspapers? Internet?_____

_____

When do you read? When you have to? Or do you also read for pleasure? _____

_____

III. Reading Experiences

What do you remember about your early reading experiences; for instance, did your parents read to you when you were a child?_____

_____

What was the last book you read?_____

_____

What are your three favorite books?_____

_____

How would you define reading? _____

_____

Do you think reading affects your life? _____

_____

NOTES

NOTES

NOTES

NOTES